WHY DID HITLER HATE THE JEWS?

WHY DID HITLER HATE THE JEWS?

THE ORIGINS OF ADOLF HITLER'S
ANTI-SEMITISM AND ITS OUTCOME IN 1941

Peter den Hertog

Translated by

Lynn Coleman

FRONTLINE
BOOKS

WHY DID HITLER HATE THE JEWS?
The Origins of Adolf Hitler's Anti-Semitism and its Outcome in 1941

First published in Great Britain in 2020 by Frontline Books,
an imprint of Pen & Sword Books Ltd, Yorkshire - Philadelphia

Typeset in India by Vman Infotech Private Limited
Printed and bound by TJ International

Pen & Sword Books Ltd incorporates the imprints of Pen & Sword Archaeology,
Air World Books, Atlas, Aviation, Battleground, Discovery, Family History, History,
Maritime, Military, Naval, Politics, Social History, Transport, True Crime, Claymore
Press, Frontline Books, Praetorian Press, Seaforth Publishing and White Owl

For a complete list of Pen & Sword titles please contact:

PEN & SWORD BOOKS LTD
47 Church Street, Barnsley, South Yorkshire, S70 2AS, UK.
E-mail: enquiries@pen-and-sword.co.uk
Website: www.pen-and-sword.co.uk

Or

PEN AND SWORD BOOKS,
1950 Lawrence Road, Havertown, PA 19083, USA
E-mail: Uspen-and-sword@casematepublishers.com
Website: www.penandswordbooks.com

Contents

Preface

Another book about Adolf Hitler? Haven't there been countless books written about this insidious man already? This is what many people will wonder when yet another book about him is published. I hold the opinion that every author that writes about Hitler should have good reason to do so.

In 1998, the first part of Ian Kershaw's monumental biography of Hitler was published. One particular sentence struck me and strongly roused my curiosity, namely: 'In truth, we do not know for certain why, nor even when Hitler turned into a maniac and obsessive anti-Semite.'

How was this possible? His deadly anti-Semitism led to one of the greatest human catastrophes of the twentieth century – and we cannot even determine when and why Hitler became such a rabid hater of Jews? I could not believe my eyes. I rushed to libraries and quickly studied many major Hitler biographies; indeed, there was no specific explanation to be found in those texts. In fact, the only related topic mentioned was the 'influence of the anti-Semitic environment'. Now, this influence was certainly an important factor, but in Hitler's time there were many people who, like him, were exposed to anti-Semitic influences who did not become anti-Semites; so why did he become one? Furthermore, Hitler did not become a 'common' Jew hater but a genocidal Jew hater, who executed 6 million Jews.

As for 'environmental influence', this could be used to explain virtually any human act. As long as this explanation is not particularised and supplemented, it is in fact inconsequential.

I knew what I had to do – seek a distinct explanation. This resulted in two books, which were published in the Netherlands, the first in 2005 and the second in 2012. These two studies offer an explanation for the origins of Hitler's demonic anti-Semitism beyond 'environmental influence'.

My books were favourably received by the press and called 'innovative'. Those who read the reviews must have gained the impression that indeed something novel was being said about the origins of Hitler's anti-Semitism.

Now, fifteen years after the publication of my first book, no new material has been published about the origins of his anti-Semitism. It seems difficult to uncover explanations for it.

I have updated my discoveries and insights (all new publications up until 2020) and bundled them into one book for an English-speaking audience. However, I still thought my own contribution to another aspect of the Hitler debate was missing. We already know what Hitler's anti-Semitism led to; however, up until now there remains disagreement on the crucial decision process in 1941: did Hitler give a clear order to kill the European Jews or not? If so, when? A multitude of answers, propositions and interpretations are presented. In the final chapters I provide my answer. I use insights into Hitler's personality that have been explored in previous chapters. The fact is that in the knowledge of why Hitler was an anti-Semitic lies important information – if well interpreted – that creates clarity about the genocidal decision process. I hope this book will contribute to the great 'Hitler debate'.

I would like to make a few more points. There are historians who strongly assert that their book is composed of primary sources. This is simply not possible. The starting point of each historical interpretation is first and foremost an explanatory story – good or bad. Without a story, the researcher cannot do anything with facts and sources. Without a story, facts and sources have no context. Once the researcher has a story – and he always does – after all, he has read countless texts on Hitler, only then can he refine it by consulting primary and secondary sources. He can also revise it, but he derives his point of departure from the tradition of the great Hitler debate. Any book on Hitler relies on previous research. If a researcher were to focus on the primary sources, he would ignore a sea of valuable information. Worse still, he would not know what to do. I am fully aware of this. Therefore, the debate – the conversation with other Hitler researchers – is particularly emphasised in this research.

The second point is this: historians are historians. Due to their educational focus on history, they draw on their own fields of study. Little interdisciplinary research takes place. Now, I arrive at the next point. Especially if one is writing about an atypical, fiendish figure such as Hitler, one should make more frequent use of social sciences. A historian must dare to look beyond their own borders. If they do, they can decipher more information about historical characters. In this study, I have employed psychiatry, anthropology, socio-biology and evolutionary theory. Indeed, Adolf Hitler was born in 1889, but we do not hesitate to – briefly – travel back to 65 million years ago.

Another curious fact: until 1998, I was not at all interested in Hitler. In fact, he always filled me with such horror that I did not even watch documentaries or read books about him. I still had to read Ian Kershaw's 1998 biography. As a historian, after all, one must know something about Hitler. I only intended to read the biography – and also part two – and then I would call it quits. But then I read the previously mentioned sentence: 'We would not know when and why he became an anti-Semite.' I have always been interested in the 'Why question'. In the field of philosophy, it is said that there is no phenomenon without reason or cause. Questions that raise the why of a phenomenon have always strongly appealed to me. I overcame my disgust of Hitler and began my research into why he became anti-Semitic. Twenty years have passed and my third book about Hitler has been published. In it one also finds – as I said before – a new proposition with regard to the decision process in 1941 that led to the Holocaust. I could never have imagined that I would take on such a subject as Hitler so thoroughly, yet it has happened.

Finally, many consider history to be boring and stuffy. Tomes have been written that produce well-founded, high-quality insights, but unfortunately they are uninteresting. I have often heard students say that they were not able to get through this or that book. Make a historical story palatable for goodness' sake. The reader will appreciate it. I am also a novelist and writer of thrillers. The story I have created about Hitler resembles a detective's tale. It was written as a search for motives. I hope that the reader will experience the tension and excitement essential in a good detective's story – but scientific criteria have always been number one.

Peter den Hertog
Emmen, The Netherlands, 2020

Chapter 1

The Riddle

No conclusive explanation has yet been given for the origins of Hitler's demonic hatred of the Jews. I am not alone in this claim, as you can see in the following quotations:

> The anti-Semitism is the only riddle of Hitler's personality that most likely will never be fully resolved. (Franz Jetzinger, 1956)

> I have never found out what was the cause of Hitler's fanatical hatred of Jews. (Fritz Wiedemann, 1964)

> Despite all the detailed knowledge, Hitler's anti-Semitism cannot be fully explained. (Werner Maser, 1971)

> We can probably no longer plumb the real cause of this ever-growing hatred [of Jews], which lasted literally to the last hour of Hitler's life. . . . Perhaps we may never be able to trace Hitler's overwhelming phobia down to its roots. (Joachim Fest, 1973)

> In truth, we do not know for certain why, nor even when, Hitler turned into a maniac and obsessive anti-Semite. (Ian Kershaw, 1998, 2009)

The last quote dates back to the year 1998 and was repeated by the author in 2009. After that, another six major studies on Hitler have appeared. We will encounter all of them later in this book. In all these publications, however, one will still not find a good explanation for Hitler's anti-Semitism. So, despite all these new studies, the question when and why Hitler's demonic anti-Semitism originated still remains. This is why I'm suggesting a sixth statement.

Until now, the riddle of Hitler's anti-Semitism has still not been resolved.

It is clear what we want to achieve in this book. We will have to see how far we are able to go. By the end of this study, readers may judge for themselves whether progress has been made towards solving the riddle – or if the riddle has even been solved.

Chapter 2

The Detective

During the 1920s, the critical English thinker Robin George Colling-wood clarified how a historian resembles a detective. Both the historian and the detective seek the truth behind events. A detective often encounters silent or evasive witnesses, yet he does not give up easily. If he asks new, surprising questions, he may still be able to force the witnesses to speak. This also applies to the historian. According to Collingwood, his sources remain silent if he asks them the wrong questions. If the historian does ask the right questions, then the sources suddenly begin to speak – sometimes very loudly and convincingly.[1]

The research on Hitler will not reveal many new spectacular sources. But the old sources can provide new insights if one asks surprising questions, as Collingwood posits. He gives us another interesting piece of advice. He says that the historian must place the authorities (in this case, the experts who have already done research on Hitler's anti-Semitism) in the witness box and submit them to a cross-examination to determine what they have *not* said.[2] Those who know what the authorities are silent about and how to describe this flaw will see exactly what is missing. It is obvious that one must know what the authorities have *actually* said. And in the case of Hitler, a proper analysis of the origins of Hitler's hatred of Jews may lie in that which has *not* been said.

Historians and the like have been researching Hitler for over eighty years. So, we will critically engage these publications, especially the more recent ones. In particular, we will consider what the authorities, harking back to Collingwood, do not mention. But how do we know what they do *not* say? Through logically evaluating an explanation one can determine why the explanation is incomplete or even false. This study intends to do this. In addition, we use an extra analytical instrument. Namely, we first explain Hitler's anti-Semitism. Through this process, we uncover a fundamental insight into Hitler's personality to understand why he was so exceptionally receptive to anti-Semitism and why he ultimately embraced it. At the same time, we gain knowledge through which we can judge explanations by other researchers; we will especially see what they do *not* say.

We also examine the period in which his anti-Semitism manifested itself – in what month or in what year? Why then in particular? At the end of the book, we will also endeavour to answer the question whether Hitler had given a clear order to murder the European Jews in 1941. And if so: when? And what were his motives?

Chapter 3

The Nineteenth-Century Background: Anti-Semitic Traditions

In the preface, I suggested that biographers mainly make use of the 'influence of the anti-Semitic environment' to account for Hitler's anti-Semitism. At the same time, I stated that it's possible to explain virtually any human act by 'environmental influences'. I even said that that is why such a statement is meaningless. To illustrate this, I pointed out that many Germans did not become anti-Semitic despite anti-Jewish influences. This shows that *nurture* provides an incomplete explanation. This in turn implies that a complete explanation requires more, *nature* to be precise, which through its interaction with *nurture* leads to different outcomes in different people. However, if there is no anti-Semitism in a culture, there will also not be anybody who hates Jews. From this, you can see that an anti-Jewish environment is still an absolute prerequisite for anti-Semites to emerge.

Hatred of Jewish people doesn't just appear out of thin air! That is why it is both understandable as well as correct, that from the earliest research into Hitler in the 1930s onwards, we keep encountering anti-Semitic influences as an explanation. In the meantime, we have, however, come to understand that this is only a partial explanation. Of course, Adolf Hitler was moulded to his core by the anti-Jewish environment in which he grew up. We shouldn't, however, forget that this is only a 'partial explanation'. The remainder consists of formative forces stemming from *nature*. So, we will be looking into Adolf Hitler and *nature*. For now, we will concentrate on the environment in which Adolf Hitler grew up. Everyone knows roughly what 'anti-Semitism' means or consists of. However, what exactly did the anti-Semitism that Adolf Hitler came into contact with consist of? What was the great diversity of anti-Semitic thoughts, ideas and assertions which informed his development? Let us take a look into this now and try to obtain a concrete picture of anti-Semitism in Adolf Hitler's lifetime.

The Jews had been supressed and hated over many centuries. They were seen as usurers and as a people doomed by God. They were subject to special anti-Jewish laws. However, as a result of the French Revolution and the dissemination of liberal ideas, an increasing tolerance in political matters and questions of faith developed. In Prussia, in 1812 Jews were guaranteed equal rights: so, they received the same rights as other religious communities. In Austria-Hungary, Jews already enjoyed legal equality from 1867.

What happened to the Jews was unique. They could leave the ghettos in which they had lived in isolation and join the rest of the population as free citizens for the first time. Now, Jewish people were given new opportunities and they indeed welcomed the opportunity. Soon they were present everywhere in society. In fact, they were an enrichment to the economy and culture.

Their social rise was remarkable. They prospered in the new capitalism. They stood out in the areas of trade and banking. They were also richly represented in politics, science, journalism and the arts. Some of them became extremely wealthy. Of course, the Jews supported the modern, democratic and liberal forces to which they had owed their emancipation. In this way, they became easily associated with the new social forces. This was a danger to them.[1]

The new freedom of the nineteenth century also had its losers: people and groups for whom social progress was virtually impossible.[2] The old middle class was driven into a tight corner by the rise of industrialisation and mass production. Officials and office workers remained in their old positions where they, in social terms, were unable or hardly able to gain promotion.

The economic slump of 1873 after the overheating of the economy and the stock-market crash was of unprecedented magnitude, especially in Germany. The Jews, who were seen as the embodiment of capitalist modernity, were blamed for the disaster. Now many of the economic losers and even more culturally critical sceptics in Germany – along with the anti-liberal conservative elite – turned against democracy, liberalism and capitalism. Some of them wanted to partially undo the emancipation of the Jews, which had been in force since 1871, while others wanted to do this completely. This gave rise to modern anti-Semitism.[3]

This is simply a case of downright envy. There was more going on with modern anti-Semitism, however – contrary to the already age-old religious anti-Judaism. Something new was added to the enmity towards the Jews, which would appear catastrophic at a later stage: one began to consider Jews a separate race. This means the Jews formed a so-called biological unit. In terms of the second half of the nineteenth century, Jews were all of the same blood and this was meant very negatively. All kinds of ugly traits emerged from their blood – we would now talk of 'genes' – whether they wanted this or not. Adolf Hitler would continue to emphasise this. On 13 August 1920, he shouted the following: 'The character of the Jew is in his blood and he has to act accordingly. No matter what profession the Jew has, he is and remains a Jew and through his blood, he only has one thing on his mind: How can I bring my people to world dominion. . . .'[4] All other conceivable and unconceivable bad qualities inevitably emerged from Jewish blood as well according to him. The Jew was determined to do evil through his biology.

This new idea, that the Jews formed a separate race ('the Jewish race' would become a typical Nazi term), did not just come out of the blue.

The concept of human 'race' had already come into fashion in the eighteenth century, under the influence of European colonial expansion and people were divided into all kinds of human races. The white race was superior. African and American races followed at a great distance. For a long time, there was confusion about primitive races such as Hottentots and Pygmies. What were they exactly, human beings or apes?[5] The general opinion was that the difference between the races had originated through geography, climate and food. One expressed vague opinions about the connection between race and culture.

Count Joseph Arthur de Gobineau, the influential pioneer of the new racism, changed this. In his 400-page book, *An essay on the inequality of human races* (1853–5), he developed a racial doctrine in which he clearly expressed his opinion about races and the connection between race and culture. A race did not originate from environmental factors but was determined biologically. And in particular: culture emerged from race. To put it in twenty-first-century terms, he says that culture stems from a race's DNA, so purely from *nature*. The white race was superior to all other races. Among the white, the Aryans (the French, the English, the Germans and North Europeans) were most high bred. Only they had the creative qualities at their disposal to produce a high culture. The Aryans were also superior physically. The Aryan body was beautiful, with blond hair and blue eyes. They resembled statues of classical sculpture. Gobineau was worried about the Aryan race. The danger was not present in the Jews, but in the crossbreeding with the lower, yellow and black races. If this crossbreeding took place, the Aryans would lose their creative powers and die a 'racial death'. Gobineau was no anti-Semite himself, but, later on, National Socialists perverted his racial doctrine and used it against the Jews.[6]

Social Darwinism also provided a strong impulse for thinking about races in biological terms. Charles Darwin had developed a powerful scientific explanation in his *On the origin of species by means of natural selection* (1859) about how the different species had originated, namely by natural selection. But the anti-Semites used Darwin to provide a 'scientific' basis for the enmity towards the Jews. Darwin had expressed himself only in terms of plants and animals in his book, but anti-Semitic Social Darwinists applied his ideas to human society and history. Higher and lower human races were distinguished by means of physical criteria. Cross-breeding was taboo on account of degeneration. They saw peoples and races fighting each other in a battle for survival. Some of them wanted to intervene in an active way and promote the so-called stronger races, based on natural selection.

Gobineau, Darwin and the Social Darwinists produced theories which served as the 'scientific' foundation for the racial superiority of the white race. Anti-Semites drew on elements from this philosophy to attack Jewish people. In the last quarter of the nineteenth century, they developed racial anti-Semitism, where heredity was the norm. The classic anti-Semitic writers and thinkers, such as Eugen Dühring (1881), Theodor Fritsch (1892) and Adolf Wahrmund (1887), published works in which the noble Aryan was viewed as the opposite of the wicked Jew, whose behaviour sprouted from immutable racial characteristics. In actual fact, this means nothing other than whatever a Jew does, it stems from his biology. In this we can see the same as Gobineau's argument, which is (now in modern terms to aid clarity): Jewish genes, DNA and chromosomes ensure that they are only able to do wicked things and never good. Later, Hitler would repeat this in his own jargon: he stressed again and again that 'the blood' of the Jew determined his 'wicked' behaviour. Here we encounter the crux of modern anti-Semitism, which encapsulates a fatal thought: due to the undermining tendencies of the Jews, which cannot be changed, and which will always exist because of heredity tendencies, Jews should really disappear. In other words: they should die. Here we see an essential difference to the much older, anti-Judaic sentiments, which rejected Jewish people because of their religion. If a Jew converted to Christianity, he was simply included in the Christian community.

In the 1870s, the term 'anti-Semitism' was used for the first time by the journalist Wilhelm Marr during his anti-Jewish campaign, in which he turned against Jewish emancipation, precisely at the time when many had lost their jobs and possessions following the economic crisis of 1873. Incidentally, Marr had also lost his job and he claimed that this was a result of Jewish actions.

The anti-Semitism of the composer Richard Wagner was authoritative for a modern art-loving elite. Wagner's own anti-Semitism had been strengthened by Gobineau's doctrine and he became friends with the French racist. He supported Gobineau financially and made his work popular in Germany. For him, the Jews were the personification of all evil, filth and wickedness. They had no inner life, were lacking in creativity and only lusted after money. In his operas, performed on an annual basis in Bayreuth from 1876, Wagner expressed a racial German ideal. In a mythical battle, the Aryans resisted the temptations of the flesh, paid for their intense joy or ignored worldly desires. This was the Aryan route to salvation. Wagner defined that which was important for the German people, namely the preservation of the purity of their blood and spirit and thus their creative powers. Although no Jews featured in his operas, anti-Semitic interpretations were obvious. The Jewish mentality had to be destroyed. After his death in 1883, Bayreuth remained an influential centre of racism and anti-Semitism. Wagner's wife Cosima introduced Houston Stewart Chamberlain to the Bayreuth circle. This thinker provided the philosophical underpinning of Wagner's ideas in *The Foundations of the Nineteenth Century* (1899).[7]

The Germans, according to Chamberlain, formed a unity through their common blood. Not all Germans looked like real Aryans, however, although they did all share the German *Rassenseele*: their noble mental condition. They were honest, faithful and diligent. The arch-enemy of the German noble spirit were the Jews. They were characterised by a materialistic, non-creative attitude. According to Chamberlain, the Germans had already been infected by Jewish blood and if this cross-breeding were to continue, 'there would be only one people of pure race left in Europe, that of the Jews, all the rest would be a herd or pseudo-Hebrew mestizos, a people beyond all doubt degenerate physically, mentally and morally'.[8] Then the Jews would achieve their desired world dominion. On the other hand, if the Germans conquered the Jews, this would lead to a revolution of the mind. The Aryan *Rassenseele* would then control the world and a new high culture would emerge. Great creators, such as Shakespeare, Michelangelo and Beethoven, would return and determine the future of the race. The new high culture would save the Germans. Chamberlain's book became a kind of bible for German racists.[9]

The concept of (Jewish) 'world domination' has already been mentioned twice in this chapter. Anti-Semites considered the social successes of the

Jews a danger to themselves. In response to the financial prosperity of the Jews – especially in response to the power of the Rothschilds' banking empire – stories also began to circulate that the Jews had been aiming at world domination. This claim returned again and again. In 1868, the hack writer Hermann Gödsche described in his novel *Biarritz* how thirteen Jewish elders gathered in a Prague cemetery. These representatives of the Jewish people proclaimed their successful ventures of the past century, gathered around a tombstone. If their grandchildren fulfilled their duties, a century later they would meet at the same cemetery and then 'they will be able to announce at that graveside that indeed they have become princes of the world and that other nations are their slaves'.[10] This Prague cemetery passage was one of the key building blocks of *The Protocols of the Elders of Zion* – describing a Jewish plan for global domination – which would, immediately after the end of the First World War – then having grown into a complete story – begin its advance in Germany.

After the economic crisis of 1873, anti-Semitism increased in Germany, reaching its provisional peak with 2.9 per cent of the votes for anti-Semitic parties in the *Reichstag* elections in 1893. After that, anti-Semitism diminished and only remained alive in a series of sectarian *Verbände*. In these circles, the word 'national' was Germanised into *völkisch*. Characteristic of members of these *völkische Verbände* was that they expressed anti-Semitic nationalism, which already showed a tendency towards destruction of the Jews and which gave the German people a special destination. Politicians who combined such radical anti-Semitism with nationalism were still exceptional.[11]

One of the first of such politicians was the Austrian Georg Ritter von Schönerer. Perhaps it is no coincidence that such a politician appeared in Austria first, as there were strong animosities and political struggles between the different nationalities in that country.[12] After gaining legal equality in 1867, Jewish people moved to the capital of Vienna in large numbers. Compared with cities in Germany, Vienna housed many more Jews. More than 50 per cent of the banks were owned by Jewish people.[13] Schönerer saw evil power in the Jews who were trying to counteract the German people. In the 1880s, he demanded a strict biological separation between Germans and Jews (no mixed marriages) to preserve blood purity. He compared Jews to tape worms and vampires who sucked the vitality out of the German people, and in 1888 he proclaimed that 'every German had the duty . . . to eradicate Jewry'.[14] Vienna became the most anti-Semitic capital of Europe.

The popular Austrian politician Karl Lueger was also a fierce anti-Semite. He was the leader of the Catholic, Christian Social Party and had been mayor of Vienna since May 1897. Unlike Schönerer, Lueger considered the Jews to be a non-race. For him, the Jews represented liberalism, capitalism and social democracy. Lueger won over both the Roman Catholics with this argument, who had labelled these movements as evil, as well as the lower middle class, because they felt threatened by the huge working class and the upper (Jewish) middle class above them. The eloquent Lueger took advantage of his voters' anti-Semitic sentiments and fears. Jews were guilty of everything. According to Lueger, they threatened the fatherland through revolutions and they were predators in human form. They belonged to the people who had killed God and who committed ritual murders of children. One of Lueger's most beloved helpers was Father Heinrich Abel. This Jesuit proclaimed that all evil came from the Jewish freemasonry. Liberalism and democracy had been founded by Satan. The wicked Jews had secretly been forming a world government. Another loyal servant of Lueger was the prelate Joseph Scheicher. According to Scheicher, the Jewish people had been ranting and raving in Austria. They had spread syphilis and committed sexual offences to try to undermine the German people. Thousands of girls had already landed in the brothels of big foreign cities because of their doing. The Jews had to disappear. If Vienna were finally to be free from Jews, the witches' sabbath of parliamentarism would also soon be over.[15]

Hitler lived in the strongly anti-Semitic Vienna from 1908 to 1913. He honoured Schönerer and Lueger. However, in *Mein Kampf*, he called Lueger's anti-Semitism a fake anti-Semitism, because it was not based on racial principles.[16] It is a fact that Adolf Hitler learned a great deal about anti-Semitism during his Viennese period. It seems obvious that he had already become a Jew hater by then. Yet, for the time being, this still remains a question that needs a well-motivated answer. We shall see.

In Germany, the disaster of the war, the defeat and the revolution of November 1918 promptly boosted anti-Semitism again. The *völkisch* Germans gained influence. New accusations were added to the list of age-old accusations of Jewish wrong-doings.

During the war, many *Ostjuden*, who looked very different from the Western assimilated Jews, fled to Germany. Due to their different appearance, the racial cliché (that Jews belong to another race) gained power of persuasion. The middle class in particular, which already felt threatened in its existence by the war, fell into the grip of fear of being dominated by strangers.[17]

In 1916, the Ministry of War even started official statistical research into the extent to which Jews would shun the front. The statistics have never been published. The truth was that, proportionately, the number of Germans and Jews fighting at the front was equal. Nevertheless, one heard this refrain everywhere: the Jew's face (*'Gesicht'*) grins everywhere but not (*'nicht'*) in the trenches.[18]

In 1917, the Social Democrats formed a majority in the *Reichstag*, which sought to end the war by negotiation. The Reich Chancellor Bethmann Hollweg was inclined to fulfill that wish. The military leadership and the conservatives were unwaveringly opposed. They were striving for overall victory. The right-wing opposition considered Bethmann Hollweg 'the Chancellor of the Jews', who sent 'the German people to the Jewish-democratic abyss'.[19]

After the fall of Bethmann Hollweg and the peace resolution of July 1917, which was called a Jewish resolution, anti-Semitism radicalised even more. In particular, the *Alldeutscher Verbänd*, a powerful *völkisch* pressure group, and the new *Vaterlandspartei*, founded in 1917, contributed to this. Jews were negatively linked to democracy once again. More accusations followed. Jews would enrich themselves from the war disproportionately and they would have secret connections with the enemy through their international financial network.[20]

Anti-Semitism took on even more evil forms through defeat and revolution. Heinrich Claβ, the leader of the *Alldeutscher Verbänd*, cried out: 'Kill them, the Day of Judgment does not ask for your reasons.'[21]

The capitulation in November 1918 would be deliberately brought about by the Social Democrats. The brave and struggling German army, which had not been defeated by any means, was brought down by a dagger in the back (the stab-in-the-back myth). General Ludendorff and General Field Marshal Hindenburg, who wanted to put the blame for their own military failure onto the Social Democrats, encouraged this legend. Accusations that the Social Democrats were Jews or that the Jews inspired them, increased. *Völkisch* Germans saw this interpretation in a wider context. Everywhere in Europe and Russia, the Jews were trying to unleash revolution through the Socialist and Communist parties in order to establish their power. Once again, it was discovered that the Jews were aiming for global domination.[22]

Shortly after the defeat, the nineteenth-century racist classics by Arthur de Gobineau, Eugen Dühring, Adolf Wahrmund, Theodor Fritsch and Houston Chamberlain were re-published in Munich by German *völkisch* publishers. A flood of anti-Semitic extracts, reviews and articles were also published. In 1919, there was a rich anti-Semitic tradition in Bavaria which influenced Adolf Hitler greatly. Adolf Hitler was not lacking in subject material to shout out his hatred of Jews.

Chapter 4

The Causes of Paranoia: The Proximate Level of Explanation

L et us now look into the proximate causes of paranoia. A problem is that little research was devoted to paranoia until 2000. Although the different editions of *The Diagnostic and Statistical Manuel of Mental Disorders* (1980–2013) define the *Paranoid personality disorder*, it only sums up its symptoms, whereas no underlying pathological psychology is mentioned. The reason for this is very simple: it is unknown or there is much uncertainty about the causes. The same applies to the delusional order with its subtype 'persecutory type': no definite causes are mentioned; they are not known either.

However, from 2000 onwards, Daniel Freeman and his research group have done innovative research into paranoia and persecutory delusions. It has been difficult to get a grip on the causes of paranoia, but progress has been made.

Daniel Freeman works at Oxford University and the Oxford Health NHS Foundation Trust. He does not use the term 'paranoia' for a simple psychiatric disorder, especially for the delusional type, instead he sees paranoia on a spectrum from mild to severe which manifests itself in the general population. So, within the population many people have a few paranoid thoughts; a few people have many. Such paranoid thinking arises mainly from normal cognitive processes.[1]

This is astonishing, as psychologists and psychiatrists have always agreed that paranoia is limited to people with serious mental disorders. It turns out this is not the case.[2]

Freeman and his staff make use of a variety of approaches, including epidemiological studies, psychological experiments, clinical trials, and a revolutionary virtual reality laboratory.[3] The virtual laboratory is a very successful invention. You can see how nicely it works and how fine-tuned it is on You-Tube. In Freeman's study *Paranoia the 21st-Century Fear* (Oxford, 2008), co-written with his brother Jason, he sums up the situations in which people may become susceptible to paranoia. In fact, this is the first time that the 'causes' of paranoia have been brought so clearly into view. Daniel Freeman and his group are known as the world's foremost scientists in the field of paranoia. In 2016, in an article in *The Lancet*, he not only repeats what he said before but also gives additional information, as he also does in his book, co-authored with Jason Freeman and Philippa Garety, *Overcoming paranoid and suspicious thoughts* (2nd edn, Oxford, 2016). There is no question of only one or two causes, instead a whole complex of factors plays its part. Even though these authors are not Hitler researchers, I am still quoting their findings. Causes of paranoia may indeed be generalised. What you see in brackets here are not quotations, but explanatory notes derived from their texts.

- The most common emotional trigger for feelings of paranoia is anxiety. . . . Anxiety is the one that seems to be most closely linked to the development of suspicious thoughts. . . . Our suspicious thoughts are simply an extension of our anxieties.
- The second major emotional trigger for paranoia is low mood. . . . For instance – feeling miserable, sad or depressed.
- [Feeling] inferior to other people . . . can lead to suspicious thoughts. Negative views of ourselves may [lead to the feeling] we're at risk [a paranoid thought].
- Worry brings implausible fearful ideas to mind. . . . Worry is a pre-dictor of paranoid thinking.
- People who respond in a paranoid way have negative feelings about themselves and others. Paranoia feeds on vulnerability. Negative self-beliefs are prevalent in paranoia.
- When we are [angry] suspicious thoughts are more likely to pop into our heads.
- Paranoia feeds on uncertainty and ambiguity.
- People who experience trauma are at greater risk . . . of paranoia. [Especially because of major life changes and events such as losing your parents, your job, experiencing a divorce.]
- The rise of distrust . . . is directly related to growing inequalities of wealth. The poorer you are, the less trusting you're likely to be and . . . the more prone to paranoia.

- An increasingly, urbanised people is likely to be an increasingly paranoid one . . . Cities are places where millions of people are lonesome together . . . Greater levels . . . of paranoia seem likely to follow as a result.
- People living alone and having less contact with friends and family are more likely to suffer from paranoia.
- [Feeling] we are special. . . . When we don't receive the recognition, we feel we deserve, we may conclude . . . that they're deliberately out to undermine us.[4]

In the following chapter, we will give a biographical sketch of Adolf Hitler from his birth in 1889 up to August 1914, when the First World War broke out. We will make use of knowledge of the circumstances, and facts which have just been quoted, which promote paranoia. We will look into the extent to which they may have played a role during Adolf Hitler's first twenty-five years. We will not, however, narrow our view by only looking at these circumstances. This sketch is intended to provide as much insight as possible into Hitler's personality and the environments in which he developed.

Chapter 5

Adolf Hitler, 1889–1914

Hitler's father was born the illegitimate child of Anna Schicklgruber in the hamlet of Strones near to the village of Döllersheim in 1837. This lay in the agrarian area of Waldviertel in Lower Austria: it was meagre, hard and rugged farming country. Initially he was known as Alois Schicklgruber, as it was unclear who his father was. This uncertainty has led to numerous speculations, particularly that Adolf Hitler had Jewish blood flowing in his veins. Hans Frank, Hitler's later governor in eastern Poland, made a major contribution to this idea during the Nuremberg trials. In *Im Angesicht des Galgens*, which he wrote at that time, he claimed that Hitler had had a Jewish grandfather. Frank's fable is still believed. Good research has, however, proved that this is completely untrue.[1] Such rumours had been circulating before Frank's publication as well. There are no indications that the politician Adolf Hitler was ever troubled by these allegations.

So, Alois Schicklgruber came from a farming background, but given the circumstances in which he was born, he carved out an impressive career for himself. He moved to Vienna and first became a shoemaker. In 1855, he entered the civil service, when he started working for the Austrian Royal Customs Office. He achieved one promotion after another. In 1876, in Braunau, he was promoted to inspector of customs. Finally, he held the highest post, which was open to him, given his education (he had only completed primary education), which was full inspector of customs. He had every reason to be proud. On the few photos which exist of him, he is portrayed as arrogant, authoritarian and rather reserved. He also had a walrus moustache of impressive proportions. He usually wore a black jacket, the uniform buttons of which shone as if they had just been polished, and his trousers were a spotless white. He was not exactly liked as a boss. One colleague from Braunau described him as unusually dislikeable.[2]

In 1876, a remarkable incident took place. Alois's step-uncle, Johann Nepomuk Hiedler, made a declaration in front of a solicitor and three other witnesses that Alois Schicklgruber was the son of his deceased brother, Johann Georg Hiedler. Johann Nepomuk probably did this to ensure that Alois would become his heir. The solicitor accepted the declaration and, a few days later, the priest in Döllersheim excised the name 'Schicklgruber' from the baptism registry replacing it not with 'Hiedler', but with 'Hitler'.[3] Thereafter he answered to the name Alois Hitler. Later, Adolf Hitler was more than satisfied by his father's 'decision'. He thought the name 'Schicklgruber' was incredibly boorish and would have restricted his political career. Indeed, 'Heil Schicklgruber' would have sounded pretty disastrous, if it had ever been called out at all!

Alois Hitler was to marry three times. His second wife, whom he married in 1883, was Franziska Matzelsberger, called 'Fanni'. She gave birth to Alois junior and Angela. When Fanni became sick and it turned out to be tuberculosis, Alois Hitler's cousin, Klara Pölz, came to help with the housekeeping. She later became Adolf Hitler's mother. Klara was twenty-three years younger than Alois and she called Alois 'Uncle'. Alois soon made her pregnant. He was not very concerned with this matter, as his wife Franziska was wasting away and would soon pass away. After Franziska's death, Alois wanted to marry Klara immediately – she was only 23 years old. Alois had to go to a lot of trouble to do so, because the Church initially refused to give its permission, because of their close family ties. Following a lot of bureaucracy, he finally obtained dispensation and married her, early one morning in 1886, at 6 am. Immediately after the ceremony, he returned to work. Klara soon gave birth to Gustav. This son died in 1887.[4]

Klara Pölz was born in the country village of Spital in 1860. This was only 35km from Döllersheim, where her husband Alois was born. Her parents were smallholders. She was a kind, gentle and submissive woman, the very opposite of her strict husband and later rebellious son, Adolf. Once married, she continued to address her husband as 'Uncle', which probably demonstrates her submissiveness and reserve towards him.

On 20 April 1889, at 6.30 in the evening, Adolf Hitler was born in the 'Gasthof zum Pommer' on 219 Salzburger Vorstadt in Braunau. It was a cold, cloudy Easter Saturday. By that time, his mother was 28 and his father was 51. Braunau was an Austrian town on the River Inn, which formed the border between Austria and Bavaria. From the very first page of *Mein Kampf*, Hitler uses this position to make a political prophecy:

fate had determined that he was born on the border of two states, which needed to be united.[5]

When Adolf was 3 years old, the Hitler family moved to Passau, which was on the German side of the border. Here he gained his typically Bavarian accent, which he would later retain. This accent was not without significance. Later, when he became a politician and agitator, the Bavarian lilt sounded charming and special to German ears. This forms one small aspect of the explanation for how he could become such an accomplished demagogue.[6]

In 1895, when his 58-year-old father Alois retired, the family moved back to Austria to the small town of Fischlhamm. The 6-year-old Adolf attended the tiny village school, which consisted of only one class. Hitler later claimed that he absorbed all the lessons that were meant for older students and so gave the impression he was precocious.

In 1897, the family moved again, this time to the little village of Lambach. Here, the 8-year-old sang in the boys' choir in the Benedictine monastery, where he gazed in wonder at the ostentatious richness of the church. He thought the church so beautiful that the young Adolf, as he later said, wanted to become a monk.[7] Later, despite his criticism of it, he praised the Church for 'magnificently exploiting the natural need of people for something supernatural. The church has understood how its mystical cults consisting of sacred music, incense and solemn rites can make an impression on people.'[8]

In 1898, the restless Alois once again decided to move. Now, the family settled in the village of Leonding, south of Linz. Their house was next to the graveyard. Adolf got up to mischievous tricks. His favourite sport was shooting with a gun. He targeted the rats that scuttled round the graveyard.[9] Even better was playing soldiers with his friends. At that time, the imperialist English were in Africa, at war with the Boers, who were fighting for their freedom. Reports appeared in the newspapers about this and Adolf followed them closely. He was the so-called leader of a group of rascals from the adjacent area, who represented the African Boers. Boys from a hamlet further away were the Brits. There was some hard fighting between them – he loved this: it was his favourite game. He didn't know how to stop: 'Playing soldiers, always playing soldiers.'[10] At night in bed and with bated breath, he read Karl May's books by candlelight or using a magnifying glass in the moonlight.[11] Even later on, particularly during the Second World War when things were proving difficult for Germany, he reread Karl May's books and went as far as to present the red-skinned Winnetou to his followers as 'the ideal example of a Kompagnieführer' (company commander).[12]

School was very little effort for the young Hitler. Learning, as he wrote in *Mein Kampf*, was ridiculously easy. That meant that he had so much free time that 'the sun saw him more often than his room did'.[13] He did in fact get very good results: he got the highest grade for every subject.[14]

In 1900, the Hitler family consisted of Alois and Klara and their two children, Adolf and Paula. Three other children had died before Adolf's birth: Gustav, Ida and Otto. Only Adolf and Paula, born in 1896, survived. Their half-sister Angela, born in 1883, was also part of the family. Angela's brother, Alois junior, Adolf's half-brother, was born into the same marriage. He had already left the parental home in 1895 at the age of 14 due to a big argument with his father. Klara Hitler's younger sister, Johanna, also lived with the family. She was probably retarded and was a hunchback. She loved Adolf, helped with the housekeeping and was a great support for Klara.

Klara Hitler had already lost three children before Adolf's birth and in 1900, her fourth child, Edmund, contracted measles at nearly 6 years old, from which he died in the same year. There has been speculation about the effect of losing all these children on Klara's attitude to the young Adolf. Was she still able to be warm and close to him after all these painful deaths? Or did she remain cool and distant to protect herself from the next loss? The well-known psychoanalyst Erich Fromm speaks of a cold relationship between the pair. He couldn't have been more wrong. All the sources suggest that Klara was a loving mother to Adolf and that Hitler loved his mother tremendously right up until her death. In fact, the term 'loving' isn't sufficient to describe their relationship, Adolf was greatly spoilt by his mother. He was her favourite and she gave him everything he wanted. Young Adolf, more than other children around him, must have felt that he was the special centre of the universe and it seems plausible that his relationship with his mother explains his later narcissistic personality, just as it does his tendency to focus on his own interests whatever the effect on others. You might also be able to conclude, from all his mother's attention, that this was also the reason why he never felt like making a great effort, he always thought he was right and tended to greatly overestimate his abilities.[15]

Alois Hitler demanded unconditional obedience from his son. If he didn't listen, he would beat him.[16] If he needed him and couldn't see him, he would stick two fingers into his mouth and whistle sharply, like he was calling a dog.[17] He wanted his son to become a civil servant, like himself. This was the last thing that Adolf wanted. If we are to believe Hitler in *Mein Kampf*, when he told his father that he wanted to become an artist, his father said, 'Artist, no, not for as long as I live, never!' In 1900, his father sent him to the Linzer Realschule; this was an education which was, indeed, a good preparation for his career as a civil servant. The young Hitler had to walk: an hour there and an hour back.

Klara was scared that her son would be beaten by his father. Adolf loved her. In his memoirs, the Jewish physician, Dr Eduard Bloch, wrote that Adolf's love for his mother was striking: 'Although he wasn't a mother's boy in the usual sense of the word, I have never seen a closer affection.' Their affection was mutual. Bloch: 'Klara worshipped her son . . . Whenever possible, he was allowed to do whatever he liked.'[18] This is confirmation of what we have already seen. August Kubizek (his childhood friend) also mentioned that Adolf loved his mother deeply. Hitler always carried an image of her with him.[19] In *Mein Kampf*, Hitler wrote that he respected his father, but loved his mother.[20] Later, Adolf's guardian, Josef Mayrhofer, said of his father: 'he was strict at home, rough, he gave his wife no reason to smile'.[21]

At that time, Linz was the most 'German' city in the multinational Austro-Hungarian Empire. Linz was almost exclusively inhabited by Germans. Less than 1 per cent of the population was Jewish and well-assimilated. German-national associations were well-supported financially by the municipality of Linz.[22] Almost all the Germans in Linz saw themselves as German nationals: They wanted to maintain the leading German role in the Habsburgian multinational state or win it back. The followers of the radical nationalist and anti-Semite Georg Ritter von Schönerer, however, took it much further: they wanted to separate the German areas from the Austro-Hungarian Empire and add them to the Hohenzollern Empire. (The Hohenzollerns had been Germany's imperial family since 1871.) The faithful followers of the Habsburgs considered Schönerer's supporters to be downright traitors. This political difference also prevailed at the secondary school that Hitler attended. Incidentally, there was scarcely any hatred of Jews in Linz, the enmity was primarily aimed at the Czechs, who were increasingly settling in the town.[23]

Most of the teachers at Adolf Hitler's secondary school were German nationals, but loyal to the Habsburgian emperor. Many pupils, however, including Adolf Hitler, supported Schönerer and therefore disapproved of the multinational state. During religious instruction, Hitler later tells with pride, he got into trouble because he had shown his sympathies for the Hohenzollerns by classifying his pencils into the Great-German colours (black, red and gold).[24] In 1924, his French teacher Huemer definitely remembered Hitler as being gifted, albeit not in every subject, also as recalcitrant and quick-tempered, and always determined to be right. He was lazy too, otherwise he would have been able to obtain much better marks, thanks to his unmistakable talents. According to Huemer, Hitler was also a gifted draftsman.[25] Hitler's performance at secondary school was indeed poor. He had to repeat his first school year in 1900. Later Hitler wrote that he had performed badly on purpose to protest against his father, who was blocking his path towards becoming an artist.[26] This was one of Hitler's many lies.

His test of strength against his father came to an abrupt end in the early morning of 3 January 1903, when his father collapsed after his first sip of wine in his favourite pub, Wiesinger, and died of pulmonary bleeding. The death of his tyrannical father probably came as a relief to the 13-year-old Adolf Hitler.

If the young Hitler had indeed been protesting against his father through bad school results, then these should have improved after his death. This didn't happen. In 1904, his scholarly performance was once again poor. The school allowed him to go up a year on the agreement that he would attend a different school. Now he was placed in a *Realschule* in Steyr, 40km away, where Hitler went to lodge with a strange family. He hated Steyr, hated the teachers and missed his mother terribly. Once again, he had to repeat the year. The beloved son managed to convince his mother to take him back in due to an illness, which he had in all probability greatly exaggerated. In the meantime, Klara had sold the house in Leonding and moved into a simple home in Linz. When Hitler's school career came to an end in 1905, he thus returned to Linz. His record showed five years of secondary education, twice repeating a school year, and zero qualifications.

Now Hitler was in charge of his own time. Later he would often say how important this was for him. He had never wanted to learn for a normal bourgeois profession, possibly because no one had made him stick to any rules since his father died and he had left school early. For the next two years, he did what he felt like: drawing, reading, painting, writing poetry and designing buildings for Linz. He also took piano lessons for three months. In the evenings he went to concerts or the opera. He continued to dream of becoming a great artist. He always went to bed late and always slept in. He despised, he remarked, having to work for a living.[27] His mother let the lazybones get on with it.

At that time, the young Hitler came across the musical and gifted pianist August Kubizek in the Linz opera, who was working as an upholsterer for his father's upholstery firm. After Hitler and Kubizek had met a few times at the opera, they talked some more but Hitler didn't think it necessary to talk about himself. After a while though, they became friends. Even when they knew each other better, Kubizek knew not to ask 'inappropriate' questions (if Hitler had a job, for example). According to Kubizek, Hitler had an inner domain, which no one was permitted to enter. A few wrong words lead to an enormous torrent of anger. He didn't have much of a sense of humour, but he could poke fun at others.[28]

Hitler always looked neat and clean; his clothes were incredibly smart. He wore a suit with impeccably ironed seams, a pristine white shirt and shiny, black dress gloves. One curious item was his black, ebony walking stick, the handle of which was shaped like an elegant, ivory shoe. He often wore a dark hat as well. He looked almost distinguished. His choice of language was extremely cultivated. His eyes, however, received the most attention: clear, blue eyes, according to Kubizek, which dominated his countenance.[29]

Hitler loved Wagner – a passion that he shared with Kubizek. The two friends discussed the composer at length. Hitler talked even more about architecture and the visual arts. He had a deep-rooted urge to change the status quo. The urban development plans that he had developed for Linz entailed a complete reconstruction. He believed that these would come to fruition. This won't be the only time that we see Hitler inhabiting a fantasy world rather than reality.

In 1905, Hitler fell in love with Stefanie, a young woman who went for walks in the Land Straße in Linz with her mother and who was two years older than he was. Her last name was Isak. If he relied on her last name, then he must have believed she was Jewish.[30] He revealed his fantasies to Kubizek about Stefanie as his future wife. She never knew that the young Hitler was in love with her, but when talking to Kubizek, he claimed that Stefanie did know because of her intuition and that she longed for him as strongly as he did for her. Actually, she was waiting until he came to ask her for her hand in marriage. He even designed a house for them in the Renaissance style.[31] However, he kept admiring her from a distance and didn't dare to vacate the safety of his fantasy world. Kubizek called him 'remarkably timid' as regards Stefanie.[32] When Hitler left for Vienna in 1908, he wrote her an anonymous letter. He went to the Academy of Arts and asked her to wait for him. As soon as he returned, he would marry her.[33] Five years later, in 1913, when he was in Munich, he inserted an advertisement in the *Linzer Zeitung* at Christmas in which he wished her good luck – again anonymously.[34] Here we see a fearful young Hitler, who does not have the courage to go to his loved one, but who remains at a distance. In the aforementioned list in the previous chapter, we read that feeling inferior to other people can lead to suspicious thoughts. Anxiety also seems to be most closely linked to the development of suspicious thoughts. Feeling inferior (due to his low social status) and anxiety seemed to have played a role with Hitler in this case. It should be clear that both feelings can be triggers for paranoia.

In 1906, the 17-year-old Hitler went to Vienna for the first time. He wanted to view the paintings in the Hofmuseum and the stately Viennese buildings. The architecture on the Ring Straße in particular stirred great excitement in him and he visited the city theatre and the opera, where he saw *Tristan* and *The Flying Dutchman*, both staged by the Jewish Gustav Mahler.[35] A year later, in September 1907, he returned to Vienna, this time to do an entrance examination for the Academy of Fine Arts. He rented a miserable room on 31 Stumper Gasse from the Czech seamstress Maria Zakreys. In the weeks before his entrance examination, he took some private drawing and painting lessons from the artist Rudolf Panholzer.[36]

The examination took place in October in the Academy building on Schiller Platz. Hitler arrived armed with a thick pile of drawings. He expected to sail through the examination. He did indeed make it to the second round, but there he floundered. His rejection was motivated by the assessment committee. Hitler hadn't drawn any people: 'Not enough heads'. Indeed, there were never any people in Hitler's drawings or paintings. There were only monumental buildings and far away in the distance a tiny mark, which may have represented a human being. These were soulless spaces. He apparently had no interest in people.

In *Mein Kampf*, he wrote that he was so convinced that he would be successful that his rejection hit him like a thunderbolt, and he left the magnificent building on the Schiller Platz deflated. The rector did tell him that his talent clearly lay in the area of architecture.[37] The rejection was a major blow to him: it was the last thing that he had expected, as we have seen. He must have suffered severe mental anguish. On our list we can read: people who experience trauma are at greater risk of paranoia. This is particularly so, if several traumas are experienced in life, which is definitely true in Hitler's case. The future had many more shocking experiences in store for him.

For the time being, he would tell no one that he had been rejected. Naturally, there has been a great deal of speculation about what would have happened if he had been accepted. Presumably, the entire twentieth century would have taken a different turn. Sometimes the flow of history depends on the tiniest of details.

After this humiliation, Hitler quickly returned to Linz, as his mother was seriously ill. Klara Hitler had been operated on at the start of the year for breast cancer. In the meantime, her condition had worsened dramatically. The Jewish physician Bloch treated her with morphine and iodoform. The 18-year-old Hitler took care of her for two months with great devotion. On 21 December 1907, she died. The young Hitler grieved deeply for her. He had lost the only person for whom he had ever felt real love. Dr Bloch still remembered the young son: 'During my 40 years as a physician, I have never seen a young man, so grief-stricken and full of suffering, as the young Adolf Hitler, the way he [. . .] approached me, to thank me for my professional care as physician, with teary eyes and a shaky voice'.[38]

There is no doubt that his mother's illness and death was a traumatic Major Life Event for the young Hitler, which, as we have read in the previous chapter, may have led to him becoming prone to paranoia, as he was also rejected by the Academy in the same period. However, for the actual development of pernicious distrust, he would have to experience even more severely negative experiences.

Hitler liked the Jewish physician Bloch. He made him a painting and later, when he was in Vienna, he sent him friendly postcards. In 1938, after the annexation of Austria, he asked after his former Jewish physician, 'Tell me, is good old Bloch still alive?'[39] He had him immediately put under the protection of the Gestapo. He called Bloch a 'noble Jew' and in the following years, the doctor enjoyed a special status. In 1940, he emigrated to the US.[40]

After the death of Hitler's mother, Josef Mayrhofer, a farmer and former friend of his departed father, from the pub, became Adolf's guardian. Mayrhofer tried to encourage him to become a baker. The young man had no interest in that, whatsoever. Mr Presemayer, a neighbour of the Hitler family, a civil servant for the postal service by profession, also offered his help so that Hitler might be able to work at the postal service. He didn't want to do this either. He kept repeating that he wanted to become a great artist. The civil servant from the postal services remarked that Hitler 'didn't have the means or contacts required to do so'. But the young man replied that 'Makart and Rubens had also worked their way up from humble beginnings'.[41] He received a more encouraging response from a neighbour of the Hitler family, Magdalena Hanisch. Her friend, Johanna Motloch, knew professor Roller, who was well known in Vienna. The professor taught at the Academy of Arts and Crafts, was a set designer at the Royal Opera and worked with the composer Gustav Mahler. Magdalena Hanisch wanted to persuade the professor to do something for Hitler's artistic ambitions, via her friend Johanna Motloch. It worked, because Roller replied in an encouraging letter to Johanna.[42]

On 8 February 1908, his neighbour Hanisch let Hitler read the sympathetic letter from Professor Roller and showed him the accompanying postcard from her friend Johanna. The professor wrote that Hitler could visit him in his office in the opera building. He should bring some of his work with him, so that the professor could assess his artistic abilities. If the professor didn't happen to be there, the young man shouldn't worry, but just return the following day.[43]

Hitler read the letter word for word, as if he were trying to remember it for ever. His face lit up with happiness. After he had read the letter, he put it down with heartfelt thanks, according to Magdalena Hanisch. The young Hitler asked her if he might write to her friend Johanna. She agreed.[44]

In Vienna, he indeed went straight to the opera house with Roller's letter in his pocket. When he approached the building, 'he lost courage and turned back. After an inner battle, he overcame his shyness and went to the opera for the second time, now he made into the stairwell – but no further. A third attempt failed as well.' Then someone asked him what he was doing there, which made him feel even less comfortable. 'Hitler came up with an excuse and went out again. To get rid of this constant tension he destroyed the letter.'[45]

He left the chance that Professor Roller would discover him as an artist unused. He did not make use of the opportunity to be admitted at the Academy of Arts – his greatest wish – through the intercession of Roller either, despite the great trouble that had been gone to, to create this opportunity. Apparently, a negative self-image had a more powerful effect than the courage to take an actual, decisive step towards his greatest desire. Above it has been made clear, people with low self-esteem and feelings of inferiority can become susceptible to paranoia. We can see a repeat here of Hitler's behaviour towards Stefanie, albeit in a different form. In both cases, he apparently felt too inferior and too anxious to approach those involved.

Hitler moved into his room in Vienna on the Stumper Gasse again. He didn't remain alone for long. In February 1908, his friend Kubizek arrived to study music at the conservatoire. Hitler had earlier persuaded Kubizek's father to allow his son to study at the conservatoire in Vienna. The father didn't like this idea very much, because his son was supposed to take over his upholstery business. The fact that Hitler managed to persuade Kubizek's father to allow his son to go to Vienna was an impressive example of his ability to convince others.[46]

Hitler and his friend lived in one room. This was once again the result of Hitler's manipulations. He had persuaded Maria Zakreys to turn over her own large living room to both young men. She herself would live in one small room.[47] We will see many more examples of his ability to manipulate others later in political contexts. We have seen that Hitler was very reserved towards authority figures such as Professor Roller, but he behaved differently towards his friend. He treated him in a stubborn, dominant way, demonstrating his strong will. Kubizek wrote that Hitler controlled his time completely and arbitrarily. He wouldn't tolerate any contradictions. He demanded one thing only: acquiescence. If Kubizek did or said anything 'wrong', Hitler would ignite with fury. Hitler could be coarse to others as well, if he felt he was their superior.[48]

One day Kubizek had a visitor in their shared room on the Stumper Gasse. It was a girl from a good family. She was one of the young ladies to whom he was allowed to give lessons, due to the advocacy of the director of the conservatoire. He usually went to her house, but this time she had come to him to ask him something about the theory of harmony. Kubizek introduced his pupil to his friend, who said nothing. The young lady had barely left when Hitler started lecturing his friend. 'Was their room supposed to become a rendezvous for this brood of musical females!' Hitler's words chastened Kubizek. Hitler angrily expounded on the fact that it made no sense to allow women to study. His message was clear: no visits from women. Incidentally, Kubizek wasn't allowed any other friends either.[49]

To the outside world, Hitler claimed, if it suited him, that he studied at the Academy of Arts. Kubizek knew that Hitler had been rejected, but he had not told his dying mother.

He had received an inheritance of about 1,000 crowns after his mother's death (his inheritance from his father had been blocked and was held by the bank; he was only to receive this on 20 April 1913). He also received an orphan's pension of 25 crowns, which was paid on the condition that he was studying, as he claimed to be doing, but wasn't. He was, in fact, committing fraud. Thanks to his inheritance and his orphan's pension, he could keep going without working in an expensive Vienna for no more than a year.[50] Despite this, Hitler stayed in bed when Kubizek left for the conservatoire in the early morning. He didn't consider getting a job. He was a great artist and needed to produce masterpieces. He said of the Academy that it was populated by 'stiff, narrow-minded civil servants, bureaucrats who knew nothing [about being an artist], stupid bureaucratic clods. The whole Academy should be blown up.' He also raged that the whole of humanity, the entire world had turned against him. He would succeed in spite of this through his own studies. When Kubizek doubted this and asked him if he was going to make it with books alone, Hitler reacted coarsely: 'I can see that you need teachers. They are of no need to me. You are a mental lodger, a parasite at another's table.'[51] As we can see, Hitler took out his frustrations and his vitriolic anger on Kubizek, the Academy and on the whole world. In our list we read: when we are angry, suspicious thoughts are likely to pop into our head. We all become angry and aggressive from time to time, but Kubizek tells of Hitler's innumerable furious attacks. For the later Hitler, too, there were few days which passed without him ranting or raving. If rage does indeed allow paranoid thoughts to develop easily, then there must have been many that emerged within him.

Just as in Linz, Hitler developed architectural plans for Vienna. Now he mainly focused on social housing. Again, he believed that his plans would be realised. He also wrote plays and operas or started doing so and he drew a great deal. He gave critiques for plays. He let Kubizek see some of his own designs. The staging was so grand and fantastic, however, that it would even have overshadowed their great master Richard Wagner. No stage manager could ever build these grotesque decorations. Despite this, Kubizek had an eye for Hitler's talents. He advised him to use them to earn some money. After all, Hitler was a poor devil. He could work as a theatre critic for a newspaper, or as a draftsman, or earn something illustrating books, or try to sell a 'modest' comedy. Hitler wasn't having any of it. He preferred to stay in his own safe fantasy world. He shied away from confronting reality.[52] Here we see, or so it would seem, behind the grand designs, which Kubizek and only Kubizek was allowed to see, lay Hitler's small, vulnerable ego and feelings of anxiety. As we have read in the previous chapter, these can be a good breeding ground for paranoia.

The two friends went to the opera almost every evening. They were continuing their habit from Linz. Hitler considered Wagner a genius. When he listened to his music, he fell into a trance. According to Kubizek, the restlessness disappeared from his eyes. Opera was his only luxury. The young Hitler didn't smoke, or drink and he didn't care for dancing. Kubizek said that young ladies clearly had eyes for him during the break at an opera performance, but he never reacted to their advances. He had no need for other friends. Apart from Kubizek he had no connection whatsoever with another human being, not even with his sister or brother-in-law in Linz anymore. He only occasionally shook hands with anyone. It even seemed, his friend said, that he was scared of physical contact with people.[53] Here again we see some characteristics which may be connected to developing excessive distrust: people who have less contact with friends and family are more likely to suffer from paranoia.

He didn't masturbate, possibly inspired by Schönerer's principles.[54] He strongly disapproved of prostitution.[55] He was probably scared of intimacy with women. Here, again, we encounter his fear.

For the young Hitler in Linz and Vienna, Richard Wagner meant more than just music or a heavenly experience. The historian Wolfram Pyta claims, on good grounds, that Wagner's opera were of great importance to Hitler's later political performance. Wagner sought a *Gesamtkunstwerk* (whole oeuvre), which combined music, the word and theatre, so that all the senses of the audience were stimulated, and they became enchanted and overwhelmed. Hitler had seen his operas innumerable times in Linz and Vienna. Pyta claims that Hitler scored better as a politician than his rivals after the First World War because he had received an education from the Linz and Viennese stage performances, which permitted him to give startling performances as a politician and agitator. In other words, he was able to make such effective use of the politician's podium, because he had absorbed Wagner's varied theatre techniques and so could conquer his public. He could go even further than that, he could enchant them. So, according to Pyta, Hitler was being educated as a politician during his time in Linz and Vienna, without even realising it.[56] It is a remarkable interpretation, which may be considered credible at the very least.

One evening in 1908, Hitler visited the rich, well-assimilated Jewish family Jahoda, along with his friend. The head of the family was Dr Rudolf Jahoda, director of a chemical plant. He was a great music lover and he was himself an excellent pianist. The entire Jahoda family – all the brothers, their wives and older children – came together regularly in the evenings to make music. Sometimes, music students were also invited to enlarge the repertoire. This is how the violinist and conservatoire student August Kubizek entered the Jahoda home. He was ardent about these musical nights and he asked the family if he could bring his friend sometime. The family agreed and Hitler went with his friend to visit the Jewish family. Dr Jahoda's library made a great impression on him. However, he behaved in a restrained way in this cultivated circle. The whole evening, he did not say anything. Though he knew a lot about Richard Wagner and talked incessantly about the composer to Kubizek, he had nothing to say in this company of true musical connoisseurs.[57] Hitler's self-esteem must have been very fragile. In the previous chapter, we read that this psychological state (especially feeling inferior to other people) can lead to people falling prone to suspicious thoughts.

After his exams August Kubizek returned to Linz. Hitler walked with him to the West station, waved him off and did not like being left behind. When Kubizek returned in November, after his holiday and a short period of military service with the reserves, Hitler was nowhere to be found in the Stumper Gasse. He had left no forwarding address, nor a message of any kind. Kubizek asked Hitler's family, but they also knew nothing.[58] They would not see each other again until 1938.

Presumably, Hitler had cut off contact so suddenly because he had been rejected by the Academy once again. Apparently, he didn't dare face his friend Kubizek, who was so successful at the conservatoire, now he had been rejected for the second time. This time, he didn't make it through the first round. Here, again, we see two experiences that are known to be possible triggers for paranoia: a traumatic event and a blow to his self-worth. Now that the door to his artistic career had been well and truly shut, this must have been an even more terrible blow to his self-esteem.

This is where his social decline began. In *Mein Kampf* he wrote that he started working as a temporary construction worker and mate at that time.[59] However, this has never been corroborated by any witness. In the summer of 1909, he moved into a shabby shelter in the Felber Strasse, near to the West station. Shortly afterwards he moved to 58 Sechshäuser Strasse. There was a newspaper and tobacco kiosk nearby, where he probably bought brochures, newspapers and magazines. He also probably read a lot in cafes. It is not known what he read. He soon moved out again, probably without paying the rent.[60] Hitler's inheritance from his mother, of approximately 1,000 crowns, had evaporated after eighteen months of lounging about and he wasn't able to live on an orphan's pension of 25 crowns. He became homeless, slept in parks and under bridges.[61] There is an eyewitness from that time, an acquaintance of Hitler's former landlady Maria Zakreys, who saw him in rags at the Merciful Sisters' soup kitchen in Gumpendörfer Strasse.[62] At that time, he was supposedly begging for a living. Hitler must have been seriously worried about his future. We have read on the list that worry brings implausible, fearful ideas to mind and that there is a close link between worry and paranoia. It is self-evident that Hitler must have been weighed down by worries; his future looked bleaker than ever before. He must have been in a low mood, feeling miserable and depressed. We have read that these feelings are the second major emotional trigger for paranoia.

By the end of 1909, he ended up in a homeless shelter in Meidling, a day care facility for paupers, vagabonds and alcoholics who had fallen on hard times. In this phase of Hitler's life, we see different circumstances and events that may promote paranoia: instead of studying at the Academy of Fine Arts, Hitler, the so-called artistic genius, drifted into a beggar's life in the big hostile city of Vienna. He had no friends and no longer had any contact with his family – he was a loner without any support in a metropolis, in which he, being penniless, must have experienced the stark contrast between poverty and wealth. The world must have seemed very threatening to him. This life in a Vienna, which offered him no safety, lasted five years; a period long enough to create a permanently suspicious mind.

In the homeless shelter, Hitler met another wanderer: Reinhold Hanisch (no relation to his neighbour Magdalena Hanisch). This was his neighbour in the dormitory. Hanisch was a dubious figure, he lived under the false name Fritz Walter and on application forms he kept giving different professions, dates and places of birth. Hanisch stated that Hitler looked sad, exhausted and starved. He had spent numerous nights outside, often being disturbed by policemen in his sleep. His feet had open wounds from walking. His clothes had taken on a lilac colour from all the rain and disinfectant. He had no overcoat and if he was outside, he would be trembling from the cold. He got a piece of bread from some of his mates and an old beggar tipped him off about where he could get free soup during the day. He took this advice to heart and went there every day.[63]

These impoverished circumstances must have been horrific for Hitler, not least because he was so fastidious about cleanliness and loved to show off his beautiful clothes.

Hitler and Hanisch went looking for temporary work together. Thanks to the early snow fall, they were able to shovel snow. They had to get up early and hurry to be at the place of work first, otherwise all of the work would already have been assigned. Because Hitler was weak and had painful feet, he was mostly too late. Hanisch and his companions, however, made sure that the supervisor gave him some work too. Hitler also tried to earn a few pennies at the Central station. He carried suitcases and bags for passengers. Hitler told Hanisch that he had been a student at the Academy of Arts. The clever Hanisch came up with an idea. Hitler could paint postcards and paintings and sell them to passers-by. Hitler objected, however. He thought he wasn't dressed well enough to sell his work and that he could get into trouble with the police without a street-trader's licence.[64]

We are already used to it, but again we see a fearful and inhibited Hitler who immediately perceived threats. The underlying emotions are feelings of anxiety which are the most common trigger for paranoia. Finally, Hanisch persuaded him and he started painting and drawing. Hanisch tried to sell the 'artistic' products. Now they both made financial progress. One of Hitler's first biographers mentions ironically that 'the independent artist and entrepreneur Hitler and his Sales Director Hanisch' were successful, because on 9 February 1910, they both moved to the much more luxurious Men's home (*Männerheim*) on the Meldemann

Straße.[65] Hitler stayed there until May 1913, when he moved to Munich. Amongst the residents of the *Männerheim* were civil servants, academics, retired officers and workers. Everyone had their own bedroom. Receiving female visitors was strictly forbidden. Incidentally, it is very unlikely that Hitler had any sexual contact during his time in the Men's home. There was a reading room there with newspapers and a library for house guests. Each inhabitant had his own room with electric light! Hitler wasn't sleeping in a large dormitory like in Meidling anymore. The now 21-year-old Hitler worked on his paintings in the reading room. He only made copies of others' work. Hanisch complained that Hitler was lazy and didn't make many drawings as a result, which negatively affected their income.[66]

A lot of discussions took place in the reading room. According to Karl Honisch (not to be confused with Hanisch), a fellow resident, Hitler mainly cursed the Reds and Jesuits (so, not the Jews). According to Honisch, the young Hitler also kept himself at a distance from other residents and let nobody get close to him. He admired the radical nationalist Schönerer, who wanted to annex German areas in the Hohenzollern Empire. According to Reinhold Hanisch, Hitler was an enemy of the Habsburgers because of their political enmity towards the Germans. Hitler rejected the federalist principle of the Habsburgers: in one nation, there should be one nationality with authority. Still, according to Hanisch, he did admire Karl Lueger, the well-spoken, anti-Semitic mayor of Vienna, who was loyal to the Habsburgs, who incidentally stated very clearly that power in Austria should only lie with the Germans. Hitler was also opposed to Social Democracy. On 1 May 1910, a factory worker came into the reading room with a red carnation in his buttonhole. Hitler jumped up and shouted: 'You should be thrown out; you need to be taught a lesson!' Hitler couldn't cope if anyone disagreed with him. That's why various residents did exactly that: it was a fun game. Hitler was then unable to control himself: he became excited, yelled and waved his arms nervously. If he was calm, however, he behaved quite differently, then he behaved in a dignified manner.[67]

According to Hanisch, Hitler didn't hate Jews at that time. In discussions he praised and admired Jewish culture and Judaism. He appreciated Jewish philanthropy. He called the claim that Jewish people committed ritual murders complete nonsense and groundless slander. He also valued the fact that they didn't engage in usury, in contrast with Christians.[68]

Hanisch's claim that Hitler didn't hate Jews at that time may well be true. Hitler had a remarkable number of Jewish acquaintances. Siegfried

Löffner and Josef Neumann, both Jewish, seem to have been almost friends with him. Hitler even went away for a week with the latter, thanks to a good commission which had earned him more than usual. He was also on good terms with the one-eyed Jewish lock-maker Simon Robins and with the Jewish Jacob Altenberg.[69] In her Hitler biography (1996), the authoritative Hamann goes through all of Hitler's good contacts with Jewish people and concludes that he wasn't as yet an anti-Semite during his time in Vienna.[70]

In July 1910, he got into an argument with Hanisch about a payment. Hitler felt ripped off. After this, the shy Hitler had to deliver his paintings himself. He only sold them to Jewish merchants such as Samuel Morgenstern, Landsberger and Jacob Altenberg, because, in his opinion, you could do better business with Jews than with Christian merchants. He also had close personal contact with the Jewish Samuel Morgenstern.[71] His 14-year-old daughter Adèle helped him in the shop. Even in front of this young girl Hitler lacked self-confidence. Adèle remembers his shyness, 'and the way he cast down his eyes and held his gaze fixed on the ground when he talked to someone'.[72] By now, his behaviour will not be of any surprise to us anymore. He constantly behaved in an inhibited and anxious manner: here we see his negative self-image, vulnerability and feelings of fear all over again.

In an early biography of Adolf Hitler by Bradley Smith (1967), the author writes a good description of how shaky Hitler's existence still was in that period. The element of threat to him is evident. Smith writes about Hitler until the First World War:

> He is a very human little boy and youth whose chief faults are his laziness and his passion for romantic games. [. . .] Even in his early twenties, following his only success in the years prior to World War I – his escape from the total poverty and humiliation of his life in the *Obdachlosenheim* to the frail security of painting picture postcards in the reading room of the *Maennerheim* – he is essentially a figure, more threatened by than threatening to the social order in which he ekes out his existence. [. . .] If the story went no further than Hitler's hegira from Vienna to Munich in the summer of 1913, it would rank only as the biography of a social failure, tragic in the sense that one man's hopes, and dreams had been shattered because of his inability to cope with his environment.[73]

The racial anti-Semitism, ubiquitous in Vienna, was, according to Smith, appealing to a bitter and ambitious young man. Personal failures could be explained as the result of Jewish intrigue. For the young Hitler, who was desperately searching for justice, the discovery of a secret Jewish conspiracy was a godsend: not he, but 'the Jew' was guilty.[74] We now know that this interpretation is not correct: in Vienna, he had not yet become an anti-Semite.

The question you may now ask is how did Hitler – psychologically – defend himself against his failures during his time in Vienna? Many researchers call him *'der gescheiterte Künstler'* (the failed artist). But is that how Hitler saw himself as well?

Birgit Schwarz, and Wolfram Pyta, inspired by the former, provide us with an answer to this question; they think it has to do with his artistic self-image.[75]

Hitler failed the entrance exam to the Academy of Arts in 1907 and 1908: two major blows, especially since he, as he says in *Mein Kampf*, was convinced it would be easy to pass the exam. He found a way to soften the blows, however. Under the influence of the nineteenth-century concept of the artist, when the cult of the genius developed strongly, Hitler began to see himself as someone whose abilities were not acknowledged, indeed: he saw himself as an unsung hero. As a misunderstood genius, he was able to turn his deeply disturbed self-esteem into the direct opposite, magnifying his own fragile ego.[76] Here we touch upon a process that is often associated with paranoia.

Greatness and insignificance are major themes with regard to paranoia. 'Magnifying oneself [. . .] is a tour de force to undo the feeling of complete smallness, eye to eye with the danger lurking around'. The author and psychiatrist Kuipers takes an additional step and suggests a possible evolutionary origin of this behaviour, namely to impress: 'Perhaps the enemies (predators) can still be persuaded not to attack by a display of power of the intended prey.'[77]

A person is no unity; opposing forces often work in one and the same person. Low self-esteem and a strong overestimation can go hand in hand. Certainly, if one feeling is a compensation for the other, both can remain present. This is exactly what we have seen in the young Hitler. On the one hand, he made grotesque works and claimed to be a great artist, on the other hand he didn't dare go public with his creations. Only Kubizek was allowed to view them. You could describe Hitler in this respect as a person with a high but very fragile self-esteem. In our list we have read something similar, to a certain degree – feeling special: if a person doesn't receive the recognition, he feels he deserves, he may feel that others are deliberately trying to undermine him. A distrustful state of mind may then emerge.

In 1913, Hitler met the four years younger Rudolf Häusler in the *Männerheim*, who was a distillery apprentice and loved painting just like he did. Hitler also went to Häusler's mother's house. Ida was happy that her son had found such a decent, older friend and backed their friendship. Rudolf's sister, Milli, gushed about Adolf and asked him to draw something in her poetry album. He said no (maybe he didn't dare draw in public) but promised to take one of his drawings with him next time, and this he did.[78]

Hitler wanted to move to Germany. He felt a strong connection to that country. There was another, very concrete reason to leave Vienna: he was being called up and didn't want to serve in the Habsburg *Vielvölkerheer* (Multi-ethnic army), which he despised. Hitler convinced Rudolf Häusler to go to Munich with him. He also convinced Ida Häusler that she should let her son go. She trusted Hitler completely and Hitler assured her that he would take care of her son in Munich. (Yet again, Hitler managed to convince someone to entrust their son into his care!) On 25 May 1913, the two young men left, waved off by some acquaintances from the *Männerheim*.[79] Suddenly, just as in the Linz years, Hitler was dressed impeccably, like a rich gentleman. He could afford this now, because on 20 April, he had received his father's inheritance, in accordance with the law.

In Munich, Hitler and Häusler rented a room from the tailor Joseph Popp at 31 Schleissheimer Strasse. Hitler lived with Häusler for nine months. Popp's wife, Anna, reported that Hitler always behaved properly:

> The young Hitler would never have thought to come into my kitchen without knocking, if, for example, he needed some water to make tea. Then I would call 'Come in loudly', he would open the door and say politely 'Forgive me', gallantly as always. I have never in my entire life met a young man with such good manners. My husband invited Hitler to eat with us on several occasions, but the young Hitler never took us up on this invitation.[80]

This was probably too intimate and anxiety awakening for Hitler, which should no longer surprise us.

In Munich he made a living, just like in Vienna, selling his paintings. Generally, he worked on a painting for a few days and then went out looking to sell it in cafes and the large beer cellars. Dr Hans Schirmer, a doctor in Munich, shared the following about this.

One evening, he was sitting at a table, drinking a glass of beer in the garden of the Hofbräuhaus. Then he saw a modest young man whom he took to be a poor student. He was walking past the tables, offering an oil painting. He looked poignant. A few hours later, Schirmer saw him again, but the young man still hadn't sold his painting. Schirmer became concerned about him and asked if he would like to sell him the painting. 'Yes, please,' he said. As soon as he had received the money, Schirmer saw him go to the buffet to buy a few sausages and a piece of bread, but no beer. Schirmer had the feeling that he needed to help him. But he noticed that the young man (Hitler) was too proud to just accept donations.[81]

From the end of 1913, when Hitler became known to a number of businesses and with traders, things started to go better for him. Sometimes he received good commissions. In that time, he apparently earned a reasonable amount. Just as in Vienna, he read a great deal, probably at the reading tables in public facilities.

We have followed Hitler to the eve of the First World War. He has experienced many painful events, but his greatest trauma was still to come . . .

Chapter 6

Adolf Hitler and the First World War

T he time that Hitler spent in Vienna was crucial for his development. After a short intermezzo in Munich, this was followed by his experiences in the First World War, which were at least as important for the development of his personality. After Germany's defeat, the revolution of November 1918 and the signing of the Treaty of Versailles in 1919, leading to dismay because of the enormous reparations and the loss of large areas of land, a political climate emerged that would make Adolf Hitler's career as a 'gifted' rhetorical agitator possible. His hate-filled words now found a willing audience via embitterment and strong feelings of resentment. The legacy of the lost war and Hitler's unique rhetoric of hate now met. That is how this insignificant individual from Vienna and the First World War could rise, firstly in Bavaria, then in Germany and, on 30 January 1933, the previously unimportant figure became Reich Chancellor.

Hitler spent the war mainly on the Western Front, particularly in the West of Flanders and in Northern France. In September 1916, Hitler and his regiment took part in the Battle of the Somme and, in 1918, in the Second Battle for the Marne, the last German offensive in the war. Hitler and his regiment ended the war where he had started: in West Flanders.

When it was becoming clear that the First World War was about to break out in the summer of 1914, Hitler was delighted. Later in *Mein Kampf*, he wrote what he experienced during that exciting time, 'I am still not ashamed to say that I, overcome by intense fervour, knelt down and thanked Heaven with an overflowing heart, that it had offered me the chance to live in these times.'[1]

The 25-year-old Hitler wanted to serve in the Bavarian army and signed up as a volunteer. He was accepted, even though he was Austrian and so had no access to the German army. His nationality was probably not determined because of the administrative load at this time. In early September, he was assigned to the 16th Bavarian Reserve Infantry Regiment. Its commander was Julius List and was therefore called the 'List Regiment'. It travelled by train to Belgium, where Hitler and his regiment experienced their baptism of fire at Ypres in West Flanders on 29 October 1914. The losses in the fight against the English were terrifying: the regiment was reduced from 3,600 to 611 soldiers, and amongst the dead was Commander List. Hitler didn't even get injured, only his right sleeve was shredded to pieces. So, he was lucky, even though this awful butchering must have been a traumatic experience for him. Incidentally, the German aim, which was to reach the Channel coast and so cut off the English from supplies and win a swift victory, had already failed by September 1914 at the First Battle of the Marne. Now the unforeseen and disastrous war of the trenches began.

In November, shortly after Hitler's dramatic baptism of fire, he was promoted to corporal and became a dispatch runner, a courier who took staff orders to the front, on foot or by bicycle. The distance between the staff to the commanders at the front was usually about 3km. Runners were mainly needed if the telephone lines had been shot down.

On 16 November 1914, Hitler's regimental commander, Philipp Engelhardt, wanted to put him forward to receive the Iron Cross Second Class. This was because Hitler had protected Engelhardt against bullets with his own body at Wijtschaete in West Flanders. Engelhardt discussed this proposal in a tent with his staff. Hitler was also present along with a few other runners. Because of the lack of space, they went outside. Barely had they left the tent, when there was a direct hit from the French. Hitler had been lucky once again. Almost the entire regimental staff died, and Engelhardt was badly wounded. Hitler said that this was the most terrible moment of his life.[2] Within barely three weeks he had experienced two intensely traumatic experiences. On 2 December 1914, Hitler did receive his Iron Cross.[3]

His new job as a dispatch runner was dangerous but was a more comfortable experience than being a soldier in the trenches. In *Mein Kampf*, he omitted to mention that he had been a runner and suggested that he had fought in the trenches, which wasn't the case: he stayed behind the actual front at the command post.

Curiously, a time of security now began for him – something he had not known until then. In October 1941, Hitler remarked during table conversations that this was the only period of his life in which he had no worries.[4] In his Hitler biography (1973), Joachim Fest even gave his chapter about Hitler in the First War the title 'Redemption by War'.

Hitler had never had his own place, good friends or a familiar family circle – in his regiment he found compensation for what he had never had. As a dispatch runner, he had a concrete and meaningful task for the first time in his life and a home to which he remained very strongly attached, right up to the very end. He was so devoted to his regiment that, according to the non-commissioned officers Max Amann and Fritz Wiedemann, he refused promotion as a result. Otherwise he would probably have had to bid farewell to the regimental staff. His superior officer Fritz Wiedemann said, 'For Corporal Hitler, the List regiment was his permanent home.'[5] It was characteristic of him that, apart from a few exceptions, he renounced the leave to which he was entitled; he preferred to remain with his regiment. Wiedemann enjoyed exchanging a few words with his inferior, the extraordinarily quiet, modest and reliable Hitler. He noticed no hatred of Jews whatsoever. Even later, after Hitler had seized power, when Wiedemann even became his Master Sergeant, he remained in the dark why Hitler hated the Jews with such fervour. According to Wiedemann, that hatred could not in any case have been rooted in his time in the war.[6] There is no single convincing document from Hitler's time in the war which shows his anti-Semitism.[7] Incidentally, all the witnesses point to Hitler being a courageous soldier.

He hardly spoke about political matters, given his reserved nature. In *Mein Kampf*, he wrote: 'I was a soldier back then and did not want to discuss politics.'[8] It was only when his comrades doubted German victory that he would erupt. Then he would become irate and say that Germany could not lose the war. Here you can see his belief in the German nation and his nationalism. Hitler's angry, stereotypical reaction provoked just such teasing remarks. Apparently, it was fun to taunt him. The only document which gives any insight into his political viewpoints during the war is a letter he wrote to Ernst Hepp, who was studying law.

He had sold several watercolours to Hepp in Munich before the war and he had been to his house on a number of occasions. Hitler wrote the letter on 5 February 1915. The style is typically Hitler, the passage is filled with complicated sentences. Some of the key sentences are:

> That those of us who will have the good fortune to once again see the Fatherland, will encounter it as purer and cleansed of foreign influences (*Fremdländerei*) . . . that because of the river of blood flowing every day against an international world of enemies, not only Germany's foreign enemies will be annihilated, but our inner internationalism will also be crushed. This would be more valuable to me than any territorial win ever could be.[9]

Here in 1915, Hitler's political development still seems to be that of the Viennese Hitler. When he speaks of 'purer and with less foreign influences', his already often-stated horror of the multi-ethnic Habsburger state shines through and he seems to be expressing the hope of a more ethnically homogenous Germany. With the term 'inner internationalism', which he hopes will be crushed, he must have been referring to socialism in Germany. These are almost the same denigrating words as those he used about Social Democracy during his time in Vienna. The German socialists may have agreed to the war loans on 4 August 1914, but that had apparently not changed Hitler's negative judgement about them. He also thinks it fine that no country is conquered, a strong Germany would be enough for him. Given his later imperialistic point of view, this is remarkable.[10] In 1947 in Nuremberg, Max Amann, Hitler's superior during the First World War, declared that Hitler had made no political tirades during war time. This is understandable, because Hitler had then not yet become possessed by fiery, new political ideas. We cannot yet find any traces of his racial dogma. We can see this from the letter to Hepp from 1915. After the war had finished, however, according to Amann, 'I didn't recognize him anymore. . . . There was an unknown fire burning within him . . .'[11]

Hitler's wartime comrades may have accepted him, but in their memories, he was the odd one out. He was known as 'the artist'. If Hitler had any time, he would sit alone in a corner, painting, drawing or reading a book. He is said to have read Schopenhauer at that time. If he took a trip with his comrades, to Lille, for example, he behaved in a reserved fashion and did not join in with the pleasures of drinking bouts or visiting brothels. When someone from his regiment suggested that he should enjoy himself with a French prostitute having got his pay, he rejected the idea indignantly. Some uncontrollable laughter ensued and one of the company said, 'Take a look at our monk!' Hitler reacted, 'Don't you have any sense of German honour at all? I would be ashamed to have sex with a French woman.'[12] Here again we see Hitler's reserve towards sex, as well as his strong nationalism.

In fact, it is highly unlikely that he ever had relations with a woman during his time at war. And even though he spent years living in a relatively constant group, he did not make friends with anyone there. There was only one relationship which awakened any deep emotions in him: that with his dog Foxl, a white terrier, which had come over from the English camp. He loved that dog with all his heart, and it was allowed to spend the night with him. Hitler was also the only one in his regiment to never receive a parcel from home.[13]

Hitler may have been a dedicated soldier, but even he was affected by the shocking mass slaughters. In *Mein Kampf* he wrote about them in a remarkably open way:

> Instead of the romance of war, came revulsion. The fervour at the start steadily cooled off and the exaggerated cheers became choked by the fear of death. The time came that everyone's instinct for self-survival rebelled against his military duty. I too was not spared from this battle. Whenever Death came hunting, an indefinable something tried to rebel, made an effort, while still presenting itself as common sense to the weakened body, but it was only cowardice, which attempted to entice an individual with such disguises.[14]

In the winter of 1915–16, Hitler had overcome his fears and had become hardened. Hitler's own regiment was thinned out in each battle and topped up by new human 'material' from the hinterland. How he finally interpreted this horror can be seen in one of his monologues at the *Führer's* headquarters in 1941: 'I went off to battle with the purest idealism. When one sees thousands being wounded and dying, one realises that life is a continuously cruel fight, where the only thing that matters is the survival of one's own species. One may perish, so the other may live.'[15] We can see Hitler's pseudo-Social Darwinist interpretation here. He might have used the word 'species' in the wrong way, but it is more important that we can conclude from this how he saw the essence of the human state, namely as an 'eternal battle between peoples'. He did not break under the yoke of barbaric violence or the mass slaughters but became immune to human suffering. His experiences in the First World War probably explain why later Hitler tended quickly to turn to violent solutions. However, among soldiers, the *Volksgemeinschaft*, where profession, position, class, education and income played no role, prevailed. Later, he wanted to achieve this throughout Germany.

At the end of September 1916, the regiment left the French village of Fromelles in Northern France, to take part in the apocalyptic Battle of the Somme, where nearly 700,000 soldiers met their death. This was the first time that Hitler became wounded: his left thigh was hit by a splinter from a grenade. He was taken to a military hospital in Beelitz, south west of Berlin. As soon as he was able to, he went to the National Gallery in Berlin to take a good look at the paintings. In December 1916, he travelled to Munich, where he had to report back for military service.[16] We do not know how Hitler reacted to the ever-present war-weariness and increasing anti-Semitism in Germany, which was now being expressed openly.

He himself was not at all weary of war, because he wrote to his superior Wiedemann that he longed to re-join his regiment and his comrades, as he did at the start of March 1917.[17] This sentiment was quite remarkable. Many would rather have stayed in Germany. There were even soldiers at the front who injured themselves, so that they could escape the misery of war.

When Hitler returned from Munich in March 1917, his regiment was stationed in Bassée in Northern France. It was sent back to Flanders in July 1917, where it suffered heavy losses in battle. The regiment was relieved on 1 August and then moved to the Alsace. At the end of September 1917, Hitler went on leave for the first time, for eighteen days. He went to Berlin, where he, so he said, had the chance to take a better look at the paintings in the museums.[18] By the middle of October 1917, he was back at the front, now in the Champagne region in North-Eastern France.

On 4 August 1918, Hitler was awarded the Iron Cross First Class at Le Cateau in Northern France, which was a remarkable distinction for a corporal.[19] Coincidentally, it happened to be Jewish officer Hugo Gutmann who had put him forward for this. He had to carry an important dispatch to the front line, because the telephone line had been cut off. He succeeded in doing so, while cycling through grenades going off to the left and the right of him. Gutmann was Wiedemann's successor. Later, Hitler would slander him and call him a coward.[20] Naturally this was because he was Jewish.

Right up until the end, he kept believing that the war would end in a victory for Germany.

From 10 September 1918, Hitler went on leave for eighteen days for the second time. Again, he spent this time in Berlin and at the end of September, he re-joined his trusted regiment, which had moved to Flanders in the meantime.[21]

During the night of 13–14 October 1918, Hitler fell victim to mustard gas at Ypres in Flanders. He was blinded and led hand in hand with other soldiers by those who could still see something – they were marched off the battlefield in single file. Without him knowing it, his time at war had now ended.

He had been wounded once before. But this latest injury, his blindness, must have been an extremely traumatic event for him. He was taken to the military hospital in Pasewalk.

On 4 November, the German revolution began with mutinies in Wilhelmshaven and Kiel. In early November, Workers' and Soldiers' Councils were set up spontaneously in many German towns. The population demanded that the war come to an end, along with hunger, misery and the monarchy. On 9 November, there was a general strike in Berlin. The Kaiser renounced his throne and the Social Democrat Philipp Scheidemann declared a republic. On 10 November 1918, Hitler heard in hospital that the war was over.

During the war, Hitler had steadfastly believed in the idea of a German victory and now, on 10 November 1918, he heard the unthinkable from his sickbed in Pasewalk, namely that Germany had lost the war. This was his greatest trauma – a Major Life Event – which opened the door to feeling despair, fear, worry, doubt, uncertainty and ambiguity, and certainly anxiety. Once again, he was stepping into a threatening world, which must have reinforced his distrustful spirit yet again.

From May 1919, he developed a paranoid conspiracy theory to explain Germany's defeat, in which the undermining Jew played a central role. From now on, he wouldn't waver from this theory, which would determine his later political and military actions. During almost all of his first thirty years of life, Hitler encountered no lack of paranoia-promoting circumstances.

Chapter 7

From Pasewalk to Lechfeld

itler was in Pasewalk, far away from the front when he heard the news of the German defeat and that the empire had been replaced by a republic. It was a circumstance which reinforced Hitler's (later) belief that the army was not defeated but betrayed by its own fatherland. Judging from Hitler's own words in *Mein Kampf*, the events in Pasewalk were absolutely overwhelming for him in the most negative way imaginable. I will summarise Hitler's account:

> On 10 November, the pastor came to the field hospital for a short address. . . . I was present at the short speech and I felt extremely touched by the words. . . . We would have been at the mercy of the victors and the war would have been lost. . . . I could not stand it anymore. . . . While everything began to go black before my eyes, stumbling, I groped my way back to the dormitory, threw myself on the cot and buried my burning head into the covers and the pillows. Since the day I had stood at the grave of my mother, I had not wept. . . . When, during the long war years, many dear comrades and friends . . . were picked up by death, it almost seemed like a sin to complain – after all, they died for Germany! . . . All had been in vain. In vain all the deprivations and sacrifices, in vain the hunger and thirst . . . in vain the hours during which we were grasped by fear of death, we nevertheless did our duty; and in vain the death of two million soldiers that died on the battlefield. . . . It had been in vain that German mothers sacrificed their sons, in vain that these mothers had let their beloved sons go with aching hearts. . . . Had all this happened so that a bunch of wretched criminals could lay violent hands on the Fatherland? . . . For me, horrible days and even worse nights followed – now I knew that all was lost. Only fools or liars and criminals could hope for the mercy of the enemy. In those nights my hatred grew, my hatred of the perpetrators of this deed. . . . Emperor Wilhelm II was the first German emperor who extended his hand to the leaders of [Jewish] Marxism. . . . While they were still holding the imperial hand in their own, the other was looking

for the dagger. It is impossible to negotiate with the Jews. . . . I, however, resolved to become a politician.[1]

What Hitler writes here, almost six years later in 1924, is only partly true. Afterwards, he wrote an understandable and coherent story of the event. In Pasewalk, he could not yet foresee the significance and the consequences of the ceasefire. The disastrous Treaty of Versailles would only become known in May 1919 and the misery in which Germany found itself would become more evident. Yes, indeed, he must have been hurt deeply in Pasewalk and have been thrown off balance. He must have felt desperate, especially since he experienced the defeat as a very personal one. It was probably no coincidence that he connected the event in Pasewalk with the grief he had felt at his mother's funeral, probably the only woman he ever truly loved, except for Geli Raubal (we will meet this woman later).

He identified himself with Germany and he had been willing to share joys and sorrows for his 'fatherland'. He did not have another life than a soldier's life: he had no wife, family, no home, no job to go to again. Other soldiers were relieved that the war was over – to Hitler, the end of the war almost meant the end of his personal life. In his pathetic writings, however, he pretended as if he fully understood the catastrophe of the defeat, that it was the Jews who had caused this misfortune and that he decided to become a politician thanks to this 'clear' insight. In other words, Pasewalk was the conscious starting point for him of a personal crusade to save Germany and to punish the 'culprits'. But nothing, absolutely nothing indicates that he had already decided to become a politician in Pasewalk. Here he acts as if he is a visionary, whereas he actually makes up a heroic story afterwards employing hindsight. Again, at that time, he could not give a consistent interpretation of what had happened and much less see what the consequences were of the end of the war. It does more justice to the truth to see Pasewalk as the beginning of a new Major Life Event, which again opened the door for him to feel despair, fear, worry, doubt and uncertainty. The situation was totally obscure to him. We know paranoia feeds on uncertainty and ambiguity. The question that arises is: when had Hitler been fed enough?

On 21 November 1918, Hitler returned to Munich in Bavaria after he was declared recovered in Pasewalk. He was assigned to the 7th Company of the 1st Reserve Battalion of the 2nd Infantry regiment. There he met his old war comrade Ernst Schmidt again.

He must have felt depressed and afraid that he would have to sell his paintings in the streets once more – in poverty and as a nobody – after the demobilisation. In Bavaria, revolution broke out sooner than in Berlin.

Soldiers' Councils originated spontaneously. Bavaria declared itself a free state on 8 November and thus rebelled against the central government in Berlin. The ancient Wittelsbach dynasty was deposed. Kurt Eisner was Jewish and now the first republican premier of Bavaria of a left coalition consisting of the *Unabhängige Sozialdemokratische Partei Deutschlands* (USPD; Independent Social Democratic Party of Germany) and the *Mehrheitssozialdemokratische Partei Deutschlands* (MSPD; Social Democratic Party of Germany). A conflict arose in the Eisner government: were the councils supposed to form part of politics in the future, or were they just a temporary solution? The USPD, with Eisner as leader, saw a permanent role for the councils in cooperation with a local parliament, whereas the MSPD was completely against it. Everyone wanted democracy – but how?

It all went very quickly for Hitler: one moment he got injured by mustard gas in Flanders, the next he heard of the defeat in Pasewalk and now he found himself in a socialist Bavaria, which had separated from the Germany for which he had fought for four years. A great, strong Germany seemed further away than ever.

According to Ernst Schmidt, you could see how much Hitler hated the lack of law and order. He would also have taken offence at the boisterous atmosphere: the dancing mania – after all the war was over – showed overwhelming proportions. Hitler did not share in the joy at all and he was happy, if we may believe his words, that he could leave for Traunstein in early December. There he had to stand guard in a prisoner-of-war camp with his friend Ernst Schmidt. If he had hoped for more order and discipline in Traunstein, he would be disappointed. Among the guards, there were some of the worst elements that only considered the army as a way to lead a care-free existence at the state's expense.[2] In early January 1919, Hitler again returned to Munich, where he was attached to the demobilisation battalion of his regiment.[3] In *Mein Kampf*, however, Hitler says that he only returned to Munich in late March.[4] This was his attempt to conceal his presence in socialist Munich.

On 21 February 1919, Kurt Eisner was assassinated by the student Arco auf Valley. As a motive for his murder, the student said that Eisner was a Bolshevik, a Jew, not a German, that he did not even consider himself a German, undermined every form of patriotism and that he was a traitor to his country.[5] The later Hitler most likely would have agreed with this, but it seems unlikely that he shared all those thoughts at that moment. On the contrary, Adolf Hitler paid tribute to Kurt Eisner because he walked along in the funeral procession on 26 February 1919 and wore the red bracelet as a sign that he had been elected to the Soldiers' Council.[6] Whether one can see genuine sympathy for the socialist republic in Hitler's behaviour is questionable. He rather seemed to have self-preservation in mind: as long as he could stay in the army, he was assured of a livelihood; in any case he did not undertake anything against the Munich Revolution, which he would later remark in *Mein Kampf* was the work of the Jewish snake. He still did not undertake anything when the revolution began to radicalise after the assassination of Eisner, moved further to the left and more and more Jewish people gathered power. On 3 April 1919, he was elected representative of his company (*Vertrauensmann*). Anton Joachimsthaler and Ralf Reuth concluded from this that Hitler sympathised with the left Soviet Republic, but Othmar Plöckinger showed that this election had no political significance whatsoever.[7] After Johannes Hoffmann's loyalist troops had unsuccessfully tried to overthrow the Soviet Republic on 13 April, the Communist Soviet Republic was proclaimed. The time of idealism was over, and violence was used against opponents. On 15 April, there were new elections for barrack representatives. Now, Hitler was elected Deputy Battalion Representative. Again, the conclusion that he harboured sympathy for the Red communist dictatorship goes too far, because the political attitudes in the barracks' councils were very divided; many soldiers did not think a lot of the Red regime. In fact, the leaders of the Communist Soviet Republic were suspicious of the barracks' councils.[8]

Ernst Toller, Erich Mühsam, Gustav Landauer and Eugen Leviné were now prominent Jewish leaders. Hitler did nothing against the things he would loathe later on, even though he probably did not think very positively about the Red regime. He could have fled to Bamberg where the ousted government of Hoffman resided, joined the many free corps who wanted to liberate Munich from the Jews or provided information as a spy to the government in Bamberg. It seems he was not yet anti-Semitic then. Probably he had not yet made his conversion. So: nothing can be discovered about the subsequent resolute anti-Semite Adolf Hitler – who knew exactly what to do – and who referred to this in a very obvious way. He kept a low profile and just waited for the things to happen. It would not be long before government troops and the free corps would liberate Munich from the so-called Jewish republic.

At the end of April, the White troops (units of the German army sent by the government in Berlin) were on their way to Munich to beat the Red Army (the army of the Munich Communist Soviet Republic). Free corps units joined the marching White Army. Hitler waited in the barracks.

On 30 April 1919, the Reds executed ten White hostages in the Luitpold Gymnasium in Munich; seven of which were members of the right-wing extremist Thule-alliance that had smuggled secret information about the situation in Munich to the Hoffmann government in Bamberg. Hitler probably only heard about this murder later on.

At the beginning of May, Munich was freed from the Reds under the direction of General Ernst von Oven. On 3 May 1919, the last resistance of the Red Army was broken. Now an unprecedented White terror followed. A hunt was unleashed on real or perceived supporters of the Soviet government or the Red Army. People were randomly executed; hundreds of completely innocent civilians were killed. People were murdered for no reason at all. And the murder in the Luitpold Gymnasium was quickly attributed to the Jews: Juda himself had allegedly given the order.[9] This so-called murder in the gymnasium by the Jews was inscribed in the city's collective memory as a symbol of the reign of the Jewish Communist Soviet Republic. This seemed to be made clear: a Jewish-Bolshevik reign of terror – never again! And again, the Jews were blamed.

From May, the power lay in Munich, in the hands of the *Reichswehr Gruppen Kommando* No. 4 ('Gruko' for short) led by General Arnold von Möhl. In fact, a military dictatorship was established in Munich, because the civilian government of Hoffmann still remained in Bamberg and had nothing to say in Munich. Political life was marked by a hysterical fear of a communist revolution flaring up again. Everyone was beset by fear because of the Judeo-Bolshevik Soviet Republic and the population was also viewed with suspicion. One of the figures who had to keep an eye on the population at all times was the convinced anti-Semite Captain Karl Mayr. He was head of the 'Information Department' (a unit of 'Gruko') and had provided a lot of information on the situation in the city to the advancing army and the free corps, earlier in Munich during the Soviet Republic.

In the liberated Munich, soldiers of the old army (so not those of the *Reichswehr*, but of *das alte Heer*) had to be demobilised. Soldiers who had lived and worked in Munich before the war had to leave the army owing to a decree by the Munich city commandant on 7 May 1919. So, Adolf Hitler had to leave the army, but he escaped demobilisation. A commission of inquiry was established, which was to examine whether soldiers or officers had joined the Red revolution. If so, they had to be arrested or re-educated. And who turns out to be in that committee according to the official instructions of 9 May? Correct, Adolf Hitler!

One can draw the conclusion here that Hitler had not actively and openly sympathised with the Communist Soviet Republic, otherwise he would never have been elected to serve on this committee. Now he was serving as a commissioner investigating the political behaviour of soldiers during the Soviet Republic. Because he knew many of the soldiers, he could draw from his own experience. He brought charges against some soldiers and he defended others against alleged Red sympathies.[10]

Through his position as an investigator, he increasingly got in touch with counter-revolutionary circles within the anti-Semitic *Reichswehr*. This is how the aforementioned Captain Karl Mayr became aware of him.

The anti-Semite Mayr was looking for politically reliable propaganda agents to proclaim an anti-Bolshevik message. Mayr's activity should be placed in a wider context. Not only in Munich, but throughout Germany fear of Bolshevism prevailed, caused by confrontation with the events in Russia since 1917, the (Communist) Spartacus uprising in Berlin in January 1919 and other communist rebellions in Western and Eastern Germany. Many repatriated soldiers had also been 'contaminated' by communist ideas.

In Mayr's view, Hitler was a good candidate for propaganda against communism; Hitler may have caught his attention due to his diligence in the committee. But before Hitler would be employed by Mayr to act as a propagandist, he had to be trained first. Mayr sent him to the third anti-communist speaker course that took place from 10–19 July in the museum association room in the Palais Porcia.[11] This was led by another anti-Semite: Karl Graf von Gottmer, who also gave lectures to students himself. Hitler was also taught by the conservative historian Alexander von Müller and still another anti-Semite: Gottfried Feder. Feder had published his *Manifesto on breaking the shackles of interest* some months before. This man was of the opinion that all interest capital was in the hands of the Jews. Jews therefore received money through interest thanks to their capital, and not because they worked for their income. Good Germans had to enter into combat against this rapacious capital. This interpretation made a deep impression on Hitler, according to his own statement. Officially, anti-Semitism was not a subject taught during the course, but its role would hardly have been concealed during the lessons.

One day, Alexander von Müller witnessed a heated discussion taking place within a group of these soldier-students. In the middle was a man with a pale, thin face and a little moustache, speaking passionately and gutturally. Later Muller asked Mayr, 'Do you know that you have a gifted person with excellent rhetorical skills among your students?'[12]

In Mayr's view, Hitler was a good student, because he sent him to the Lechfeld military camp shortly after the end of the speaker course. According to the commander there, the repatriated soldiers in Lechfeld were already under Bolshevik influence. Moreover, a worsening of the situation was feared due to the arrival of German repatriates from Russia.

On 19 August 1919, Hitler arrived in Lechfeld as an anti-communist officer. He would have pointed out the dangers of Bolshevism, but he also talked about the Treaty of Versailles and that of Brest-Litowsk. We do not know whether he already saw the 'treacherous hand' of the Jews in the Treaty of Versailles. But he already spoke of the Jews in Lechfeld. And he raged against the Jews in the presence of the soldiers to such an extent that the commander of the Lechfeld camp, Oberleutnant Bendt, felt called upon – for fear of charges – to ask him to temper his anti-Semitism. This is evidenced by a written notice by Bendt, dated 25 August 1919. At the same time, the report is the first reference of anti-Semitic statements made by Hitler in public.[13] Hitler had thus become an anti-Semite – by August 1919 at the latest.

Hans Knodn, one of Hitler's colleagues, did not agree with Bendt. Knodn wrote a furious letter to Mayr in which he strongly criticised the call to be cautious about the negative role of the Jews. If one could not talk about the Jews the way Hitler did, German interests would be grossly damaged in favour of an alien race. Knodn's letter provides a good insight into the atmosphere in which Hitler moved.[14]

Presumably Hitler's first public verbal attack on the Jews, *Oberleutnant* Bendt had reported on, came to the attention of Captain Karl Mayr. This is supposed to be the reason why Mayr had Hitler write a reply on a question by Adolf Gemlich, also a propagandist, just like Hitler. On 10 September 1919, Gemlich had asked Mayr how Jewry relates to social democracy. Hitler answered in writing. This was Hitler's first written report on the Jews and this letter to Gemlich – dated 16 September – would go down in history as the famous Gemlich letter. In it one sees for the first time several basic elements of Hitler's *Weltanschauung* (ideology). 1. The Jews are an alien, non-German race; 2. The Jews are behind all evil: they intrigue behind the scenes of the social democracy in favour of themselves and at the cost of the German people; 3. Only a powerful government of national unity is able to pursue an effective policy against the Jews; 4. One cannot resolve the problem of Jewish evil by an 'emotive anti-Semitism' (this only leads to pogroms), but by an 'antisemitism based on reason', that is, the privileges of the Jews should be abolished by laws and after that they should come under the Alien Acts; 5. The final undisputed purpose is *Entfernung* (the removal of the Jews).

The later Hitler would not distance himself from these 'principles' even a little bit. However, he would aggrandise them and integrate them in one system. Incidentally, here he meant by *Entfernung* – in these early days of his career – not killing but removal from Germany. Hitler was considered a natural-born and high-spirited orator in Lechfeld who enthused the soldiers with his views. He received a lot of applause. It was already the second time that Hitler was considered a gifted orator. During this time, he must have discovered his rhetorical gifts. During the period he spent with Kubizek in Vienna, he had already showed narcissistic traits. Now Hitler reaped success as an orator, even more: he proved to be unparalleled in his success in this respect, which must have stimulated his narcissism.

Chapter 8

The Method

In 1965, the American historian Richard Hofstadter wrote the essay *The paranoid style in American politics*. In this essay he detaches the concept of paranoia from pathology and uses the term *paranoid style* as a description of a type of behaviour by politicians and their supporters, who verbalise paranoid political views. In various historical periods, Hofstadter explains, there is often corresponding behaviour in politics by individuals or groups characterised by a distinctive attitude and reaction towards a hidden danger. The characteristics of these groups and their leader are: they discredit movements or other groups, claim that they are conspiring, they greatly exaggerate the consequences of the dangers of these hostile groups. The groups that are demonised have often been put in a bad light for a considerable time already, sometimes even for centuries. Hofstadter uses the term *paranoid style* to indicate this type of suspicious behaviour and suspicious ideas. He does not attribute clinical significance to this kind of paranoia. In fact, he makes a clear distinction between clinical paranoia and the political paranoid and his followers who are normal human beings and mentally healthy; the paranoid style has nothing to do with a mental disorder.[1]

The paranoid style can be easily recognised. The one that puts it most emphatically on the stage, the political paranoid, claims that there is a giant conspiracy. This is aimed against the whole nation, culture, way of life – against millions of people. Negotiations or attempts to reach a compromise do not make sense, because the conspirators represent absolute evil. There is not much time left. The absolute and irreversible triumph of the conspirators is near. Against this danger, the political paranoid wants to start a crusade: 'what is at stake is always a conflict between absolute good and absolute evil . . .'.[2] The battle that must follow is apocalyptic according to this politician.[3]

Hofstadter only provides descriptions. If political behaviour of a leader and his group have these characteristics, then Hofstadter classifies it under the paranoid style. He limits himself to the history of the US and to illustrate this style, he provides a series of examples from the American history of social movements and their paranoid style leaders (Joe McCarthy and his followers is one of them). But if we look at Hitler's paranoid statements about Jews, we see the characteristics of the paranoid style: Hitler saw: 1. A giant Jewish conspiracy, in fact, against all mankind; 2. Jewish conspirators represented absolute evil; 3. Hitler unleashed a crusade against this evil; 4. This evil was so strong and well organised that it (the Jews) might still prevail.

The *Diagnostic and Statistical Manual of Mental Disorders* (DSM) does not necessarily see an expression of pathology in these types of ideas. The manual states that, hostile statements legitimised by culture can be understood as normal expressions for the socio-cultural environment in which the personality finds itself.[4]

However, the strict boundary that Hofstadter draws between paranoia against a group legitimised by a long, hostile tradition on the one hand and, on the other, clinical paranoia feels artificial. It seems like a construct. So, this clear division exists more in his mind and less in reality where the border is more erratic. Of course, there are people and politicians that will not be paranoid in the clinical sense, but still express themselves in a paranoid style. At the same time, there are of course also people who do have paranoid traits in the clinical sense and, perhaps for that very reason, express the paranoid style as well.

How do we find out now if Hitler was not only a representative of the paranoid style, but also a man with strong paranoid traits? It must be clear that this is what I suspect. I particularly want to show his paranoid traits by *not* taking into account what Hitler claimed about the Jews, which are, after all, expressions of the paranoid style, expressions of his socio-cultural environment, but by trying to work out if Hitler distrusted members of his own circle, such as his friends, acquaintances and employees. So, we are going to study the side of Hitler's behaviour that has *nothing* to do with the Jews and the hostile anti-Semitic tradition. Now, if it appears that Hitler often showed unjustified and pervasive distrust and suspiciousness of others in private circles and in all kinds of different situations, then Hitler was a paranoid in a clinical sense and simultaneously a verbaliser of the paranoid style. In fact, in that case he used his own paranoia to enforce the paranoid style, which was accepted in anti-Semitic circles. And, more importantly, his extremely lethal anti-Semitism can be well explained from its clinical and patho-logical paranoia: paranoids have no opponents but enemies to be destroyed.[5]

In this respect our approach differs from other researchers who also concluded that Hitler was paranoid. In 1992, Edleff Schwaab published an outstanding book on Hitler's paranoia, namely *Hitler's mind, A Plunge into Madness*. Schwaab only considers Hitler's anti-Semitism and, on that basis, he concludes Hitler was a deadly paranoid. According to Schwaab, Hitler's paranoia was the madness that culminated in the Holocaust. In fact, in 1997, Robert Robins and Jerrold Post did likewise in their book *Political Paranoia: The Psychopolitcs of Hatred*. These researchers also only look at Hitler's anti-Semitism. In 1999, once more it is concluded, now by the psychiatrist Fritz Redlich, in his study *Hitler, Diagnosis of a Destructive Prophet*, that Hitler was paranoid. However, again his conclusions are based on Hitler's anti-Semitism. I repeat: formally Hitler's anti-Semitic statements, however radical they may be, are expressions of his socio-cultural environment; they stem from the individual's culture in which he is living. They don't necessarily entail a mental disorder.

To find out if Hitler was indeed paranoid, we must first ignore his remarks which stem from anti-Semitic traditions. We will examine Hitler's behaviour in his daily life. How did he behave towards his friends, acquaintances, secretaries, generals? How suspicious was he? Did he clearly cross the limits of normality?

To make the reader a little more familiar with the features of paranoia, I provide him with some quotes from the Freemans. Paranoia occurs in the case of 'the unfounded belief that someone is out to hurt us'. 'Paranoia . . . is all about believing others to intend us harm'. Or that without good reasons, it is believed that someone wants 'to ruin or to get rid of us'.[6] And the DSM summarises: 'The essential feature of a paranoid personality disorder is a pattern of unjustified pervasive mistrust and suspiciousness of others such that their motives are interpreted as malevolent.'[7]

If we find a series of examples of paranoid behaviour in the sources, we can immediately form an opinion as to the degree to which Hitler showed clinical paranoia; this way we can place him within the paranoia spectrum. The Freemans have provided us with a good scale for this. If it turns out that Hitler had a high score for paranoia, we will try to articulate its significance for the origins of his anti-Semitism and show how his paranoia does lead to lethal anti-Semitism. We will go into particulars of this in the final chapters.

Chapter 9

Hitler and Paranoia

The anti-Semitism that manifested itself in Munich and Bavaria during the chaos immediately after the end of the First World War is also a form of paranoia. In those days, it was zealously proclaimed in the region that the Jews were perilous enemies. This was a continuation, activation and intensification of an age-old tradition. Hostility towards the Jews was an accepted standard within that tradition. This way, anti-Semitic Germans in Bavaria could aim their hatred and frustration at the enemy legitimately. With this development of hostility – if we go by Hofstadter's description – there was a paranoid style in the first place; in other words, there was no clinical paranoia. But we, as I have said, are looking for any clinical paranoia in Hitler, so we are not looking at his behaviour towards and utterances against the Jews.

We'll start with some examples from Hitler's Viennese period, which may indicate paranoia in development. August Kubizek was worried about his friend's mental state. The 18-year-old Hitler lived under stress and he was full of blame. He was rejected by the Academy of Arts, barely had any money and had no chance of developing a relationship with his – more or less imaginary girlfriend – Stefanie. About Hitler's feelings of frustration, Kubizek notes that '[his] indictment became an indictment against time, against the whole world. In torrential tirades of hatred, he railed against the present, alone and lonely, against all mankind, which did not understand him, which did not do justice to him, by whom he felt chased and cheated'.[1]

What the young Hitler is saying here, is almost perfectly in line with paragraph 1 in the DSM-5 on the paranoid personality disorder: suspects, without sufficient base, that others are exploiting, harming, or deceiving him or her.[2] We also see one of the descriptions of the Freemans in this, namely that others want to ruin him. In addition, one can also interpret the tirade of hatred as the expression of a narcissistic Hitler who feels aggrieved: he, the brilliant Hitler, felt under-appreciated, the harvest of

Arthur de Gobineau
The influential pioneer of the new racism. He claimed that culture emerged from race. (Public domain)

Charles Darwin
Anti-Semites used Darwin to provide a 'scientific' basis for the enmity towards the Jews. You often find pseudo Social-Darwinist interpretations in Hitler's statements. (Pixabay license)

Richard Wagner Hitler loved this composer and considered him a genius. Wagner's theatrical operas may have influenced Hitler's own performance as an orator and politician. (Pixabay license)

The young Adolf Hitler Here, he is 10 years old. This picture is part of a class photograph from primary school. (Public domain)

August Kubizek Hitler's friend in his youth. They were both enchanted by Richard Wagner and went to his opera innumerable times. (Public domain)

Childhood home This is where the Hitler family lived between 1898 and 1905. The house was opposite a churchyard. Now it houses a funeral home. (Photograph by author)

Hitler's parents' gravestone Hitler's father died when Hitler was still young, in 1903. He probably did not mind that much. The death of his mother in 1907, however, was traumatic for him. (Photograph by author)

Impoverished Vienna This small courtyard at 31 Stumper Gasse, gave access to Hitler's and Kubizek's room. He lived here between 1907 and 1908. (Photograph by author)

Front view of the Academy of Arts In 1907 and 1908, Hitler failed his entrance examination. These rejections badly affected his self-esteem. (Photograph by author)

The *Männerheim* on the Meldemann Strasse. This is where Hitler lived in a small room between 1910 and 1913. He sold postcards and small paintings, which he had painted himself, in order to make ends meet. (Photograph by author)

German trenches Hitler didn't fight in the trenches himself. He was a dispatch runner. The violence of the First World War had an enormous impact on him. This probably explains why later on Hitler would so quickly turn to violent solutions. (Attributed to Everett Historical, royalty-free stock photograph)

Hitler with his fellow dispatch runners in Fournes in 1916 His dog Foxl is also in the photograph. (Attributed to Everett Historical, royalty-free stock illustration)

Hitler in the early 1920s
He became a rhetorical phenomenon in Bavaria at this time. His self-image changed in this period. He began to view himself as a Messiah, who had been given to the German people by God. (Public domain)

Hitler in Potsdam
On Potsdam Day, 21 March 1933, Hitler bowed to the Reichs President Hindenburg. This was his way of making clear that he was not striving for absolute power. Hitler was good at using gestures to lie with. Just behind him is Göring and Goebbels is on his left. (Attributed to Everett Historical/Shutterstock.com)

appreciation was long overdue and, as a result, he expressed his frustration in a hateful manner.

There is an overlap between the narcissistic and paranoid personality disorders: both characters quickly feel aggrieved. It is possible that in this case Hitler's behaviour arises from both paranoid and narcissistic traits.

Moreover, Hitler often used the word 'deceit'. When he had bought a lottery ticket with Kubizek and he did not win the first prize, he lashed out angrily at the state lottery because it committed 'overt deception' at the expense of well-meaning citizens.[3] Sometime later, the young Hitler saw treacherous opposing forces again. When Kubizek was prospering at the Academy of Music and, through the intercession of one of his teachers, was even allowed to give extra lessons and earn money, the contrast between him and his friend became even greater. Kubizek said in this connection that Hitler, 'spoke of traps that were slyly plotted on his way – I remember exactly this sentence! –, only with the sole purpose of thwarting his social progress [. . .] everyone and everything had conspired against him, for him there was no way to earn a penny'.[4]

This interpretation of Hitler strongly resembles what is said in the DSM-5 on the paranoid delusion, namely: the individual believes that he or she is being conspired against, cheated or obstructed in the pursuit of long-term goals.[5] In fact, one already sees a prefiguration of Hitler's subsequent grotesque anti-Semitic conspiracy theory in this quote from Kubizek. We also see, as we read further in Kubizek, that Hitler often reacts very angrily. We have seen this before. Now we go into it a bit deeper. The humble Kubizek already knew he had to be careful with the easily offended Hitler. As a result, he did not dare to ask his friend 'inappropriate' questions, such as whether Hitler had a job. Hitler would immediately consider such a question as a humiliation and he would throw a huge tantrum.[6] After Hitler had failed the entrance examination for the Academy of Arts, and did nothing but sleep late, lounge and nose around in textbooks, Kubizek yet once summed up the courage to ask his friend if he could manage alone with just his books. Hitler immediately sensed disapproval and responded very rudely, 'You need teachers, I realise that. To me they are unnecessary. You are a spiritual boarder, a parasite that sits at a table where he does not belong.'[7] According to the DSM-5, it is typical of an individual with paranoid personality disorder that he perceives attacks on his or her character or reputation that are not apparent to others and is quick to react angrily or to counterattack.[8] Hitler clearly seems to qualify for this as well. And the Freemans say: Anger: when someone is angry suspicious thoughts are likely to pop into his head (how many times did Hitler get angry? Countless times!). In particular,

Hitler's highly vitriolic and haughty counterstrike draws attention. At the same time, one can also consider the statements of the young Hitler as megalomania of a narcissist: he, the unique Hitler, needed no ordinary teachers of course.

This type of reaction – very sensitive to criticism and insults – is also noted by Konrad Heiden, Hitler's first biographer. Heiden followed Hitler in the 1920s and 1930s and interviewed acquaintances from the *Männerheim* in Vienna (where Hitler lived from February 1910 to May 1913). Heiden notes that Hitler already saw a defeat in an unpleasant question.[9] The Freemans also say something like this: the paranoid feels that others want to hurt him or do him down. In this context, the observation of Ernst Hanfstaengl, his press secretary and confidant of whom he was very fond, is also relevant. Hanfstaengl says Hitler was constantly on the alert and suspicious once anyone wanted to know anything about his past, his character or his private life.[10]

According to the DSM-5 and the Freemans, a paranoid feels belittled quite quickly, is vindictive and unforgiving.[11] Gottfried Feder taught Hitler economics in the summer of 1919. He was aware that Hitler felt attacked quickly. In 1921 or 1922, Hitler was visiting him and Feder saw his brother-in-law, the renowned historian Professor Alexander von Müller, arrive. He rushed into the garden where he caught Müller and said that Hitler was already inside. Feder whispered a warning to his brother-in-law, 'Do not use a Latin quote that he does not understand! He will never forgive you!'[12] A narcissist could have responded the same way. We have already seen that narcissists also feel quickly aggrieved.

Now let us look at even clearer indications of paranoia in Hitler's actions showing explicit unfounded mistrust, which we consider less in terms of narcissism.

In 1922, Hitler went by car to Berlin with Ernst Hanfstaengl to get money for the ailing party funds. Then, a year before the putsch, Hitler was hardly known in Berlin. He did not have a drop of blood on his hands yet either. But after Hitler had spoken privately with a collector of addresses of potential donors, a van arrived. And Hanfstaengl tells that:

> To my dismay I learned what I had to do at that moment. To escape any danger of being spied, I had to make a tour of the listed addresses with Hitler, hidden in the interior of the vehicle. Duly stowed away, I was transported criss-cross through Berlin the hours after that, without having the faintest idea where Hitler made his every pitch to get financial support for the party. . . . After being finally freed from my

dungeon, Hitler said goodbye to me on one street corner or another, with the instruction: 'Now, our meeting point tomorrow will be in the arsenal, on the first floor, near the display case with Frederick the Great's uniform, at ten o'clock!'[13]

Hitler's exaggerated fear of being seen by an enemy is conspicuous. Hanfstaengl even speaks of being spied on. What is also striking, is that Hitler only tells his confidant Hanfstaengl – apparently for security reasons – where to meet again the next day at the very last moment. Hitler seems to live in a paranoid world.

On 20 April 1923, Hanfstaengl went to Hitler to congratulate him on his birthday. After Hanfstaengl had congratulated him, he pointed out the splendour of cakes and pies and said how nice they would taste. But Hitler thought otherwise,

> 'Yes, if one can be sure, that not much of it is poisoned!' 'Poisoned? But, Mr Hitler,' I countered, 'you surely do not aim to aggrieve your friends and admirers that want to pleasure you with these rare delicacies with such suspicion?' 'I do not know,' was the reply. 'Remember that the owner of this house is a Jew and that nowadays it is very easy to let poison seep along the walls to eliminate an opponent. In any case, I do not touch food in this house for reasons of principle.'[14]

The fact that Hitler was afraid on that very 20 April 1923, that there was poison in the cake, can be justified. After all, in April 1923, he was indeed well-known in Bavaria and had already made many enemies. But his fear of poison which could easily seep down along the wall and the fact that he, for reasons of principle, never ate in his own house out of fear, is exaggerated. As is known, the fear of being poisoned is one of the most prominent symptoms of paranoid delusion. Usually this fear is mentioned in the same breath in psychiatric textbooks where the person concerned assumes conspiracy and deceit, with the assumption that he is spied on and vilified and that his long-term goals are thwarted. Hanfstaengl may have exaggerated here. It is in the nature of man to ridicule someone who was once a friend, but later became an enemy in an extreme way (Hanfstaengl fled to the US in 1937). If so, then Hanfstaengl will have started from a 'true core', that is an observation of paranoid behaviour in Hitler.

In this context, another comment of Hanfstaengl's is relevant. He says that it was characteristic of Hitler that he never had a notebook with him, that he never wrote down a single sentence, because Hitler feared that information about him would fall into the wrong hands.[15] This is also demonstrated by the following example.

In April 1923, Hitler was in Berlin with Hanfstaengl. He suggested visiting the Lunapark to Hitler. Hitler agreed. The three (a certain Lauböck was also present) went there. When the three climbed the stairs in the park to a restaurant, a photographer took a snapshot of them. Before Hanfstaengl noticed what was happening, Hitler rushed to the photographer as if he wanted to arrest him. Hitler claimed that he was dealing with a photo reporter who tried to eliminate the German freedom movement by taking a photograph of him, the spokesman for the national cause, before the stage set of a Jewish entertainment centre. He claimed the film in a threatening way, after which the photographer disappeared in the bustle of the crowd. Hitler started to chase him. After about half an hour, he came back more peacefully: he had destroyed the negative that had made him feel so threatened.[16]

As has been said, Hitler was afraid of being poisoned. This fear always played a role in Hitler's life. Heinrich Hoffmann, Hitler's personal photographer, mentions another incident of this sort of Hitler's distrust. In about 1930, he made a trip to Feldafing at the Starnberger See with Hitler and others. They saw a smart car by the side of the road, having broken down. Hitler ordered his chauffeur to stop. The unlucky person, a Romanian envoy, could not fix his car himself. Within a short time, Hitler's chauffeur had repaired the vehicle. The next day, Hitler received a package containing three cans of caviar and a charming letter of thanks from the Romanian embassy. He was fond of caviar. Yet, he returned the gift by mail. In an equally charming letter, he stressed that it was the duty of every driver to help someone in need. This matter of course, as Hitler put it, did not justify such a precious gift. But to Hoffmann he remarked, 'You can never be too careful!'[17]

Do people with a paranoid streak also behave differently from normal people with respect to their (sexual) partner? The DSM-5 reads, 'Has recurrent suspicions, without justification, regarding fidelity of spouse or sexual partner.'[18]

It is interesting in this context to examine how Hitler behaved in relation to Geli Raubal, probably the only woman he ever really loved, not taking his mother into consideration. Geli Raubal was his half-sister's daughter, so his niece – and nineteen years younger than he was. In 1929, Geli came to live with Hitler in his spacious apartment at the Prinzregenten Platz in Munich. Geli was outgoing and lively, she cheered everyone up and she initially felt flattered that her important uncle was fond of her. Hitler was immensely jealous and suspicious, however, and no man was allowed to approach the girl. She had to account for every hour if he was not there. When Geli wanted to go to a ball in 1930, it cost her an extraordinary amount of persuasion to get permission from Hitler. Finally, he agreed, but he did not agree with the bold dress she had chosen. Then he bought a more modest one for her. And she was not allowed to go out alone. Heinrich Hoffmann and Max Amann, the latter an old war comrade of Hitler, were sent by Hitler as watchdogs (*Tugendwächter*). Hoffmann bluntly expressed his opinion to Hitler the next day, 'The compulsion under which Geli lives . . . bothers her to such an extent that she feels extremely unhappy'.[19] Hoffmann was right. On 19 September 1931, the girl shot herself in Hitler's apartment. This was how she tried to free herself from her uncle's jealous stranglehold.[20]

When Hitler was staying at the Hotel Kaiserhof in Berlin in 1932, Mrs Goebbels came to bring him food through the back door. Hitler was afraid of the hotel's kitchen.[21] Fear of an attempt on his life by poisoning was conceivable. But the following example (the incident must have taken place after 1933, because the example shows that Hitler was already Reich Chancellor), which also expressed this fear, his suspicion and mistrust, seemed yet again very exaggerated, so paranoid in nature. The source is again Heinrich Hoffmann; he told a comical anecdote that one day Hitler received a delegation from Turkey, a country he had a good relationship with. When the delegation had returned, they sent him a big box with the most delicious sweets, candied fruits, the finest chocolates made of marzipan, honey and chocolate from Turkey, all exquisitely wrapped in colourful boxes. Hitler considered it a wonderful gift but did not accept it. He ordered the box to be closed and buried (!) with its precious contents in the garden of the Reich Chancellery. Hoffmann asked Hitler why he did not distribute the goodies among his staff. 'I cannot give something to my people that I reject myself.' A few days later, Hoffmann saw some workers in the vicinity of the 'chocolate-grave'. They consumed the marzipan crescents with gusto. As if he knew nothing, Hoffmann inquired where they got those delights. 'We dug up the coffin,' said the men. 'It tastes great. Our kids will enjoy it as well.'[22]

Otto Wagener, a prominent National Socialist who belonged to the private circle of Hitler from 1929 to the early summer of 1933, also talked about Hitler's exaggeratedly suspicious mind. Wagener was Chief of Staff of the *Sturmabteilung* (SA) in the beginning, then he led the economic department of the *Nationalsozialistische Deutsche Arbeiterpartei* (NSDAP). In 1932, he joined the *Stab des Führers zur besonderen Verfügung*. In 1933, he was Reich Commissar for the Economy from April to mid-July. Hitler was, according to Wagener, very interested in the assassination of Julius

Caesar (Caesar was killed by dagger thrusts in the Roman Senate in 44 BC), and in the fate of Queen Elizabeth I of England (Elizabeth felt threatened by her rival to the throne, Mary Stuart, and had her beheaded in 1587), in the means by which Napoleon secured his power and in the vicissitudes of Czar Peter the Great. According to Wagener, Hitler studied their history with breathless zeal and this interest had affected the way Hitler perceived his own environment: he saw the same daggers and intrigues aimed at himself, uninterrupted and everywhere.[23]

Hanfstaengl had already noticed much earlier (in 1922) that Hitler 'almost anxiously separated the individual circles of his acquaintances, he said to no one where he was going or with whom he had spoken . . .' and that he 'kept the people from his surroundings separated as by watertight bulkheads . . . and this remained typical of him to the end'.[24]

Friedrich Hoßbach, adjutant to Hitler from 1934–8, judged on the basis of his personal encounters, 'Distrust was one of Hitler's dominant traits. He demanded confidence but responded with distrust.' On the battlefield, according to Hoßbach, distrust of the enemy was justified, but 'as the foundation of life in a state, distrust negates the basis of good faith; mistrust causes subversive and disintegrating effects – it is not protective and stimulating'.[25] Mistrust can be a helpful response, but in the paranoid the adaptive response is perverted into destructive behaviour.[26]

Of course, dictators are justifiably suspicious. However, in these cases people in Hitler's inner circle were still surprised. It seemed they thought that Hitler's reactions were exaggerated.

In June 1934, Hitler felt threatened by the conservatives and also by Ernst Röhm and his SA; there was actually a threat from that organisation, but it is certain that Röhm was not planning a putsch. Hitler probably did believe in it. Anyway, on 30 June he had the head of the SA executed, but he went further. He seized the opportunity to settle scores with a series of old enemies. One of the diagnostic criteria for the paranoid personality disorder in the DSM-5 is: the person concerned 'bears grudges (i.e. is unforgiving of insults, injuries or slights)'.[27] If one looks at the old enemies who had nothing to do with the SA, whom Hitler ordered assassinated, he went even further than being vindictive. Robins and Post have noted it already: a paranoid has no opponents, but enemies to be destroyed.[28]

Otto Ballerstedt was chairman of the Bayernbund in the 1920s and came into conflict with Hitler in 1921 (!). Hitler had caused him physical injury, for which he was punished with three months' imprisonment. In 1934, the Bayernbund had long been forgotten and Ballerstedt had withdrawn from politics more and more since 1925 and since the 1930s he wrote books on the cultural heritage. But Hitler had not forgotten his old 'enemy'. Otto Ballerstedt was murdered on 1 July 1933, on his orders. We see the same with Gustav von Kahr. Kahr had only supported the Putsch of 1923 for a few hours and then said goodbye, which caused Hitler's revolutionary actions to fail. Kahr had long since abandoned politics as well, but ten years after the Putsch the vengeful Hitler still found it nevertheless necessary to murder him. Others who saw Hitler as an enemy were eliminated as well: Fritz Gerlich, Bernhard Stempfle, General von Schleicher and Gregor Strasser.[29] A paranoid's memory never seems to forget an enemy or a perceived enemy. It seems precisely what the DSM-5 states: he bears grudges and is unforgiving.

In an incident dating back to the second half of the 1930s, Hitler's fear of poisoning is again apparent. The example is based on *Winifred Wagner oder Hitlers Bayreuth*, published by Brigitte Hamann (München, 2002). Hitler often stayed with his very beloved Wagner family, who obtained a glimpse into his household as a result.

> The head of the household Kannenberg complained how difficult it was to cook for the Fuehrer, because he was always afraid of being poisoned: 'You have no idea how careful we must be. If my wife prepares his meals, no one is allowed to approach to a distance of ten meters away from the pans. . . .' 'Even when Hitler was a dinner guest at Wahnfried, one of his bodyguards always made sure by closely monitoring us that we,' said Lieselotte, 'did not put poison in the food!!!!'[30]

Note that the last sentence of the quote refers to a Hitler who was staying with a family close to his heart, but even in this familiar circle his distrust still dominated. The four exclamation marks at the end of the quote are Lieselotte's, Winifred Wagner's secretary and right hand, who thus expressed her amazement at Hitler's peculiar behaviour.

All the examples so far have been incidents in the semi-private sphere. Although they often have a political dimension, they do not cover major political and military matters. If we dwell on what the DSM-5 says about personality traits, it becomes clear why Hitler's paranoia also manifested itself in areas other than those of the private sphere. I quote, 'The personality trait expression is relatively inflexible and pervasive across a broad range of personal and social situations.'[31] Characteristic of a personality with its traits is that it always responds *the same way* in all sorts of very different conditions. Therefore, it will not be surprising that Hitler also showed unfounded distrust in the field of major politics. Some of the following examples relate to that.

Hitler's distrust of the nobility and royal families is a constant in his perception. Hitler's reaction to the upcoming wedding of Prince Bernhard and Princess Juliana of the Netherlands is typical. Goebbels wrote about this in his diary on 5 January 1937, 'The Fuhrer has dismissed Prince Bernhard. But the Fuehrer welcomes the whole event because the princes show their true face as a result.'[32] What that true face was is shown by what Friedrich Hoßbach wrote about Hitler. Hitler feared:

> Reactionary rebellion. . . . A reactionary uprising was the object of constant concern of Hitler . . . although a monarchist reaction was neither available, nor did she pose any threat to the Third Reich. . . . It was remarkable how the idea of monarchist intrigues preoccupied Hitler again and again, although there was no danger from this side.[33]

The last sentence of this quote shows that Hoßbach concluded that Hitler's suspicion was unjustified.

It seemed that Hitler usually considered groups as cliques, the danger of which he grossly exaggerated. It will come as no surprise that he also saw a much greater danger for his policies in churches than was the case. For Hitler, churches were the cruellest institutions one can think of, which, if one was not careful, might be fatal. If they would tolerate anything unpleasant about someone, they did so only in order to, when it suited them, use it as blackmail.[34]

In 1938, General Franz Halder already said about Hitler that 'no one can demand confidence, when he does not inspire confidence himself. Hitler is too suspicious of the general staff.'[35] A few months later, on 22 May 1939, the *Stahlpakt* with Italy was signed in the presence of the German military leaders and accompanied by celebrations. What the generals did not know was that negotiations had taken place, initiated by Hitler, and the outcome was attached to the *Stahlpakt* as a secret protocol. That secret protocol included far-reaching obligations for the *Wehrmacht*. It meant that both countries would support each other in case of war and that they could only conclude joint ceasefires or peace. In retrospect, general Walter Warlimont called the withholding of this information by Hitler evidence of a complete lack of confidence in his troops.[36]

The following example is even more baffling. On 23 August 1939, Germany (Von Ribbentrop) and Russia (Stalin and Molotow) concluded a non-aggression pact in Moscow. This convention also included a secret protocol. According to this protocol, Germany and Russia would divide Poland along a clear line of demarcation. Again, Hitler did not inform his generals. When he invaded Poland on 1 September, the military leaders had still not been informed about that division. Stalin invaded Poland on the night of 16–17 September to claim his part of the territory. There were bloody clashes between Russians and Germans. This confrontation was inevitable because the Germans, who knew nothing of the demarcation line drawn by Von Ribbentrop and the Russians, had already exceeded it by 200km. Even Generals Keitel and Jodl were not yet aware of the secret agreement at that time. Warlimont wrote in this regard, 'One of them might even, when he heard of the first message that the Russians were advancing, have asked the following question in a terrified way: "Against whom?"'[37]

The next morning, Stalin called Von Ribbentrop and sharply reproached him with the fact that the Germans occupied the oil field in Drohobycz in violation of the secret agreement of 23 August. The Russian military attaché appeared to speak to Warlimont. Warlimont, who knew nothing of the collusions either, emphasised the German claim to this oil field to the Russian. Hitler, who knew everything, came up with the excuse that 'the diplomats' were to blame. Finally, the Germans retreated.[38] The actress and filmmaker Leni Riefenstahl happened to be a witness to this tragedy. She had flown to Warsaw by military plane to shoot films. She was highly surprised at what she heard from some German officers. The oil-rich region, conquered by the German army, was to be given back to the Russians on Hitler's personal orders. After this command, flags that marked the front line, were moved to the back. One of Leni Riefenstahl's comrades heard an officer say on that occasion, swearing loudly, 'German soldiers have conquered these territories with their blood. Now Hitler gives this land to the Russians as a gift.'[39] Hitler's secrecy seems ill thought out. It failed in its original purpose and led to the loss of German lives.

On 24 May 1940, Hitler ordered his advancing armoured divisions to halt near Dunkirk. Later, Hitler's *Haltebefehl* provoked a lot of speculation. After all, he had the chance to destroy the defenceless British army there. Churchill called this *Haltebefehl* 'The Miracle of Dunkirk'. Wolfram Pyta gives a striking interpretation of Hitler's behaviour here. He robbed his generals of a shining victory. If they had managed to utterly defeat the British down to the last man at Dunkirk, they would have harvested eternal fame and he, Hitler, would not.[40] If it is interpreted correctly by Pyta, then you could indeed see an extreme form of narcissism here. It is also possible to interpret this in terms of paranoia: the DSM-5 reports that it is a characteristic of the paranoid personality disorder that the person concerned quickly perceives his honour or reputation threatened.[41]

The cocktail of a paranoid narcissist or a narcissistic paranoid is extremely dangerous.

On 30 January 1942, Speer flew to the Russian industrial city Dnepropetrovsk. It was his task to restore the train routes and intermediate stations in the East. These were thoroughly destroyed by the retreating Russians. Speer visited the construction workers and troops in Dnepropetrovsk. In the evening, they tried to entertain themselves by singing songs. Some of the songs released by the army were melancholy: they sang about the desire for the Heimat and the desolation of the Russian extensive steppes. Yet, they were the soldiers' favourite songs. A week later, Speer flew to the Wolfsschanze at Rastenburg, Hitler's East Prussian headquarters. When Speer told Hitler about the gloomy songs, it strongly attracted his attention. He asked about the contents. Speer gave him the lyrics. Hitler read them and drew his own conclusion. Speer says, 'Hitler was, however, immediately convinced of the malevolent actions of a certain opponent. He believed that my story led him to this opponent.'[42] Speer did not consider the songs harmful. However, according to Hitler, the publishers wanted to undermine the fighting power of the German units in the East through those melancholy songs. Because of these 'evil motives', Hitler even had them prosecuted. This response was, as Speer said, typical of Hitler. He hoped to draw important conclusions from unusual observations. When Speer characterises Hitler in his book in general terms, he notes that Hitler's distrust was an element in his life that could haunt him in the smallest of details.[43]

The following example illustrates how Hitler suddenly perceived corresponding threats in his own country due to incidents in Italy. Some kind of paranoia seemed to be awakened in him based on parallelism. On 24 July 1943, the Grand Council of Fascism came together in the Palazzo Venezia in Rome and adopted a resolution with a large majority, in which Mussolini was instructed to ask King Emmanuel III to take over the actual command for the well-being of the country. The next day, Mussolini went to the king, who let him know that he had already appointed Marshal Pietro Badoglio as Prime Minister. Subsequently, the Duce was arrested. Immediately, Hitler had all the delegates of the German *Reichstag* put under surveillance. He feared a similar danger – coming from these delegates – as that of the Grand Council of Fascism for Mussolini. This was an exaggerated fear, because the German delegates were barely comparable to the members of the Great Council with regard to their power. Even stranger was that Hitler suddenly expelled all relatives of the German princely houses from the *Wehrmacht*! He assumed that the noble families would rob him of his power as well as the king of Italy (also a representative of the nobility) had done with Mussolini. The German nobility suddenly became a fifth column in Hitler's perception: an utterly paranoid fantasy.[44] Hitler was seeing ghosts.

After Mussolini's downfall, Hitler distrusted his Italian negotiating partners in an exaggerated manner and was afraid that the German delegation would be poisoned by the Italian deputation. On 6 August 1943, the Germans and the Italians met each other in a train carriage at Tarvis. The Minister of Foreign Affairs of both countries participated. General Keitel and Major General Warlimont represented the German army command and General Ambrosio represented the Italian supreme command. Hitler feared the Italians would leave the Axis. He did not trust the allies an inch. To ensure the safety of the German participants at the conference, Hitler gave special instructions, 'Only perform joint action, do not conduct separate negotiations and under no circumstances eat or drink as long as the hosts themselves have not eaten.'[45] But the German participants were not afraid of poison in the food. They had more sense of reality than their leader. They ate fearlessly with their Italian colleagues. Warlimont wryly noted that the Germans totally forgot Hitler's warnings against the Italians during the delicious, communal meal in the dining car.

Hitler's increasing distrust of his own general staff was disastrous. On 19 December 1941, Hitler himself took over the command. He interfered with all matters, large or small, a plague for the German warfare. When setbacks followed, Hitler began to intervene in the leadership of the military operation. Because he tended to believe front officers rather than his generals, the particular officers (*Sendlinge*) had to appear at the headquarters regularly.[46] General Heinz Guderian, Hitler's best expert in the field of tank warfare, wondered whether Hitler still trusted one single general by 1943. His answer was 'No'. Hitler did not believe anyone anymore. He assumed that he was lied to in advance. That distrust obviously worked counterproductively. In his memoirs Guderian describes, just before the Battle of the Bulge in late 1944, Hitler carrying through the secrecy of the attack to such an extent that neither the staff nor the troops were given timely notice, so that supply was inadequate.[47] In the beginning of 1944, Hitler was devoid of any realistic perception. In a detailed analysis in April of that year, Hitler blamed the great German military crisis on a series of betrayals, which had started in September 1939. First, the betrayal of the Italian monarchy in 1939 made the war possible for England. This betrayal was followed by further treacherous acts on nearly all fronts. North Africa was lost due to treason. The military undertaking around Tunis failed due to treason. Rommel had to stop his campaign due to betrayal. Stalingrad was lost because of treason.[48]

In this analysis of the military situation in April 1944, Hitler's distrust is systematically and radically present, the separate elements come together here to form a major paranoid delusion.

The words of Albert Kesselring, the Luftwaffe General Field Marshal in the South and later in the West, also showed Hitler's radicalising distrust. Between 10 March and 12 April 1944, he visited Hitler four times. Kesselring, a Nazi at heart, told, not without pride, that Hitler completely trusted him at that time and that he took decisions in accordance with his proposals. He praised Hitler's resilience at that time. There is no doubt that Kesselring was an ardent admirer of Hitler. This makes what Kesselring said about him in the final phase of the war, all the more remarkable, 'Because of his morbid distrust – in the end actually more or less toward all – Hitler bit off more than one can chew, by handling all government affairs himself.'[49] Finally, even the pathologically faithful Goebbels, who supported Hitler until the last moment and almost never uttered a word of disapproval about his genius Fuehrer, directs some criticism towards him in the diary entry of 28 March 1945. Goebbels wrote in response to Hitler's conclusion that the system of the bunkers around Trier were abandoned, that Hitler indeed had the right views, but he rarely drew the right conclusions from them.[50]

In the last year of the war, Hitler's radicalising and growing distrust was also apparent in his attitude towards his faithful supporters. The first example is taken from Christa Schroeder, one of Hitler's secretaries, and dates from 1944. Hitler's personal physician, Dr Morell, prescribed tablets for flatulence. The physicians Professor Brandt and Professor Hasselbach felt that the strong shaking of Hitler's left hand and the deterioration of his eyesight were caused by the side effects of these tablets. They held the opinion that Dr Morell's treatment was irresponsible and reported this to Hitler. Christa Schroeder describes Hitler's reaction this way:

> But Hitler did not tolerate one word of condemnation about his personal physician. He depended on Morell to such an extent that he was unable to see the sincere intentions of the physicians Professor Brandt and Professor Hasselbach, who entered a protest against Morell's treatment. He only saw the intention in everything to remove Morell and, he further concluded, because they knew exactly that he could not live without Morell, they were after his life in an indirect way.[51]

Therefore, Hitler thought that Brandt and Hasselbach wanted to murder him. However, his suspicions had no foundation whatsoever. By the end of the war, he also began to distrust his personal physician Morell.[52]

This is remarkable because there was 'a strong relationship based on mutual trust with his physician'.[53] As late as October 1944 he said about Morell, 'He is and remains my only personal physician and he has my full confidence.'[54] But the stress of the last weeks caused his paranoia to conquer his confidence. When Morell wanted to give him a glucose injection on 21 April 1945, which he had done a hundred times before, Hitler held him and:

> Was inflamed with anger and told me that he knew exactly that I wanted to inject him with morphine. He knew, said Hitler, that the generals wanted to sedate him to get him to Berchtesgaden. When Morell had assured him that he knew nothing of the plot, Hitler screamed at him, 'Do you think I am a fool?' Hitler threatened Morell to have him shot. Finally, he dismissed Morell with the words, 'Behave yourself as if you had never met me.'[55]

After Morell had left on 22 April 1945, Hitler showed distrust with regard to *every* physician. His private chauffeur Erich Kempka, who stayed at Hitler's side until the end and then helped to burn Hitler's and Eva Braun's bodies, says:

> Following the dismissal of Dr. Morell, the chief said that he did not want to consult any physician again, since he no longer trusted anyone anymore. He felt that one of his physicians could administer a morphine injection to remove him from Berlin in an intoxicated state and against his will.[56]

In the final stage of his life, Hitler's distrust had a remarkable character: now it did not refer to an attempt on his life anymore, but to saving it. His paranoia fully evolved in those last days. Heinz Linge, Hitler's personal servant, confirms this:

> Hitler still only accepted medicine handed by me. His suspicion could not be surpassed anymore. Although he could hear whispered conversations again. . . . [following the attack on 20 July 1944, Hitler had become quite deaf]; but that did not make his suspicion disappear, which not only made his life hell. If I had not had such strong nerves, I would not know what I had done.[57]

Ironically, the following anecdote was told by Traudl Junge, one of Hitler's secretaries. Just before his death, Hitler distrusted the poison pills he was given by Heinrich Himmler to commit suicide. Then he thought that Himmler deliberately did *not* put poison in them in order to let him fall into the hands of the Russians. He tested a pill on his dog Blondi, which died immediately.[58] On 22 May 1945, an officer of the US intelligence asked Christa Schroeder if Hitler had ever entered into a personal correspondence with friends. She responded with, 'No. He has always stressed that it was his power that he had never written any letters, even in the *Kampfzeit*; if they had fallen into the wrong hands, one would have made improper use of everything.'[59] One of the diagnostic features for the paranoid personality disorder is that the person involved expects that information coming from him will be used against him in a malicious manner.[60] Hitler seems to qualify again for this criterion.

Many forms of distrust are well-founded in times of tension and war, certainly when it concerns an active and dictatorial head of state. There were many attacks on Hitler and the one on 20 July 1944 was almost successful. Hitler's paranoid perception was definitely pathological. The historian Peter Hoffmann conducted extensive research on all personnel and material measures taken to protect Hitler against attacks. Hoffmann described exactly what measures were considered justified and deemed urgent by Hitler's security agents. Hoffmann recognised that many of them were rightfully taken. Nevertheless, in his final chapter he concluded that Hitler's concern for his own safety had to be classified as strikingly deep, morbid and irrational.[61]

So far, Hitler's (paranoid) anti-Semitism has been deliberately ignored in this chapter and other behaviour was considered to determine whether Hitler acted from his own paranoid tendencies, because the anti-Semitic tradition can camouflage individual paranoia. Yet, we also encountered anti-Semitic remarks by Hitler, showing such a foolish character at the same time, that we can immediately perceive the effect of individual paranoia. On 3 April 1929, Goebbels, for example, wrote:

> In assessing the Trotsky matter, I cannot agree with Hitler. He does not believe in a contradiction between Trotsky and Stalin but believes that they are all dirty tricks of the Jews to bring Trotsky to Germany and thus to introduce him to lead the *German Communist Party* (KPD). In my opinion, he sees ghosts (*Das ist mir zu spökenkiekerisch*).[62]

The highly dedicated Goebbels therefore believed that Hitler saw things that were not there, even with regard to the Jewish nemesis. With this example we finish the search for Hitler's paranoid manifestations.

The examples collected here are very similar. They are from different – and independent – sources and from different periods of Hitler's life. Therefore, they substantiate the presumption that Hitler was essentially a man with strong paranoid traits. The story of Adolf Hitler as a paranoid can also be graphically summarised in three links. It looks like this:

Assertion: Adolf Hitler is a man with strong paranoid traits.

↓

A series of examples demonstrate that Adolf Hitler showed pervasive distrust and deep suspicion from his adolescence to his death, where this was not justified.

↓

A paranoid is someone who often demonstrates a penetrating distrust and deep suspicion when there is no good reason for this.

The third link is valid; for it is simply a definition of a paranoid. So, the assertion in the first link is proved and safely anchored.

Chapter 10

The Anti-Semitic Turnaround

So, what exactly is the significance of Hitler's paranoia for the emergence of his anti-Semitism? It is one of the central questions of this study.

Paranoia must materialise and it does so depending on circumstances of time and culture. Around the end of the First World War, the Jews in particular were 'discovered' by *völkisch* Germans in Bavaria as those who undermined what Hitler pursued most passionately: Germany's victory and a strong German state. Anti-Semitism (in particular, the claim that the Jews tried to undermine and destroy Germany) was recognised by Hitler, given the power of paranoia working in him, as the essential truth about the political world. So, Hitler's paranoia manifested itself in anti-Semitism. If there had been no paranoid traits in Hitler, he might have become an anti-Semite, but never such a deadly, fierce and rabid one – as we noted before: paranoids have no rivals or opponents but enemies to be destroyed – or he would not have become an anti-Semite at all. One can see that in the identification of Hitler as a man with strong paranoid traits lies a considerable explanatory power. We have now made a step from Hitler's paranoia to anti-Semitism. Has the matter been completed now?

No.

Above, I strictly separated Hitler's paranoia from his anti-Semitism (first paranoia then the manifestation in anti-Semitism). However, paranoid thoughts, feelings and behaviour do not just drop out of the sky. They arise in constant interaction with the environment. In his Viennese period Hitler became thoroughly acquainted with anti-Semitism, although he had not embraced it yet. Later, probably in the war, especially during his days on leave, he must have heard of all kinds of anti-Semitic concoctions again. All these experiences were good pioneers for the concretisation of his paranoia into anti-Semitism. He had not reached this point yet, in spite of the fact that he (as we saw in the previous chapter) already had paranoid traits. The question that comes up is when did Hitler get in touch with anti-Semitism intensely enough that it became so attractive to him that his paranoia took on its conclusive form. From November 1918 (losing the war, deposition of the emperor, start of the Republic) Hitler entered another very insecure period. Paranoia thrives in uncertain and ambiguous times – and this was especially true for Germany from that illustrious month of November in 1918. Conspiracy theories were buzzing about; people who had a tendency towards paranoid thinking, simply became even more paranoid by uncertain or downright paranoid incentives (such as conspiracy stories).[1] Hitler must also have been subject to this process. Whether and how this interaction process worked in Hitler during the Munich Revolution, we do not know, but from the period after 3 May 1919 – and this is a fact – a strong interaction between Hitler's paranoia and the environment must have developed; he came under the direct influence of the anti-Semitic *Reichswehr*: his paranoid traits now had clear direction and content. And from July 1919, that interaction between his paranoia and anti-Semitism became even stronger: Hitler was then educated by the highly anti-Semitic *Reichswehr*: he was trained to become a spokesman by anti-Semitic teachers. During this period, Hitler's disorientation ended. Former anti-Semitic knowledge now got an emotional charge for him more and more and it (the anti-Semitic knowledge) began to provide crucial answers for him. In a report of 25 August 1919, written by Hitler's boss Bendt, the commander of the Lechfeld camp, we hear of public anti-Semitic statements by Hitler for the first time.[2] At last . . . (he was already 30 years of age), his paranoia had become concrete as extreme anti-Semitism: he embraced it with his heart and soul, and he would never let it go. One could formulate the interaction and its result as follows in three sentences: 1. Hitler had paranoid traits and expressed them in anti-Semitism; 2. Anti-Semitism in its turn stimulated Hitler's paranoia and vice versa; 3. So, there was a mutual reinforcement that resulted in a rabid anti-Semitism by the summer of 1919.

The outlined interaction is actually the story of the origins of Hitler's anti-Semitism in short and also accurately indicates the time of his anti-Semitic turnaround. We would now like to add some extra depth and meaning to this short account.

In the first part of sentence 1, it is mentioned that Hitler had paranoid traits. We have anchored this assertion in detail and solidly in the previous chapter. We don't need to repeat this, so now we can look at the second part of the same first sentence. Here, it is claimed that Hitler's paranoia expressed itself as anti-Semitism, which means a completely anti-Semitic world view.

I suggest some interpretations concerning this aspect.

First, we look at the concept of personality. According to the eminent Theodore Millon, personality can be characterised in psychology as 'a complex pattern of deeply embedded psychological characteristics that are expressed automatically in almost every area of psychological functioning. That is, personality is viewed as the patterning across the entire matrix of the person.'[3]

The DSM-5 formulates approximately the same. It says about personality traits, 'Personality traits are enduring patterns of perceiving, relating to, and thinking about the environment and oneself that are exhibited in a wide range of social and personal contexts.'[4]

This means there is a stable pattern of thought, feeling and acting, which is expressed in many different situations. If you assume a stable pattern, then you can also assume that a personality will often respond in the same way in all sorts of different conditions. This is called the 'effect of the personality'. For a disturbed personality – for example, a paranoid personality – something else is added. Contrary to the normal personality, the enduring pattern of its traits is less flexible and more pervasive: the invariance of the paranoid personality is even more prominent and more striking. What has been established is that 'they create vicious circles by repeating their pathology again and again in all facets of life'.[5] So, in this case the effect of the personality has a narrowed focus and works even more strongly. Based on the 'effect of the personality' we can conclude that Hitler probably developed his overall anti-Semitic world view from deeply embedded paranoid tendencies. This statement is crucial; the notion it contains expresses the relationship between Hitler's paranoia and anti-Semitism. That is why I am repeating this sentence with slightly different words for emphasis: Hitler expressed his paranoia as anti-Semitism, including a whole anti-Semitic world view, via the effect of the personality.

Now, let's move on to the next sentence. The assertion in sentence 2 refers to a mutual reinforcement. This assertion seems a common sense presumption; and 'common-sense presumptions state what is normally to be expected, but are [only] rebuttable in their applications to a particular situation if it can be shown to be abnormal in some relevant aspects'.[6] You see roughly the same in people who have an anxious nature. If you place them in frightening situations, they become even more anxious. This is obvious to everyone. The Freemans have also confirmed and demonstrated this self-reinforcing process. They point to at least three studies, based on figures showing that the level of paranoia in men increases under the influence of paranoid stories whether they are true or not.[7] I believe that the aspect of mutual reinforcement has now been safely confirmed.

We can now go one step further: Hitler's clinical paranoia quickly became mainly anti-Semitism and his anti-Semitism mainly his clinical paranoia.

Moving onto the second statement in sentence 3, where it is said that rabid anti-Semitism manifested itself in the summer of 1919. There is a reliable source for this. Hitler's first anti-Semitic statements were contained in a report written by Hitler's superior Bendt. We have already referred to this source in this chapter. It is completely authentic and reliable. There is no reason whatsoever to doubt the authenticity of this source.

It does not necessarily follow, however, that Hitler only became a hater of the Jews in the summer of 1919. This is because if someone says something for the first time, they might have been convinced of what they are saying for a long time beforehand. Still it seems that Hitler only became a hater of Jews in the summer of 1919. Some months earlier, namely during the Munich Revolution from November 1918 until the beginning of May 1919, Hitler exhibited behaviour which was hardly compatible with that of a fierce anti-Semitic. Some months later, however, in July 1919, he was trained by the strongly anti-Semitic *Reichswehr*, as we have already seen. This is why it is probable that his anti-Semitic turnaround occurred in the summer of 1919.

Chapter 11

The Lethal Consequences of Hitler's Paranoia

There is still an unanswered question, namely the degree of paranoia: how high does Hitler score on the paranoia scale? The DSM writes about the severity of a mental disorder, then the manual mentions: mild, moderate, severe. They are three benchmarks that one can extend randomly, for example, by creating a scale of 1 to 100. It is the merit of the Freemans that they, with regard to paranoia, have made a clear classification. I have already touched on it. They place paranoia on a sliding scale, so they use a dimensional approach. They divide people into five groups and give an explanation of each group, so that the reader knows what to expect; as the severity increases, the group decreases; group 1 is therefore the largest, group 5 is the smallest, I quote:

1. Negative views of oneself and others (e.g. fears of rejection, feelings of vulnerability, feeling that the world is potentially dangerous)
2. Ideas of reference (e.g. people talking about you or watching you)
3. Mild threat (e.g. people trying to cause you minor stress, such as irritation)
4. Moderate threat (e.g. people going out of their way to get at you)
5. Severe threat (e.g. people trying to cause you significant physical, psychological or social harm; conspiracies known to the wider public)[1]

Based on the examples of Hitler's behaviour as described in Chapter 9, everyone can classify Hitler himself. I myself have counted many examples that fall into group 5. If this is true, Hitler falls into the 'select' group of people who score the highest for paranoia. But there is something else. Thanks to the Freemans, we can now say something more about Hitler and *the paranoid style*. We can now weaken the strict limit Hofstadter drew between non-clinical and clinical. According to Hofstadter, someone who believes in (political) conspiracy stories is not paranoid in the clinical sense. The Freemans, however, provide a more nuanced answer by means of the following example: if someone believes that there has been no moon landing, that the event was therefore a fake and if the person in question does no longer care about it, he is not paranoid. But if he believes that the unscrupulous and deceitful government deliberately withholds information to give a false impression to him and other civilians, he is indeed probably paranoid.[2] So paranoia only begins to play a role if the person involved is afraid that someone wants to hurt him secretly and consciously when that fear is unjustified. If someone believes in *paranoid style* conspiracy stories, he is not paranoid if he does not feel threatened by these stories and if they do not play a role in his life. He is paranoid, however, if he perceives a strong threat to himself and his country.

There is no doubt that Hitler believed in the anti-Semitic conspiracy stories and perceived a catastrophic threat in them. Anti-Semitism formed the basis of his overall *Weltanschauung*. The Jew was not only Germany's enemy, but of all mankind. In Hitler's eyes, the Jewish danger is so great, so comprehensive, so huge that he sometimes doubts whether or not it can still be warded off. In *Mein Kampf*, he wrote: 'If the Jew triumphs . . . then this planet will again move through the ether without people, like millions of years ago'.[3] The disaster that Jews threaten to cause therefore has apocalyptic proportions. Hitler's 'logic' is this: the Jew lives as a *Völkerparasit*. After the death of his victim (the nations on earth) this vampire (the Jew) will also die, as the vampire can no longer suck blood.[4] But Hitler would make every effort to prevent this cosmic disaster. On 1 January 1942, Hitler proclaimed, 'the Jew will not exterminate the peoples of Europe (*ausrotten*), but he will be the victim of his own attack'.[5] A month later, on 30 January 1942, he repeated this statement more comprehensively for the *Reichstag*.

> We are well aware that the war can only end by eradicating the Aryan peoples, or by the disappearance of Jewry from Europe. I have already expressed it in the German Reichstag on 1 September 1939 . . . that this war will not end the way the Jews envisage, namely that the Aryan peoples will be eradicated in Europe (*ausgerottet*), but that the result of this war will be the destruction of Jewry. For the first time, the real ancient Jewish law will be performed this time: an eye for eye, a tooth for a tooth.[6]

While he said this, the first death camp, Chelmno, was already fully operational. The construction of Belzec, Sobibor and Treblinka was planned, Auschwitz was being prepared. It is inconceivable that Hitler commissioned the genocide without being entirely convinced that Jewry was conceivably the most demonic enemy. Hitler never doubted his anti-Semitic beliefs for one moment. A day before his suicide he prophesied in his will: 'Centuries will pass, but from the ruins of our cities and monuments, the hate will renew against the people who are ultimately responsible and to whom we owe everything, namely the international Jewry and its helpers.'[7] In fact, Hitler implicitly calls here for the continuation of the struggle against the Jews for centuries after his death. The persistence of his paranoid delusional enmity can hardly be clarified in a better way than in the last example.

When the Freemans write about conspiracy theories and paranoia, they call the people who believe in it, and in whose lives these stories play an important role, paranoid. Now we can conclude from Hitler's anti-Semitism that Hitler falls into group 5, because what he believed in posed the most serious threat imaginable. Actually, you could argue there should be a category 6, because what Hitler implemented implied more than a 'severe threat'. If one looks at aspects of his formulations, in particular his belief that, possibly because of the Jews, the earth will move through the ether without people, like millions of years ago, and that the Jews want to exterminate the peoples of Europe, one sees no expression at all of 'ordinary' anti-Semitism, but an apocalyptic anti-Semitism stemming from the strongest possible paranoid delusions, scarcely even imaginable for most of us. So, to prevent 'these catastrophes' he had to kill the Jews. In 99 per cent of the biographies of Hitler, only external anti-Semitic influences are mentioned as an explanation for Hitler's anti-Semitism – not his powerful paranoia from within. It is, I repeat, an omission.

Chapter 12

Nature and Paranoia: The Deepest Roots of Paranoia

Now we want to try and answer the last question about the origins of paranoia. We have already learned a lot about Hitler. It has become clear that he was exposed to almost all of the circumstances which promote paranoia during the first thirty years of his life. We have also seen that he became a full-blown paranoid. The link between his paranoia and his anti-Semitism has been clarified by the 'effect of his personality'. There is a lot to be said for the idea that his paranoia coincided entirely with his anti-Semitism. In addition, we have established that Adolf Hitler was very probably in a category of people who score the very highest for paranoia. It has also been made apparent that his paranoia was of the deadly kind. At this point we arrive at an essential question, which almost no Hitler researcher has ever thought about in fundamental terms. The question is this: how is it that people ever become paranoid? The answer may seem self-explanatory, but the deeper explanation is beyond almost everyone. The answer is: because distrust and its sickly variant, paranoia, are indisputably linked to the human spirit. But why is that? To gain insight into this, we will have to travel back to a distant point in time.

The rise of mammals occurred 65 million years ago. They had already existed, but as the result of the sudden extinction of dinosaurs, belonging to the class of reptiles, many new habitats emerged for them. Therefore, they were able to start a widespread differentiation. Thus, all kinds of new mammals arose in different niches. Suspicion will already have been present among them. Suspicion, after all, has survival value and preserved or strengthened itself in different degrees in the origination of new mammalian species over the last 65 million years. What played a role in this was the extent to which predators became a threat and a threat of members from their own group or kind: mutual competition was always important; sometimes it could be so strong that one or the other was killed.

False alarm occurs much more often than a real alarm. Prey flees immediately, even when there is a very low risk of deadly danger. This is called 'the smoke detector principle': animals are likely to demonstrate higher levels of anxiety than is strictly necessary since, like a smoke detector, the cost of reacting to a false alarm is much lower than the cost of not responding to a real alarm.[1] This phenomenon occurs practically all the time, but the degree of fear varies per individual. Animal lovers can tell you this from experience. For example, every pigeon fancier knows that one pigeon is more suspicious than the other by nature. Most of them can easily be tamed, but there remains a small number of pigeons that will not lose their suspicion towards their keeper. Here, there is the natural trait variation within one population.

Man has descended from mammals. We do not descend from the great apes, as is often said, but we have a common joint ancestor. Genetically, we are most closely related to the bonobo and the chimpanzee. With them, we share just as many common genes. If we travel back to the past: 5½ million years ago, we will find the common ancestor of human beings, the bonobo and the chimpanzee, somewhere in Africa. This dating is based on the analysis of DNA and blood proteins and is therefore very reliable.[2]

What our common ancestor of 5 million years ago looked like we do not know; he lived in rain forests and in that humid and warm environment, everything rots quickly and makes fossilisation virtually impossible.[3] It is, however, certain that he had feelings of suspicion, fear, anguish and aggression. After all, they are feelings that have survival value; these occur in all mammals and continue to be maintained when a younger species develops from an older species. Moreover, our common ancestor that lived 5 million years ago was most likely already able to imagine what other members of his kind felt or thought. We think this because this has often been found to be the case in chimpanzees. This ability is called the 'Theory of Mind' and it is a very distant and general foundation for paranoia: someone with paranoid traits, after all, makes mental images about what others think about him and what harm they want to do to him. Probably this ability is already older than 5 million years; the outcome of research into gorillas says that 'gorillas seem to be taking account of the thoughts of others'.[4] But the common ancestor of man and gorilla lived 7½ million years ago. It seems that this even earlier ancestor has passed on his theory of mind to the gorilla, bonobo and chimpanzee. Be that as it may, the empathic ability must have developed as far back as the earliest stages in the development of homininae.

Who do we resemble most: the bonobo or the chimpanzee? This question is legitimate, because the genetic distance of humans to the other two is equal, but the differences between the societies of these human anthropoids are substantial. Bonobos live peacefully together in groups, hardly argue and if they get angry with each other, they never kill each other.

In chimpanzee groups, on the other hand, there is constant enmity that regularly results in the death of one of the chimpanzees; there is always an Alpha male who demands the best for himself: the best food and he mates with most females. He owes his power not only to himself but engages in coalitions with other males. This is a real bully, but he is never sure of his position, because a coalition can be built against him just like that, removing him from power. Chimpanzees also wage war against other groups of chimpanzees. The highly respected Jane Goodall described this event for the first time. It took place in the Gombe National Park.[5] She was accused of anthropomorphism. Later studies supported her interpretation, however.

It is obvious that we look more like chimpanzees. In other words, like chimpanzees, we, people, have more reason to be suspicious and to be careful.

So far, some general comments about the survival value of suspicion and the very old evolutionary past. For us, the more recent past is more interesting, in which early homo species evolved and where we can become more concrete about our ultimate explanation of paranoia.

At the start of the Pleistocene, approximately 2½ million years ago, the effects of the climate change began to become noticeable. It grew dryer and cooler. Sections of the wide-ranging tropical jungle disappeared. Savannahs developed with some trees here and there.[6] Unlike the chimpanzees and bonobos who stayed in the remaining rain forest, several hominids evolved, who walked upright, who exploited new kinds of food outside the rain forests. They were hunter-gatherers.

This must have been a time of a turbulent and rapid evolution. *Homo habilis* lived in East Africa about 2 million years ago. *Homo erectus,* whose origination is dated somewhat later, left Africa and spread deep into Asia and Europe. There have been many more hominids since 2 million years ago, but the exact pedigree of mankind is currently not clear.

Early modern human originated in Africa 300,000 years ago. For a long time, it was thought that early modern man had only appeared on the stage 200,000 years BP. But due to the surprising discovery in 2017 in Jebel, Morocco (based on highly reliable dating methods), it was established that the rise of modern humanity lies another 100,000 years deeper into the past.[7] The conclusion that can be drawn is that the cradle of modern man was not in Ethiopia (East Africa) – as we always thought – but that modern man had already spread throughout Africa 300,000 years BP. 'This indicates a complex evolutionary history of our species, possibly involving the whole African continent.'[8] And what should one think when talking about a complex evolutionary history of our species?

The answer is that early homo developed from a semi-selfish being that essentially worried about its own kinship (so those who are genetically related to him) into a being that began to connect with the unrelated members of his own kind more and more. The group grew.

There are various reasons for this. About 500,000 years ago, early mankind developed more advanced hunting methods. An example of this is improved quality of spears. Now they could organise hunting parties, which yielded more food. Meat contains much more protein and many more calories than fruits. This allowed their brains, in particular, to grow. In addition, about 500,000 years ago early homo learned to use fire. This meant they could cook and consume much more food than was possible previously. Here we can see another reason why the group was able to grow, and their brains could also grow in size. According to the eminent researcher Robin Dunfar, there was another additional reason: the development of language, which he dates back to 500,000 years ago. According to him, a group would have a size of 115 to 120 members.[9]

Spoken language had a revolutionary effect. Being able to exchange information swiftly made it possible to work together more efficiently, particularly when hunting. At this point, human beings shot to the top of the food chain. In spite of this 'high' position, they were still afraid of large predators, which had been hunting them for such a long time.

Language allowed the group to formulate all kinds of rules, which made the group more cohesive. Anthropologists Peter Richerson and Rob Boyd argue that this led to a gene-culture co-evolution. This happened in the following way: culture selected genes and vice versa and in such a way that cohesive group formation was promoted. Imagine that a type of cultural behaviour is good for the unity of the group, then this behaviour can selectively work upon genotypes, which increases the unity of the group even more. This way, cultural selection can favour an innate psychology.[10]

There will always have been characters who wouldn't work together and who ruthlessly pursued their own interests. They dodged, were cowards, deserted, stole meat or fruit, committed betrayal or tried to take the lead. At the same time, such undermining figures could be discovered by the loyal members of the group in a timely manner. Those perpetrators could then be avoided, they were gossiped about, or stricter measures were taken such as denying access to the territory as well as access to sexual partners; in extreme cases they were put to death.[11]

This is how liars and losers were treated, those who plucked the fruits of working together, but who didn't pay the price for them. This was a danger from within the group, so feelings of distrust against some group members were justified. In this, a predecessor of paranoia can be seen.

The Israeli historian Yuval Noah Harari dates the emergence of language much later than Robin Dunfar. Harari dates it to between 70,000 and 30,000 years ago.[12] The difference between his dating and Dunfar's is more than 400,000 years. Clearly, there is a lot of uncertainty about the exact dates of the decisive steps which human beings took during the Pleistocene period.

Through language, Harari remarks, humans were able to exchange more information with one another. On this point he is saying virtually the same as Dunfar. As a result of language, they were able to draw up joint plans and carry out complex actions, such as making use of new techniques to hunt whole herds of animals. An example is surrounding wild horses and driving them into a gorge, so that they could be slaughtered en masse. Archaeologists have even found sites where fences and obstacles were placed in order to cause whole groups of animals to fall over and send them to a slaughter site.[13]

The pressure in a group or tribe to remain unified and to show cooperative behaviour was even more important where there was the threat of danger from an enemy tribe. If they were unable to form a strong unit, an enemy tribe could exterminate the entire group and take over their (rich) hunting and foraging grounds. This was the greatest danger imaginable.

Wars between tribes and the resulting slaughters did take place, as witnessed by the massive damage to skeletons in the Ofnet cave in Bavaria or the slaughterhouse at Jebel Sahaba in Sudan, where entire groups of hunters and gatherers were exterminated.[14]

Cooperation and loyalty towards the entire group at the expense of other groups or tribes had survival value and this will have influenced selection. This type of loyalty shows strong similarities to what we would now call in-group favouritism. If that is the case, then in-group favouritism relies on a long and old evolutionary developmental process and has become part of our human nature. Indeed, in-group favouritism seems to be in-born, as it can be seen in all cultures. In extreme cases, the out-group is seen as a representative of pure evil and the Devil and ungrounded distrust emerges – that is paranoid delusional thinking.

We can thus see both internal as well as external threats in the hunter-gatherer groups: freeloaders from within the own, domestic group and other enemy tribes from outside. It was not a carefree life. Everyone had to remain on guard and distrust was necessary for survival.

In the *Evolutionary Psychology* textbook by Lance Workman and Will Reader, it states the following about threats coming from the domestic group, 'there are researchers who acknowledge that the mind may well contain a large number of innate, domain-specific mental modules for detecting contamination as well as cheating'. And: 'given the strong evolutionary pressures on us to detect free riders, it would be somewhat surprising if natural selection had not played some role in the development of cheat detectors'.[15] Here the suggestion is that cheat detectors – just like in-group favouritism to the exclusion of out-groups – is part and parcel of the human experience. That is to say, it is part of human nature.

We can safely assume that people's ability to dispose of 'cheat detectors' is inherited from the distant evolutionary past. The ability to discover 'cheats' is useful in everyday life. However, if someone is exposed – especially during his formative years – to too many 'cheats' and other kinds of threats, cheat detectors may, after the real threat subsides, remain active to such a degree that delusional thinking arises; that is, threats are perceived even though they no longer exist. Here, one observes a rising unjustified mistrust (paranoia) and the clear interaction between nurture and nature.

Now we have some more background information about the long history of suspicion and mistrust, we can return our focus to Adolf Hitler, but now from a different perspective. We now understand how aspects of human nature, such as those which have developed over a long evolutionary period, could have manifested themselves within Hitler. He had a predisposition to distrust out-groups, but at the same time he also had innate cheat detectors towards the in-group – just like everyone else. Hitler, however, had been strongly exposed to threatening conditions during his first thirty years and these were incentives to delusional thinking. An extreme form of paranoia emerged within him, where nature and nurture combined in a morbid fashion.

It may be clear that I do not think it is a good thing that historians who write about such an immensely influential figure as Hitler completely disregard the connection between Hitler's behaviour and evolution and biology. Culture, politics, economics and traditions play an immense explanatory role in history, but let historians not forget that nurture and nature are deeply connected and if nurture is only taken into consideration, only half the story is told. In fact, the most profound explanations are ignored if we do not involve nature. In other words, historians can no longer afford to neglect other social sciences in their research. If used properly, evolutionary psychology and socio-biology, psychiatry and anthropology can give in-depth and additional explanations for human behaviour.

In the course of the time I worked on this book, experts have counselled me not to write about heredity. Their advice proved to be an incentive for me to do exactly that. However, it became clear to me why they had recommended not to write about heredity. One can say little about how much behaviour is inherited and how much is determined by the environment. But what we can do is place human behaviour within a broad and ancient perspective of hundreds of thousands of years ago. This is what I have done. This way, mistrust and suspicion were placed in different functional contexts and their development provided insight. Mistrust and suspicion were thus adaptive and fitness enhancing, but as always with emotional adaptations, dysfunctional variations occur.

Mental properties occur in the population on the basis of normal or Gaussian distribution. Francis Galton, a pioneer in the field of psychology, was the first to claim in 1869 that the statistical normal distribution also applies to psychological traits. This statement has been reaffirmed time and again.[16] Normal distribution is single-peaked, symmetrical and has a graphical form shaped like a bronze church bell. In case of mistrust and suspicion, this means that a large group has a normal amount of sound suspicion. But at both ends of the curve, the distrust increases or decreases drastically as the group gets smaller. The decreasing group of highly suspicious people can be characterised as paranoid. Their suspicion is so exaggerated that it is dysfunctional. As said before, if a person has experienced threatening circumstances too often, there is a chance he may continue to perceive them even if they are no longer there. And as long as mistrust and suspicion have existed in humans, dysfunctional variations must also have occurred. This makes it understandable why paranoia, the disposition for it and varying degrees of paranoia occur in all ages. Indeed, paranoia belongs to human nature. However, a dysfunctional variant such as the one observed in Adolf Hitler seldom leads to such a huge catastrophe, though it originated from 'normal' human nature.

So far, much has been discussed. I will summarise the subjects.

Suspicion is of all time and has survival value. Mammals that are also animals of prey have more reason to be suspicious. Man descends from the same ancestor as the chimpanzee, bonobo and gorilla. Chimpanzees' society is quite violent, however, that of bonobos is not. Chimpanzees even wage wars. It is clear that we are more similar to chimpanzees than bonobos. Modern man originated 300,000 years ago and lived in groups of hunter-gatherers, just like his human-like ancestors. Mistrust and suspicion were required to survive; they enhanced fitness. Threats always followed from within the tribe and from outside: other tribes could form a deadly threat and within the own, domestic group there were threats from deceivers, thieves, liars, traitors, predatory free riders and bullies. Over the span of evolution, an innate distrust has developed towards other groups. When it came to the own group or tribe, a cheat-detecting module developed. So, a predisposition to distrust other people as well as other groups is part and parcel of human nature. For the first thirty years of his life, Adolf Hitler was consistently exposed to traumatic circumstances. These can be incentives to delusional thinking. Unfortunately, this proved to be the case with Adolf Hitler, where we see a diabolic form of paranoia emerging.

I hope that I have been able to show which role nature played in the emergence of Adolf Hitler's paranoia.

Chapter 13

Paranoia, Morality and Emotions

Hitler placed the Jews in a moral perspective as soon as he started talking about them; that is to say: he disqualified them as purely evil. Why does a moral perspective develop so quickly? It has to do with the typically interpersonal functioning of paranoia. If someone is depressed, he feels dejected, loses weight, his thinking slows down and he suffers from insomnia. There is such individual suffering that the behaviour of others is not automatically disqualified. Fear of cats, fear of wide or narrow spaces or fear of leaving your own home do not lead to rejection of other people either. This applies to many other psychiatric disorders. To name just a few examples: sleep-wake disorders are not relevant to politics and neither are dissociative identity disorders. Precisely because paranoia, on the other hand, relates so strongly to other people and to groups, from feelings of fear, hatred and suspicion, a morality of violence is created. One sees here that the negative ethical valuation derives from those emotions and its related cognitions. Here I would like to repeat what Robins and Post say about paranoia: only paranoia is the quintessence of political psychopathology: political paranoids have no opponents or rivals, but enemies and enemies must not simply be defeated – they must be destroyed! There is no other mental disorder that will continue to have such a profoundly destructive effect on human affairs.

Charles Darwin, Emile Durkheim and more recently Jonathan Haidt generalise the connection between emotions and morality. They say that morality, whether it is good or bad, derives from archaic social instincts and emotions. If they are right, then the morale of most people does not appear to be a counterpart of emotions and instincts as is claimed so often, but they more or less emerge from it in a disguised manner. In this regard, Darwin, Durkheim and Haidt take a stand against Plato, who claims that justice comes from values that transcend the individual. In fact,

Christians also completely separate morality from human emotions: good morality is all that God forbids or approves for that matter.

Jonathan Haidt did thorough, empirical research into the emergence of moral positions instead of assuming a priori that morality is something that is separate from human instincts and emotions. In his book *The righteous mind* (New York, 2012), he examined the reasoning process through which people reach the most diverse ethical judgements; he concluded that moral judgements are determined by feelings in 99 per cent of cases and that the remaining 1 per cent stems from intellect, which, afterwards, still gives a rationalisation of the underlying intuitions. Haidt did not just claim this. In his 500-page book, his statement is repeatedly and empirically substantiated. To illustrate his findings, he consistently uses the same metaphor. He represents the human mind as an elephant and his rider, where the elephant represents feelings, intuitions, instincts and where the rider represents reason, but in this metaphor the rider is not the one who steers, but the elephant is. And it is the rider's duty to *serve* the elephant. In other words, feelings come first, strategic reasoning second. From an evolutionary perspective, feelings are much older than the ratio, by which moral views are formulated. What was first and what contributed considerably to survival apparently continued to have its effect. The well-known primatologist Frans de Waal clarified this as well. In his book *The Bonobo and the Atheist: In Search of Humanism Among the Primates* (2014), he made clear that morality is older than humanity. It may sound a little provocative, but no one can dispute the fact that in the communities of chimpanzees and bonobos there are strong building blocks for our moral systems. It is likely that feelings, even when a human being is thinking about non-moral issues, play a role. In fact, it is impossible to reason without feelings. In his book *Descartes' Error* (1994), the well-known neurologist António Damasio clarified this mutual dependency explicitly. He gave a set of examples of patients who, through brain damage, did not get any input anymore from the circuits where feelings are generated and whose intellect had remained intact at the same time (they score well on IQ tests, memory tests and the like), but they were no longer able to reason in such a way that they could make sound decisions for their personal and social well-being. They quickly deteriorated. Without emotions to control their mental processes, if not determine them, they were unable to think well.

Hitler praised himself because he did not consider himself a representative of anti-Semitism based on purely emotional grounds, but of anti-Semitism based on reason. He writes this in his Gemlich letter of 16 September 1919, which was his first anti-Semitic written text. He could not be more off target: his anti-Semitism primarily emerged from his feelings; with the help of his mind, he gave them a 'rational' form. (We looked at the Gemlich letter at the end of Chapter 7.) However, Hitler's feelings were closely linked to his paranoid traits. By translating his feelings rhetorically and extremely well into credible political ideas, an agitator for the extreme right wing *völkisch* groups was created, who could lead them all into a 'morally responsible' future in which everything would be good for the German people . . .

Chapter 14

Provisional Incantation of Fear and Narcissism

We have indicated that the defeat Hitler heard about in Pasewalk was the start of one of Hitler's new Major Life Events. From then on, Hitler again reacted with fear, uncertainty, doubt, just as he had in Vienna in 1908–13. When did the existentially intense uncertain Hitler become more confident? When did this Major Life Event come to an end? We can now answer this question.

What Bradley Smith said about the Viennese Hitler, namely that the discovery of a hidden Jewish conspiracy was a godsend, does not seem to apply to the Viennese Hitler but to the Hitler in Munich from 3 May 1919. From that time onwards, he began to acquire the proper 'insights' into the reasons for the embarrassing German defeat, which was made known to him in Pasewalk and appeared so puzzling to him at that time. He could somehow restrain the resulting fears and uncertainties by his new insights. After all, the enemy was no longer invisible but had a clear face: The Diabolic Jew.

Hitler discovered more and more areas where the Jewish archenemy was supposed to be active; as a result, the world became more and more black and white and predictable to him. Finally, how comprehensive Hitler's anti-Semitism was, appeared from what Eberhard Jäckel said about it. Jäckel talked about the Hitler in the early 1920s, so when the NSDAP was significantly on the rise in Bavaria. 'Jewish was,' as already mentioned, 'the revolution of 1918. And the whole Weimar republic was Jewish, Marxism was Jewish and of course the Bolshevik blood dictatorship in Russia; the international stock capital was Jewish as well. The leftist parties were also Jewish – they were the troops of Jewry; finally, democracy, parliament, the term "majority" and the League of Nations were also Jewish.'[1] Jäckel forgot to mention one of Hitler's central thoughts, namely that the Jews were already preparing for global domination. If you read Hitler's teachings of the 1920s, you can ascertain that he saw the work of the Jew behind every evil. This way, Jews also held power over prostitution, the press with which they manipulated public opinion, they were behind every revolution and war, also behind famines, and they tried to bastardise peoples, so that they would lose their power, and so forth, and so forth. In fact, the Jew was an anomaly in the natural order and therefore he had to disappear.

The feelings of fear and insecurity, which had resurfaced with the Major Life Event of Pasewalk in November 1918, decreased after May 1919. Now, Hitler experienced social stability and began to realise successes. He made himself useful to the *Reichswehr* with his propaganda and became the star speaker of the NSDAP. In the early 1920s, he was already known as 'the rhetorical phenomenon of Bavaria'. The oracle was a curiosity that people loved to attend. Hitler's self-confidence increased. He saw himself as a drummer until the Putsch in November 1923, after which he regarded himself as the God-sent leader for future Germany. At the same time, the more or less isolated anti-Semitic phrases disappeared; he saw the possibility of increasing cohesion between all the so-called evil of the Jews. In *Mein Kampf,* written in 1924 and 1925, and in his *Zweites Buch,* written in 1928, his anti-Semitism consists of a firmly constructed and strong worldview. Then his fears succumbed as a result of his social successes and so-called deep paranoid insights into world events: he knew the eternal truths, they created an inner balance, and a sense of well-being arose.

When Hitler wrote his *Zweites Buch* in 1928, his party, the NSDAP, did not yet amount to much. The party only had two seats in the *Reichstag*. As a result of the economic crisis, which broke out in the US in 1929 and spread to Europe, greatly afflicting Germany, Hitler's NSDAP for the first time became a party which could not to be ignored. In 1930, the number of seats had grown to 107 and, in 1932, Hitler won 196 seats in the *Reichstag*. On 30 January 1933, the unthinkable happened. The former nobody from Vienna and First World War corporal was confirmed as Reich Chancellor by President Paul von Hindenburg, the former great First World War general.

It is debatable if Hitler's narcissism grew as a result, for in about 1924, he already viewed himself as a God-given dictator to save Germany. In Hitler's case, however, he could always go a step further.

His successes did not stop in 1933. He achieved one peaceful victory after another in international politics. Saarland was returned to the Reich in 1935, following a referendum, which Hitler attributed to himself. In 1936, he occupied the demilitarised Rhineland, seriously violating the

Treaty of Versailles in the process. The Western forces went no further than verbal protestations. Hitler's peaceful conquests continued. In 1938, Germany's strength increased through the *Anschluss* (annexation) of Austria. In September of that year, he welcomed back the Germans from Sudetenland through the Treaty of Munich.

In the spring of 1939, Hitler invaded and annexed Czechoslovakia, going against all international agreements. Now, this supreme liar was showing his true colours. A shiver of intense fear crossed Western Europe. Now, people realised, war was on its way, this man was not going to stop of his own accord. Hitler did indeed continue. On 1 September 1939, he attacked Poland. England and France felt forced to declare war on Germany. By 1940, Hitler controlled Western Europe in its entirety. Then he was called the Greatest General of All Time, '*Größter Feldherr aller Zeiten*' by Gröfaz.

Hitler's narcissism was exploding. His sense of self-worth had become extreme, but his old fears still existed, however deeply they were buried. In 1941 they resurfaced when he was about to lose the war in Russia. Then he initiated the genocide of the Jews.

Chapter 15

Other Interpretations

We have submitted an interpretation-proposal for Hitler's anti-Semitism. However, there are other stories about Hitler that can explain his anti-Semitism and its consequences. What is the best story? We had to compare it to our story. But how? One aspect of a story is its anchoring. If it is deficient or incomplete, then there is the question of no good explanation. The advice from Collingwood resembles this. He says, 'Work as a detective and put the authorities [as said: the experts who have already been doing research into Hitler's hatred of Jews] on the witness stand. Cross-examine them and find out what they have *not* said.'[1] Collingwood does not use the 'soft-approach' with regard to this witness hearing. He declares, 'The scientific historian puts them to the torture.'[2] He wants to force the witnesses to speak the truth by means of the torture chamber. Now, torture is – usually – not a good method of getting to the truth. But Collingwood speaks in metaphors to further emphasise that the historian must be insistent and critical (the torture) to discover weaknesses in other stories. A good explanation is in-depth, answers all the questions and does a better job of explaining than the others. This is how we obtain an instrument to compare.

Chapter 16

The Viennese Interpretation

The Hitler investigation began with Konrad Heiden. This journalist was a contemporary of Adolf Hitler. He visited his mass meetings in the 1920s and also interviewed people who lived together with Hitler in the *Männerheim* in Vienna from 1910–13. In 1933, he published a book on the history of National Socialism and, in 1936, the first Hitler biography, *Adolf Hitler. Das Zeitalter der Verantwortungslosigkeit* written by Heiden, appeared. Joachim Fest says that this biography has stood the test of time. Anton Joachimsthaler awards it the value of a primary source.[1] Not unjustly, because most of the later Hitler biographers go back to this source. Heiden, however, provided no specific interpretation for the origins of Hitler's anti-Semitism. This is understandable. He had already published his work before the Second World War. So, the genocide of the Jews had not yet taken place: the urgency to give a good explanation for Hitler's anti-Semitism did not exist yet. This urgency would only arise after the war. In his book, Heiden only indicated 'anti-Semitic influences' to which Hitler would have been exposed in the *Männerheim*. Hitler supposedly developed his hatred of Jews there during the years 1910–13. When Hitler finally left the *Männerheim* in Vienna and travelled to Munich in 1913 he, according to Heiden who based his ideas on this topic on *Mein Kampf*, complained about all races that were present in Vienna, especially the Jews. He saw Jews everywhere, 'divisive elements of mankind'.[2]

After the Second World War, Sir Alan Bullock in particular quickly wrote a biography about Hitler. This was one of the most successful commercial Hitler biographies and was considered a standard and masterpiece for a long time.[3] What was Bullock's explanation, now there was the urgency to explain Hitler's anti-Semitism? Bullock disappoints the reader: he explains nothing at all. He copied Hitler's own – very unreliable – statement from *Mein Kampf* and noted – characteristic of the then Freudian climate – that a tormenting sexual jealousy was possibly one of the roots of Hitler's anti-Semitism as well.[4]

Between the Bullock (1952) and Fest (1973) period, biographers such as Franz Jetzinger (1956), Hans Bernd Gisevius (1963), Bradley F. Smith (1967), Friedrich Heer (1968), Ernst Deuerlein (1969) and Werner Maser (1971) tried to gain insight into the origins of Hitler's anti-Semitism. All of them indicate that Hitler's hatred of Jews already originated during his Viennese period (1908–13), or even earlier, but now we know that, during that time, he was more of a friend of the Jewish people than a Jew hater. In fact, it is almost certain that the Viennese Hitler was as yet no anti-Semite.[5] Yet, all the above biographers gave an explanation for Hitler's anti-Semitism in those early years. How can this be? Their assumption was created by hindsight bias. From 1919, when Hitler became active as a politician, he proved to be a radical anti-Semite, so he had to have become a Jew hater in the extremely anti-Semitic Vienna, if not before. Then, without them knowing it themselves – the power of the confirmation bias does its work, in other words: they searched for arguments that confirmed their own assumption, while ignoring the arguments that refuted it. They did not question their a priori starting point.

Why is that?

Raymond Nickerson aptly described the phenomenon in an extensive overview article, 'Confirmation Bias' from 1998: The basic idea is that:

> Once one has taken a position on an issue, one's primary purpose becomes that of defending or justifying that position. . . . Once a belief or opinion has been formed, it can be very resistive to change, even in the face of fairly compelling evidence that it is wrong. The effect of the confirmation bias can hardly be noticed: [people] can be quite facile at explaining away events that are inconsistent with their established beliefs. . . . It seems that people generally select test items that are consistent with the rule they believe to be correct and seldom select items with falsification in mind. So, there is a natural defence to falsification.[6]

I would like to place two remarks about my critical observations with regard to Hitler researchers mentioned above.

It's easy to criticise them afterwards, but all of them have written good biographies and made important contributions to the Hitler research during this period. On the other hand, they could have been more critical during this period. Thus, none of the researchers, with the exception of Smith, paid serious attention to sources that make mention of Hitler's good relations with Jews. Reinhold Hanisch, Hitler's business partner, for example, was ignored by all in this respect. They also disregarded the evidence from the period 1914–18, indicating that Hitler was still not a Jew hater in Vienna. During the war at the front, he scolded everything that was 'foreign' and 'international', but he did not breathe a word about the Jews. This, for example, is evidenced by Hitler's letter to Ernst Hepp of 5 February 1915.[7] Also war comrades, with whom Hitler dealt daily, claimed that they hardly noticed anything of his anti-Semitism.[8] And his entire correspondence until 25 August 1919 does not mention a single word about Jews.[9] Most of these sources were already known during their lifetimes. Little was known in their time about Hitler's behaviour during the 'Jewish Munich Revolution' in 1918/19, which is difficult to reconcile with that of a fierce anti-Semite. So, one cannot blame them for not taking that into account.

Thus, the researchers that noticed that Hitler had already became an anti-Semite in Vienna use the sources selectively. In any event, we do not see a tendency to falsify among these researchers. On the other hand, one sees how strong the verifying power of confirmation bias works. Because there are no good sources that show that Hitler was an anti-Semite in Vienna, researchers just figured out an explanation that seems credible. Their arguments can be reflected as follows:

1. Adolf Hitler became an anti-Semite in Vienna.

↓

2. Hitler became impoverished in Vienna, in which anti-Semitism was extremely pronounced and he blamed his abject poverty on the Jews.

↓

3. Therefore he became an anti-Semite.

Point 1 is what they want to prove. Point 2 is partially correct: Vienna was the most anti-Semitic capital city in Europe at that time. It is also correct that Hitler became greatly impoverished during 1908 and 1909: he had no roof over his head, hardly owned any clothes, slept in parks and under bridges. Finally, he ended up staying in the Vienna homeless shelter in Meidling. There is no evidence in any of the reliable sources at all, however, that he blamed his poverty on the Jews. On the contrary: reliable sources show that Hitler praised the Jews in Vienna and that he got on very well with them. Point 3 therefore has no meaning whatsoever.

What would George Collingwood observe about these researchers? He would probably say: what they do *not* say is that there are no reliable sources from which it appears that Hitler was already an anti-Semite in Vienna.

Chapter 17

More Recent Publications

In 1996, an impressive biography about the young Hitler – written by Brigitte Hamann – was published. Thanks to her research it has finally become clear that Hitler had not become a hater of Jews in Vienna;[1] his anti-Semitic transformation, according to her, 'has to be placed during the time of change in 1918/19'.[2] Hitler was already 30 years old at that point. Now other questions come to mind. How is it possible that of all people Hitler, who later became the most rabid and deadliest anti-Semite of all times, did not become a Jew hater in the extremely anti-Semitic Vienna? We will answer this question when we discuss Sir Ian Kershaw.

And the second question is: if Hitler became a fierce anti-Semite in 1918–19, why did he only become one in those years? Hamann is clearer in an article in *Der Spiegel* about the date of Hitler's change: it was no wonder that 'during the poignant revolution in Munich, all the fragments of Hitler's Viennese experiences and all that he read in Vienna merged into one system just like on a magnetic field'.[3] She explains her metaphor and her interpretation becomes plausible. Hitler, so she says, had learned a lot of useful things in Vienna. The essence of it was the Jews are guilty of everything. However, he did not give credence to this yet in Vienna but had only taken note of it. In 1919, however, the Jews, so the story goes, were often the leader of the left-wing revolutions and therefore the provokers of all the revolutionary misery, death and shedding of blood. Moreover, they also thwarted Germany becoming a strong national state. In post-war Munich, the things Hitler had heard so many times before in Vienna, seemed to be confirmed by empirical facts. And so, the anti-Semitic fragments were merged into a system.

Those who read carefully discover an assumption in Hamann's explanation, namely: someone who had already taken note of anti-Semitism and is subsequently exposed to confirmatory anti-Semitic influences, becomes an anti-Semite. This assumption is not valid in the general sense: not everyone becomes an anti-Semite after extensively taking note of the 'doctrine' of anti-Semitism and after this doctrine seems to be confirmed by certain events. However, this could actually be true in Hitler's case; Hamann's interpretation is at very least a good story, which is partially true as well. However, the interpretation is not complete.

Hamann's story is characteristic of a historical story about a character. One only takes nurture – all sorts of environmental influences – into account and hardly any attention is paid to *nature* – inherited qualities – interacting with *nurture*. This is understandable. It is extraordinarily difficult to be specific about historical personalities in terms of *nature and nurture*. A tool to measure this is simply missing. At least, it appears that way.

For example, consider a family in which two sons grow up under virtually the same conditions. One joins the Boy Scouts and loves it, whereas the other does not like it at all. Why?

The question is difficult to answer. This question seems a little easier to answer if we consider the choice of football when one son has an exceptional talent for this sport and the other does not. The talented son will perform well, have fun and gets lots of praise. Here one can see that *nature* plays an important role in pursuing football.

Hamann only tells us about nurture.

And what she tells us about nurture, namely the question of confirmatory anti-Semitic influences that fell on fertile ground because Hitler had previously acquired anti-Semitic knowledge in Vienna, is tenuous. We cannot blame her for this. When she published her book an earlier version of the DSM, admittedly, was to hand; however, the manual did not mention causes of paranoia because they were still unknown. So, even though she looked into the DSM and read about *paranoid personality disorder*, she would still not have been able to tell a story about Hitler that integrated the causes of paranoia. It was only after 2000, thanks to research by Daniel Freeman and his research group, that the causes of paranoia were clarified based on good empirical examination. Hamann was not able to comment about this. Hamann tells us, as previously mentioned, nothing about *nature*. This is also understandable. Evolutionary psychology hardly ever belongs to the domain of knowledge of the historian. In addition, all that I have said about *nature*, especially how *nurture* may work upon *nature*, and how natural selection has created the forerunners of paranoia into innate tendencies, is founded on studies that were published ten years after Hamann's book was issued. Recall that Collingwood said, 'Look after what they do *not* say.' We have shown this in this case and immediately noted that Hamann actually could not have mentioned them. Nevertheless, she has written the best biography about young Hitler.

It is now over two decades since Hamann's 1996 publication. Due to new research, we can, if we make the effort to do so, observe more aspects of stories about historical personalities who have been of exceptional importance. In this respect I would like to emphasise the following.

A historical narrative is a record of events showing how one event emanates from another. A thousand-and-one forces play a role in this, including the course of action of the characters. Some historical figures are so unique that – despite the fact that they have only been able to develop under specific social and political circumstances – they have transformed history. In Hitler's case, his 'unique' personality even caused the Second World War, and he made his mark on the rest of the twentieth century. Almost all historians do in fact agree with each other: 'without Hitler no Holocaust'. An evil genius such as Hitler, who exerted such a great influence, should not only be 'explained' as one does in traditional historical stories. In this case, one should also take an in-depth look into his personal traits which made him receptive to anti-Semitism. We have seen that these traits were paranoid, and that Hitler scored, in that respect, the highest possible. For their part paranoid traits can also be analysed. One sees in these traits: suspiciousness, hostility, anxiety and psychoticism. With regard to the last trait, I emphasise that it does not, in any way, mean that he was psychotic. The counterpart of psychoticism is lucidity. Hitler did not have the lucidity to look at the phenomenon of anti-Semitism critically; to a certain extent, delusional thinking plays a role. Psychoticism only counts in that sense and its concrete meaning is that through his delusional thinking his suspiciousness became unjustified and unfounded.

It is beyond dispute that the mentioned traits contain a hereditary component in one way or another. That is the reason why one sees those traits among people, always and everywhere. We also took a big step into the past in Chapter 12 and paid particular attention to the development of suspicion in the Pleistocene period towards members of the own group and distrust of other tribes. This means we have gained better insight into the hereditary background of paranoia. This has allowed us to employ *nature* in our explanation. In other words, the tendency to paranoid traits which were so characteristic of Hitler are the result of natural selection. Please note I am only speaking about 'tendency' here. This tendency will only come to fruition as a result of sufficient stimulation. We have tracked this in Chapter 5.

In 1998, the first volume of Sir Ian Kershaw's monumental biography appeared. His biography is seen as a landmark historical work. Many consider it the best Hitler biography since Joachim Fest.

Kershaw stresses the morbid side of Hitler's personality. When he writes about the Viennese Hitler, he asks himself the following question:

> Why and when did Hitler become the fixated, pathological anti-Semite [. . .]? Since this paranoid hatred was to shape policies that culminated in the killing of millions of Jews, this is self-evidently an important question. The answer is, however, less clear than we should like. In truth, we do not know for certain why, nor even when, Hitler turned into a manic and obsessive anti-Semite.[4]

Here are a few comments on this important passage in his work. In my opinion, Kershaw is the first 'ordinary' historian who uses the word 'paranoid' and then consistently maintains this term throughout the rest of his work about Hitler. In all 'ordinary' biographies I will discuss later on in this study I have not come across the term. However, there is a contradiction in Kershaw's words. On the one hand he says that Hitler's paranoid hatred underlies Hitler's anti-Jewish politics and that it is pathological. On the other hand, he notes that we do not know why Hitler developed his manic-obsessive anti-Semitism. Without Kershaw being aware of this, he has more or less given the answer to the why-question: the extremely hostile anti-Semitism stemmed from Hitler's paranoia. The question might have been better posed if he had wondered what the link was between Hitler's paranoia and anti-Semitism and what Hitler's paranoia might have stemmed from; he would immediately have mentioned the main causes of Hitler's anti-Semitism. Why did he not do this? Here the same applies as to Hamann. In the time he wrote his biography there was hardly any knowledge about the causes of paranoia. So, he couldn't elaborate on this with regard to Hitler. Intuitively, he must have felt that he was right whenever he qualified Hitler as 'a paranoid anti-Semite'. Kershaw provides the reader only with words such as 'paranoid antisemitism', 'paranoid anti-Semite', 'pathological antisemitism', 'manic obsession'; they remain labels and the reader has to figure out for himself what they mean. In Chapters 9 and 10 we have shown Hitler was a real paranoid and clarified the relationship between paranoia and his anti-Semitism. To speak with the voice of Collingwood: there it is told what Kershaw couldn't yet tell.

It is remarkable that Kershaw does not agree with Brigitte Hamann's conclusion that Hitler was not yet an anti-Semite in Vienna (according to Kershaw, he was), especially because he often refers to her work with consent. In addition, he emphasises that there are no reliable testimonies of Hitler's paranoid anti-Semitism from Hitler's Viennese era; and he mentions that Hitler's close comrades from the First World War did not remember any anti-Semitic remarks from Hitler later on.[5] It does not end here: Kershaw also mentions Hitler's good contacts with Jews in his Viennese period, yet he states, 'However, it is difficult to believe that Hitler of all people, given the intensity of his hatred of the Jews between 1919 and the end of his life had remained unaffected by the poisonous anti-Semitic atmosphere of the Vienna he knew – one of the most virulently anti-Jewish cities of Europe.'[6] That Hitler did not yet become an anti-Semite in Vienna, be it somewhat moderate, is unthinkable for Kershaw. It is quite possible, however, as previously noted, that, due to his faithful relationship with the Jewish physician Dr Bloch, the young Hitler was not very receptive to anti-Semitism. Dr Bloch was the Hitler family's physician; and he was the first Jewish person Hitler got to know. Dr Bloch was well-known in Linz, especially to poor people. Everyone knew that he was always willing to visit the ill at night too.[7] After his mother's death, Hitler showed his gratitude by giving Dr Bloch handmade gifts. Hitler still sent him friendly messages from Vienna as well. A postcard from January 1908 states, 'With the most heartfelt wishes for the New Year, your ever-grateful patient Adolf Hitler.'[8] In addition, Hitler had probably been in love with Stefanie Isak for years (1905–13). If he had relied on her last name, he might well have inferred she was Jewish. This interpretation has been confirmed by the German historian Anton Joachimsthaler, who claimed in a BBC interview that Hitler actually thought she was Jewish.[9] First impressions are often difficult to change, which is called the 'primacy effect' in social psychology. Dr Bloch could have worked as a kind of Jewish prototype for Hitler, just like Stefanie Isak, and, as a result, could have made the young Hitler insensitive to the Viennese anti-Semitic malignancy. Otherwise stated: the first conclusion colours and brings into conformity with itself all that comes after.[10] This possibility was not considered by Kershaw.

Kershaw tends to see an anti-Semite in the Viennese Hitler. So why, he wonders, did no one notice that in his surroundings? His answer is, and he calls the answer very banal: in Vienna, anti-Semitism was so common that Hitler's anti-Semitic expressions were possibly not noticed.[11]

One might, of course, wonder what people in the very anti-Semitic Vienna would notice and remember. That must be something very exceptional. So: someone who expresses himself positively about the Jews. This is exactly what we find in the sources: a Hitler who speaks with appreciation of Jews and Judaism.

If Kershaw is indeed right about the fact that Hitler already expressed himself in an anti-Semitic way in Vienna, then at least he did not stand out as a rabid anti-Semite. Such fierce and intense anti-Semitism would surely have been remembered by Hitler's comrades from the *Männerheim*, namely Hanisch, Anonymous and Honisch. For example, Honisch points out that Hitler was only opposed to the 'Jesuits' and the 'Reds', but apparently, he did not speak a word about the Jews.[12]

Kershaw also doubts whether Hitler was really friends with Jews. He argues that Hitler had remarkably few friends in his life and that he even concealed his feelings to people in his immediate circle. In his dealings with Jews, Kershaw said, maybe it was just his own interest that was at stake: the Jews Robins and Neumann helped him with money, Siegfried Löffner acted as an intermediary between him and Jewish traders. Perhaps Hitler was simply pragmatic: as long as he benefitted from them, he could swallow his abstract dislike of Jews.[13]

However, showing that pragmatism and that swallowing were not necessary in his friendship with Rudolf Häusler. Hitler knew this friend from the *Männerheim*. He left Munich with him in 1913. Their connection was so close that they spent time with each other in Munich for nine months and lived together in the house of the tailor Joseph Popp, longer than Hitler stayed with Kubizek at Maria Zakreys' house in Vienna. Yet, Häusler did not notice any anti-Semitism in Hitler's attitude. Häusler was even disconcerted when he got to know the later Hitler as a fierce anti-Semite. Häusler's daughter shows how surprised her father was about this: in Vienna, her father had not noticed any anti-Semitism.[14]

Later, during the First World War, Hitler did not need the pragmatism Kershaw spoke about either. However, he did not express himself in an anti-Semitic way, not even at times when one would expect it, as in his letter to Ernst Hepp of 5 February 1915. Hitler interpreted the Viennese platitudes in this letter: he expressed the hope that Germany would be freed from *Fremdländerei* and that *unser innerer Internationalismus* would also disappear. The word 'Jew' is not mentioned, his later racial dogma is not yet visible.[15] By the end of the war, when he was attacking pacifists and slackers, he did not mention the word 'Jew' either.[16] So, it remains to be seen whether Kershaw's pragmatic interpretation is correct.

Finally, Kershaw concludes from the pros and cons: it is likely that Hitler had already hated Jews in Vienna. He blamed the Jews for all the setbacks he had suffered. It is possible that his hatred did not reach much further than the rationalisation of his personal circumstances.[17]

Indeed, Hitler's personal circumstances in Vienna, especially at the beginning, were miserable: no access to the art academy, no clothing, he was homeless, suffering from hunger and cold. But why did he blame the Jews for this? In addition, he made use of Jewish charity at that very time!

Later in Munich, when he witnessed and interpreted the years 1918–19, especially the months after 3 May 1919, in Hitler's view there was indeed a relationship between Jews and revolutionary events, which he found horrible. Then, in other words, Hitler indeed had sufficient 'empirical evidence' to make the Jews into a scapegoat. He did not yet have this evidence in Vienna. It is more likely that Hitler gained a lot of knowledge about anti-Semitism in Vienna, but that he had not yet embraced it; as mentioned above, the primacy effect prevented this. In Vienna, Hitler had not yet aimed his hatred at the Jews. His abhorrence was probably still very diffuse, unfocused.

Kershaw considers it likely that Hitler adopted radical views on the Jews during his first leave as a soldier in Germany in 1916. The Munich of 1916 shocked him. Anger, dissatisfaction, cursing, people who had lost courage determined the atmosphere. Hitler saw the work of Jews in this. Hitler also noticed that 'almost every clerk was a Jew and every Jew was a clerk'.[18]

Here Kershaw relies on Hitler's own allegation in *Mein Kampf*. In 1924, Hitler was already such a rabid anti-Semitic, that his statements about what he observed about Jews eight years before, do not seem very reliable. There are no other sources that confirm a radicalisation in Hitler in 1916. Therefore, his statement is supported by meagre evidence.

When Hitler heard about Germany's defeat and revolution in Pasewalk in November 1918, he felt this to be, in Kershaw's opinion:

> An absolute and unpardonable betrayal of all he believed in. . . . But if there is any strength we have put forward in the suggestion that Hitler acquired his deep-seated prejudices, including his anti-Semitism, in Vienna, and had them revitalised during the last two war years, if without rationalizing them into a composite ideology then there is no need to mystify the Pasewalk experience through seeing it as a sudden dramatic conversion to paranoid anti-Semitism. Rather, Pasewalk might be viewed as the time . . . when his own rationalisation fell into place.[19]

As explained by Kershaw, Hitler must have seen a confirmation of the ideas he had cherished from the Viennese years with regard to the Jews and social democracy in the revolutions that took place in Munich, Berlin and elsewhere during this period.[20]

The process that Kershaw describes seems correct. It corresponds to Hamann's description. There was a state of stress (the defeat and revolution in Germany). Hitler was searching for culprits. In doing so, he made use of knowledge, which was already present in him in a fragmented way, but now – that is, during his stay in Pasewalk and during the Munich Revolution – this knowledge fell into place permanently, which led to him finding *the* answer. Only the question is, just as in Hamann's case, if Kershaw's date is correct. The only thing that is known about Hitler's experience in Pasewalk is what he says about it himself in *Mein Kampf*. So, we actually do not know anything about that period. Moreover, after Pasewalk, Hitler participates in the 'Jewish' revolution of Munich, albeit with little enthusiasm. Why, for example, did Hitler not join the free corps units and *Einwohnerwehren* that were popping up like mushrooms everywhere and that called on every right-minded German to fight against the Jewish revolution in Munich? It seems more obvious that Hitler did not make his conversion to anti-Semitism until the months after the fall of the Soviet Republic on 3 May.

Let us now look at Ralf Reuth's findings in his book *Hitler's Judenhass* from 2009.[21] As the title indicates, he focuses entirely on Hitler's *Judenhass*. It is also interesting that it is a recent publication: he was able to include seventy years of research on Hitler. It is a rare and good book on all anti-Semitic influences upon Hitler from 1919 and in the 1920s. If one looks at all those factors, it seems almost impossible that Hitler did not become an anti-Semitic. From Ralf Reuth's perspective, just these influences seem to be the causal forces.

Who will deny that these influences had a major formative effect on Hitler? What is entirely missing in his interpretation is the answer to the question: why was Hitler so receptive to anti-Semitism? We have seen Hitler scores high for paranoia and have understood that his sensibility for paranoia had come into existence during his first thirty years due to a series of traumas and painful experiences. We have also seen that the precursors of paranoia remain a part of human nature as a result of a long evolution.

It is inevitable that Hitler's personal idiosyncrasies played a role in his anti-Semitic turnaround. Not a word is mentioned about this – now we are almost accustomed to this omission – while true personality traits can explain a lot with respect to someone's choices, behaviour and ideas. Interestingly, neither the word 'paranoid' nor 'paranoia' appear in Reuth's book. Apparently, he has not attached any value to the statements made by Kershaw, who consistently uses the term 'paranoid', as we have seen. Yet, Reuth seems to have an eye for a certain pathology in Hitler, because he recognises Hitler had delusions and immediately provides the well-known statement of 'the influence from the environment', namely, 'Eckart had provided the pseudo-scientific basis for Hitler's anti-Bolshevik and anti-capitalist motivated hatred of Jews, thereby contributing decisively that for him the illusion of the "Jewish conspiracy to gain world domination" could become the ultimate truth. Hitler now included everything in this delusion, even though the results were totally nonsensical.'[22] Whatever inner impulse made Hitler accept this illusion so enthusiastically so that he subsequently included 'everything' with conviction is not touched upon. I repeat once again: no attention is paid to pathological traits that are a substantial part of Hitler's identity and that made him receptive to anti-Semitism. No mention is made of the fact that traits are the result of both *nature* and *nurture*. It is then quite understandable that Reuth doesn't consider at all how these traits could have developed as a result of the interaction between *nature* and *nurture*.

In 2013, Othmar Plöckinger published his impressive study *Unter Soldaten und Agitatoren*. Plöckinger is a historian who clearly enters the debate – he should be an inspiration to every historian. He successfully participated in the debate because he has made convincing corrections to the *Hitlerforschung*: he deconstructs and presents a better interpretation for assumptions that have been accepted as fact on the basis of new sources. However, no one single book is perfect. The back cover of his work states, 'with the diligence of a detective, the author reconstructs in detail, for the first time, how Hitler, who returned from the war, became the leader of the National Socialistic German Labour Party (NSDAP) and a radical anti-Semite'. The subtitle contains the words 'Hitler's formative years', and in the preface Plöckinger notes that the book is partly biographical. However, Plöckinger also only looks at the external circumstances. Although he records them wonderfully, there is no description of Adolf Hitler's personality during the period of time before the anti-Semitic influences began to affect it. In fact, he does not discuss Hitler's character at all, not even for a moment. Hitler's personality is more than vague and nebulous with Plöckinger: it is completely intangible; Hitler remains an empty shell. The assertion that the book clarifies why Hitler became a radical anti-Semite is a half-truth; yes, again the influences – they are repeatedly presented in a very detailed way – but Hitler's typical reaction to them – from within – is missing. Nature isn't mentioned.

What would the critical Collingwood have said about Reuth and Plöckinger? Collingwood insists that one has to look at what historians do not say. Of course, we do not know if he had any knowledge of the effects of nurture and nature and how much they fuse as a person develops. Imagine, however, that he did have this knowledge, then he would agree with me that they tell half the story. They do not take Hitler's first thirty years of nature interacting with nurture resulting in strong paranoid traits into consideration at all.

Shortly after Plöckinger's publication, another new and major biography about Adolf Hitler appeared again, in the same year: 2013. More than thirteen years had then passed since the publication of Ian Kershaw's masterly work. The new biographer is Volker Ullrich, who published part one of his scheduled two-volume biography: *Die Jahre des Aufstiegs 1889–1939*. In his foreword Ullrich already speaks approvingly about Kershaw, who uses the words 'delusional ideological fixations'.[23] This is, in fact, not correct, because Kershaw always speaks of 'paranoid' and not of 'delusional'. Ullrich notes here that Kershaw does not underestimate the 'delusional' fixations.[24] But what the reader is supposed to make of this remains unclear. The same applies when Ullrich writes on p. 59 that the Viennese Hitler – although he already shared a few anti-Semitic prejudices and clichés (with his Viennese contemporaries) – was still far from his later <u>paranoid</u> hatred of the Jews. Now Ullrich uses the word 'paranoid' nevertheless, but he does not explain it, even though you can attach many meanings to the word.

When Hitler did indeed develop this paranoid hate, namely from May after the fall of the Munich Soviet Republic, while he was working for the *Reichswehr*, it is not mentioned by Ullrich, let alone explained. We only read that 'Hitler absorbed the prevailing anti-Jewish mood and scattered cries in nationalist anti-Semitic brochures and flyers like a sponge'.[25] The metaphor 'sponge' does not provide any clarity here; on the contrary: the metaphor obscures what actually happens. Hitler is like a sponge absorbing anti-Semitic information – but why is he so eager? The answer lies in the peculiarity of Hitler's psychology, which has developed itself until that stage, as we saw. Ullrich does not utter a word about this – the well-known omission. In the meantime, more has become known about paranoia. However, a historian is a historian.

Ullrich devotes his Chapter 13 to 'the human being Hitler'. At the beginning of this chapter, he draws attention to a difficulty in describing Hitler as a human being and the reason for this, so he says, is his unfathomableness. Even for his closest followers, he remained a mystery and as a means of support he names: Otto Dietrich, Ernst Hanfstaengl, Albert Speer, André François-Poncet and Otto Meissner – all these figures express, in one way or another, that Hitler cannot be properly assessed, that he remains a sphinx, an enigma.[26] But suppose that this enigmatic feature is exactly a characteristic of Hitler's personality – then what? A characteristic of a paranoid is that he wants to remain impervious to others. Such a person protects his private world. Ullrich cites Meissner, who notes about Hitler that he 'suspiciously closed himself off and granted only a few – and only occasionally – a glimpse in his inner self'.[27] Point 3 of the DSM-5 checklist on *paranoid personality disorder* says: is reluctant to confide in others because of unwarranted fear that the information will be used maliciously against him or her.[28] The trait suspiciousness is present here. If we focus on the paranoid trait 'is reluctant to confide in others', it sounds rather moderate if we take Hitler into account. In fact, Hitler was never inclined to confide in others. So, the thing Ullrich considers a problem to get through to Hitler could actually be the feature of the man in the sense that it primarily refers to a paranoid inner self. If this is the case, Hitler becomes a lot less mysterious. In fact, Hitler's so-called unfathomableness would just belong to his paranoia. And nowadays a lot is known about people with paranoid traits. It sounds a bit ironic, but actually they are more or less an open book, so Hitler as well – thanks to the fact that the paranoid personality is excellently defined in the DSM-5 and to the work of Daniel Freeman and his research group.

In the spring of 2015, Wolfram Pyta published *Hitler, der Künstler als Politiker und Feldherr*. The study commands attention because it provides a totally new view on Hitler's personality, political performance and his role as a strategist. The emphasis in Pyta's interpretation is on Hitler's self-image: he primarily saw and continued to see himself as an artist – from his time in Linz until the end of the Second World War and the way he saw himself determined the specific nature of his politics.

It is unfortunate that he pays little attention to the inception of Hitler's hatred of Jews in 1919. He mentions it briefly and indicates anti-Semitic influences – the famous *nurture* effect. He points to all kinds of anti-Semitic writings that Hitler must have read and uses the metaphor of 'the seed of a dragon' [anti-Semitism], which was implanted into Hitler in 1919 with disastrous consequences.[29] The metaphor does not seem well chosen to me: 'seed' is an organic entity in which all hereditary characteristics are locked up that will only be expressed after germination and influence of the environment. But Pyta refers to environmental influences with 'dragon seed' here. The question that immediately arises is why the anti-Semitic environmental influences had such an impact on Hitler. What was so typical of Hitler's being that made him so receptive to anti-Semitism? To use the metaphor correctly, one could ask the question like this: from what seed (inherited characteristics) did the personality traits develop in interaction with the environment, making the impact of anti-Semitism so intense? We now know the answers. We also know what Collingwood would have said about Pyta.

In autumn 2015 another Hitler biography appeared, written by Peter Longerich.[30] A second such title to be published in 2015: a fruitful year, seventy years after the end of the Second World War. Longerich is a rare and eminent expert in the field of the Holocaust research. He has published a great deal about Hitler and the Holocaust, and he is someone who always emphasises the bigger picture and the broader context, even to such an extent that the character Hitler is sometimes in danger of disappearing behind major social processes and political developments. But in this publication, the character Hitler must be at the centre – and this is definitely so. Longerich consulted a group of psychiatrists, psychologists and psychotherapists; he refers to this in his word of thanks. Therefore, one expects that Hitler's psychology is profoundly dealt with. In particular, one expects that his conversion to anti-Semitism in 1919 will get a thorough psychological explanation. This expectation is not really met, however. In the chapter 'Hitler schooling by the Reichswehr' (in July 1919), the anti-Semitic influences are mentioned in particular.[31] Longerich also stresses that Hitler's letter of 16 September 1919 to Gemlich was typically created under the influence of contemporary anti-Semitic writings. However, it is clear that Hitler's embracing of anti-Semitism was psychologically functional for him. Anti-Semitism provided Hitler with an explanation for the catastrophic situation in which Germany found itself. I quote, 'The defeat, which seemed to him as inexplicable and undeserved, and the rapid political radicalisation subservient to the revolution, by which he was dragged along as well – all this was now considered to be a premeditated manipulation that had been going on for a long time [by the Jews].'[32] With a bit of good will one can see a psychological explanation in here. The phrase 'already premeditated manipulation' has a paranoid connotation, but Longerich does not specify from what innermost feelings or pathological traits Hitler gave this interpretation. Does he refer to the influence of the environment once more? Or to paranoia from within? It remains uncertain. He could have done. In the year of his publication a lot more about paranoia was known. However, that knowledge has not yet penetrated Hitler experts, even if they are advised by psychiatrists and psychologists.

Longerich briefly mentions the morbid aspect of Hitler's anti-Semitism; Hitler 'imagined' himself in a 'dangerous situation' – a dangerous condition 'that not only applied to the German people but to all mankind' and 'in his distorted perception this threat was of an apocalyptic proportion'.[33] In particular, the words 'imagined', 'distorted perception' and 'an apocalyptic proportion' seem to indicate a pathological condition. But which?

The reader may think of a paranoid state again, especially of the aspect of delusional thinking, but Longerich does not use the word 'paranoia' or 'paranoid' here. Only 900 pages later he mentions the word for the first and last time as well. Meanwhile, the reader has arrived in May 1943. Hitler's harangue in front of Goebbels, Longerich calls a tirade, 'a paranoid Tour de Force' but immediately puts this description in perspective by noting that behind this 'paranoid Tour de Force', there was a clear political calculation.[34] It is obvious: Longerich does not think much of any kind of paranoia. In this respect, he contrasts with Ian Kershaw who consistently speaks in his writings about Hitler as the 'paranoid anti-Semite'.

When Longerich talks about Hitler in the 1920s, he notes 'that he was capable of formulating his own threats and fears as collective fears and at the same time he could suggest destruction scenarios, which one could use to eliminate the dangers in the world . . .'.[35]

Here we look into Hitler's head and we see threats and fears in him. But which ones? Longerich does not provide an explicit answer here, but it is likely, if one looks at what he had written earlier (p. 72), that he is referring to the Jewish danger. The question, however, of what the source of these internal fears and threats was that he changed into collective fears is not answered. It is true that the character of Hitler is looked at closely: his psychology comes somewhat into view, but the real roots of his fears are still ignored.

Occasionally, Longerich seems to suggest a genetic predisposition for the Hitler phenomenon. He speaks of Hitler's successes of which the causes 'were *deeply hidden in his personality*'; he speaks of 'raging anger and megalomaniacal refusal to accept reality [as] the expression of his psychological *disposition*'.[36]

Although Longerich gives initial impetus to the explanation of the origins of Hitler's anti-Semitism – he also implicitly refers to a genetic predisposition, more questions are raised than answers provided. In Chapters 8–10 and 12 we have tried to give the answers. Let the reader judge whether or not they are good ones.

Chapter 18

Freudian Psychohistory

It is striking that researchers who have been reviewed here have hardly looked at the person of Hitler and instead have emphasised anti-Semitic influences. Those who have done so (regarding Hitler's psychology) were the 1970s Freudian psychohistorians.

Both the famous speech of the historian William Langer, 'The next assignment' in 1958, in which he called on others to deepen historical knowledge through the use of psychoanalysis, as well as the publication in 1958 of *Young Man Luther* by Erik Erikson are seen as the formal beginning of psychohistory. Yet, historical figures had already been analysed at an earlier stage. Freud himself, for instance, analysed Leonardo da Vinci. It was an encouragement for future psycho-historians: psychoanalysis could therefore also be applied to people from the past. Freud's analysis of Leonardo could have been a warning as well: although his analysis was sublime – he elucidated Leonardo's entire artistic and intellectual development in an ingenious way – none of it made any sense whatsoever. Freud started from an early memory of Leonardo's of a vulture. This vulture was crucial, since, according to traditional beliefs, it could only exist as a female bird and was fertilised by the wind. Freud got all the information from this, but he used German translations in Leonardo's notebooks in which his 'nibbio' was wrongly translated into 'vulture' instead of 'hawk'.[1]

Originally, psychoanalysis was a doctrine and treatment method to cure patients. In the 1960s and 1970s, however, it became a theoretical weapon against the establishment in the hands of critically educated scientists who were schooled according to the Marxist and Freudian doctrines. Prominent philosophers and psychologists such as the neo-Freudians Wilhelm Reich, Herbert Marcuse, Jacques Lacan, Erich Fromm and Robert Laing exposed the hidden interests of those in power. It seems that this intellectual climate stimulated the development of psychohistory as a supplement and correction to the traditional historical sciences. In any case, more and more psychohistorical works appeared in the US during these turbulent years. In 1976, *The Journal of Psychohistory* was founded.

Psychohistory is the science of 'historical motivation'.[2] The psycho-historian tries to discover the motives and unconscious motivations of historical characters. This is the most important aspect of his historical research. He usually makes use of Freudian theories. Because these historians are so focused on the analysis of unconscious motives, they often use sources other than customary ones in the historical sciences. They involve fantasies and metaphor use of historical characters, mistakes, comments aside, jokes and the like in their analysis. Most psychohistorians are not historians by profession, but psychiatrists, psychologists or psychotherapists.[3]

Hitler was also the object of the psychoanalytic approach. Psycho-historians believed they had uncovered Hitler's unconscious roots of revenge and destruction for the first time. Some traditional historians indicated a favourable attitude towards the research results. The famous German Hitler researcher Andreas Hillgruber, for instance, was really enthusiastic about the possibilities of psychohistory.[4] In the 1970s, four psychohistorians wrote about Hitler: William Langer, Erich Fromm, Rudolph Binion and Robert Waite, who explicitly applied Freudian analysis.[5] After his analysis, Langer drew the conclusion that Hitler was a neurotic psychopath. Fromm, on the other hand, considered Hitler a necrophile. Binion came up with an entirely different explanation: Hitler murdered the Jews in order to take revenge on the Jewish doctor who had 'killed' his mother, in other words: he had not treated her properly for cancer. Waite shifted towards Hitler's father; Hitler wanted to kill his so-called half-Jewish father but took the Jews instead.

The different outcomes of their analyses are striking. They say more about psychoanalysis and its practitioners than about Hitler, namely: psychoanalysis as applied by the analysts is a doctrine for which it's hard to claim validity.

Remarkably, the word 'paranoid' or 'paranoia' is hardly mentioned, if at all. Why didn't the psychohistorians come up with the idea that Hitler was paranoid? The interpretations of those historians are strongly associated with Freud's views and within the context of Freudian thinking the interpretation of Hitler as paranoid does not fit. Freud dealt chiefly with people who suffered from neurosis. These people are not abnormal: it only affects part of their personality and their perception of reality is only mildly distorted.

Sometimes Freud touched upon paranoia and only once he published extensively on paranoia: 'The Case of Schreber' (1911). This article concerned a man, Paul Daniel Schreber, who suffered from a severe psychosis: he thought he was already dead and decaying, yet he ached for death (in psychiatry this is called a 'bizarre thought') and for hours he sat stiff and motionless looking ahead. Freud related paranoia closely to psychosis in this case (characteristics: bizarre thoughts and hallucinations). The authority of this Jewish founder of psychoanalysis, who fled from Vienna in 1938, only developed fully after the Second World War. The psychohistorians were totally influenced by him, therefore they couldn't see any paranoia in Hitler. He didn't suffer from a psychosis after all: his thoughts were neither bizarre nor was he hallucinating.

Nowadays psychologists are convinced of the fact that it is not possible to explain a human personality by only looking at his infancy and childhood; so, it is not enough if one focuses solely on the relationship that the growing up child had with his father and mother. Freudian psychohistorians do exactly this, they limit themselves to early home surroundings. An exceptional and preponderant level of attention is paid to this, notably if traumatic events have taken place, whereas hardly any note is taken of later significant social and cultural influences.

Again: there is hardly any foundation for that basic assumption. Therefore, in our explanation, we have looked much farther than the relationship of the young Hitler with his parents. We have gone through his first thirty years of life and noticed what traumas he went through, which made him receptive to paranoid delusional thinking. We have also taken a giant step back into the past and, in this way, we have included *nature* in our interpretation; we understand that a genetic disposition to paranoia must have played a part. There is a further criticism concerning the Freudian approach. The psychohistorians of the 1970s emphasise repression and the unconscious: typical Freudian notions. However, there is scant evidence that these core elements of Freud's theory exist. The famous American memory and often expert witness Elizabeth Loftus concluded that there is hardly any evidence for the phenomenon of repression and also therefore not of repressed memories, which suddenly emerge later; the unconscious as formulated by Freud can therefore not exist.[6] There is no doubt about that. David Stannard also checked whether there is scientific evidence for Freudian repression. He says that a very psychoanalytic web is spun around the phenomenon of 'repression' – and thus the typical Freudian unconscious, which, after many years, is still nothing more than speculation – a speculation that contradicts the results of a mountain of scientific research.[7] (There is, of course, an unconsciousness in which processes are going on that anticipate conscious thinking, feeling and acting – but that is not the Freudian unconsciousness.) It is correct that psychoanalysis no longer has a place in historical research. After all, one cannot base valid interpretations upon an invalid theory. One can say that the anchors of the psychohistorians are simply false, incorrect, not valid.

Chapter 19

More Modern Psychological Research

We have seen that Freud's analysis is unreliable, as discovered in the course of the 1970s. Psychiatric diagnoses appear to differ for the same patient; there is no mutual reliability, and there are no uniform criteria for the same disorder. For six years, American researchers worked to eliminate these deficiencies. They relied on a formidable amount of empirical data. The result was the publication of *The Diagnostical and Statistical Manual of Mental Disorders III* in 1980. Two major innovations, intended to make diagnostics more reliable, caught the eye. The first was the exit of theories concerning the efficacy of causes – mostly including Freudian theories. That is to say, presumed underlying psychopathological processes used to make a diagnosis, were disregarded. The reason was that psychiatrists did not agree on what was the most viable psychological theory and conducted a school-of-thought battle. The DSM sought a taxonomy that was separate from that battle. The manifest symptoms were now the starting point – nothing else. This was the second innovation. So, no causes were mentioned for each disorder, but only a list of symptoms and it was agreed how many symptoms the patient must have to qualify for the relevant diagnosis. This is called the check-list method. Thus, the diagnosis was no longer linked to subjective views and theories and was standardised and simplified at the same time.

In concrete terms, this means – if a diagnostician only looks at the symptoms through applying the check-list-method – he is not taking account of someone's life history, the importance of the family in which he has grown up, the influences of society and culture and his neurobiology. But therein lie the causes in most cases. If one, for example, looks up *paranoid personality disorder*, one would find a good definition of the disorder and an accompanying list of seven symptoms. The patient must have four or more symptoms to qualify for the diagnosis (the check-list method). However, and in the meantime, this may have become clear, one would find nothing about the causes! There are a few exceptions, concerning neurocognitive disorders, for which the causes are often clear.

It is a pity these diagnostics fail to mention possible causes. However, if they are not yet known, it is sensible to not include them. It is a strong point, indeed.

There has been much criticism of the DSM binary approach: either one has a particular mental disorder or not; another outcome is not yet possible. In 2013 (in the DSM-5) a first move was made towards the dimensional approach, which introduced a sliding scale as an alternative to the binary approach. I believe the dimensional approach is more reliable than the check-list method. The point of departure is that every human has personality traits – which cannot be disputed. From there, we can look at the extent to which a person has these traits. There are fifty traits divided into twenty-five pairs.[1] Each pair consists of two polar opposites. One is pathological, the other is not, but they are connected to each other through a continuum.

Let us consider the pathological personality trait 'callousness'; it is described as lack of concern for the feelings or problems of others; lack of guilt or remorse about negative or harmful effects of one's actions on others.[2] Its polar opposite is 'kind-heartedness' at the other end of the spectrum. Kind-heartedness brings to mind sympathetic concern for the well-being of others, and being empathic, kind, tender and warm. *Every* human can be placed somewhere between these two poles. The polar opposites of the pathological traits are generally healthy and adaptive traits, but that is not necessarily the case. Take the above-mentioned example kind-heartedness: there are individuals who, due to extreme kind-heartedness, repeatedly allow themselves to be taken advantage of by unscrupulous others.[3] Again, every human can be placed somewhere on this spectrum of callousness versus kind-heartedness. The same also applies to the other twenty-five spectra with their two extremes. One may see extreme paranoia as one polar opposite, the other is trust. Here, one sees there is clearly no question of a binary approach. It is an improvement, but alas the entire DSM-manual from 2013 is strongly dominated by the binary method. It is expected that in the upcoming DSM, the binary approach will completely disappear and in its place the dimensional approach will be used for all mental health disorders.

In spite of its shortcomings, the DSM is a standard work. It is probably correct when it claims about itself that the current diagnostic criteria are the best available descriptions of how mental health disorders are expressed.[4] If we just look at all the behaviours and cognitions that are considered diagnostic criteria, it may be concluded that it is the richest encyclopaedia and largest reference book of psychiatric behaviour. There is no better catalogue of psychiatric abnormalities. It is also relevant what the DSM-5 says about a disorder in general, that it produces significant distress or disability in the person concerned. The degree to which a person is suffering from the disorder is also important for the diagnosis.[5]

Historians who wanted to say something about the psychology of Hitler, were equipped with a better diagnostic tool from 1980 onwards than the previous Freudian theories. However, this better tool only provided, as we have noted, information about the symptoms of a mental disorder. Historians who are not familiar with psychology and psychiatry stayed in dead water with the DSMs. If they, however, paid attention to the manual, they could identify Hitler as a man who had a paranoid personality disorder, especially if they looked at the list of behaviours that characterise this disorder. Thanks to the manual, they would be able to establish that Hitler had a delusional disorder too and they would have been able to further specify that Hitler particularly qualified for the persecutory and grandiose sub-types. As no causes have been mentioned in this case, they couldn't look for them in Hitler's life and integrate them into an explanatory story. Psychiatrists and psychologists, however, from the period after Freud obviously had more knowledge of paranoia than we read in the DSM. We are now going to take a look at researchers who conducted psychological research into Hitler in the 1990s.

Hitler has been diagnosed with many mental disorders. We are limiting ourselves to those researchers who have highlighted paranoia. There is a clear reason for this, namely paranoia is that form of psychopathology – in contrast to other disorders – which is particularly relevant to politics. There is another reason as well, which we might easily forget, because it has been mentioned and explained at the beginning of this study: a debate with other researchers is required for a good investigation.

Edleff Schwaab grew up in Germany when the Nazis were in power. His father was an active member of the party and a high-ranking Nazi official. The young Schwaab fought in Russia. After the Second World War, he emigrated to the US where he studied psychology. At a later age, he started to reflect on what had happened in his home country, especially on what kind of man Adolf Hitler had been. In 1992, he published *Hitler's Mind. A Plunge into Madness.*

The title is quite revealing, he views Hitler as a madman. The man had a paranoid mind and ultimately became a paranoid psychotic. In Schwaab's biography, Hitler's paranoia is at the core of his analysis; he distances himself completely from the Freudian approach and emphasises that later events were more crucial than those of his childhood. Yet, his statements about these later events are imprecise and vague. Nevertheless, Schwaab does not tell a just-so-story.

Schwaab describes Hitler's sick mind rather than explains it. He ignores the *paranoid style*, he does not mention this concept, but he does recognise that Hitler had been greatly influenced by the anti-Semitic tradition; however, he discounts it as *the* explanation. The driving force of all his actions was his paranoia hidden behind his hatred of Jews. Hitler's anti-Semitism was so all-consuming, extreme, powerful and obsessive that it cannot be considered an anti-Semitism of the average anti-Semite. Hitler thought the Jews wanted to destroy mankind, and if the Jews succeeded then this planet would again move through the ether without people, like millions of years ago. Such bizarre thoughts can only stem from a sick mind, and these precise thoughts formed the core of Hitler's paranoid mode of thinking. Hitler, as told by Schwaab, was absolutely sure that a mysterious mandate had been conferred on him to avenge and to heal. According to Hitler, it was beyond question that he was the Redeemer and the Messiah; all downright psychotic thoughts. Here one sees, according to Schwaab, a kind of grandiosity that often goes along with paranoia. This paranoid grandiosity is also exhibited in Hitler's words: 'I believe today to act on behalf of the Almighty Creator. By warding off the Jews, I am fighting for the Lord's work.'[6] One sees in these words the delusional conviction of a man who works for God as a prophet in biblical times.[7] With his pathological ideas he couldn't see through his unrelenting cruelty and appreciate the enormity of the catastrophe of the Holocaust. Hitler didn't have the ability to learn something, which fell beyond his pathological ideas. His world view yielded to a pathological one: a set of ideas frozen in unyielding obsessions, which are nothing more than totally insane convictions; they 'reflect the powerful mind-distorting effect of his paranoid condition'.[8]

From the beginning of his political career, Hitler demanded the removal of the Jews, but in a speech in front of the *Reichstag* on 30 January 1939, he spoke about this subject in very ominous words; it concerns his notorious prophecy, which he would repeat again and again. 'Today, I will be a prophet once again: Should the international financial circles of Jews outside Europe succeed once again to involve the nations in another war, the result will not be a Bolshevistic triumph and a victory of Judaism but the extermination of the Jewish race in Europe.'[9] This prophecy stemmed from his paranoid belief that the powerful Jews (the *Drahtzieher*) were behind the government of England and especially the US. By threatening to kill the European Jews, Hitler thought he could stop the *Drahtzieher* from conspiring against Germany to save their tribesmen in Europe. So, Hitler hoped to continue his policy of conquest without intervention. Schwaab calls this type of thinking a kind of reasoning that made the Holocaust possible.[10] The conquest of Russia and the killing of the Jews emanated from one and the same interpretation.[11] With this, Hitler came into the final phase of his paranoia.

Driven by the thought of conquering the Jewish Russian Colossus, he also felt emboldened to murder the non-Barbarossa Jews. As the war progressed, more Jews came into his domain. For Hitler's paranoid mind, this was unacceptable. By killing the European Jews, he wanted to control a situation that was getting out of hand.[12] 'He felt sure the world would be pleased.'[13] These were all strongly paranoid ideas.

Schwaab mentions the anti-Semitic Vienna where Hitler lived from 1908–13. In that time, Hitler became all too familiar with anti-Semitism. Schwaab views the First World War as a crucial experience for Hitler. This period taught him to use violence, to be cruel and unscrupulous as a means of attaining political goals.[14] However, the fact that Hitler became a thoroughbred paranoid is not explained through traumatic events. It is only by showing Hitler's thoughts and deeds that Schwaab can demonstrate that the man was blatantly paranoid in a powerful way. He himself says, 'It is more plausible to assume that it was a regressive, vicious, innate tendency towards sadistic behaviour than a reaction to an emotionally shattering experience in childhood. [. . .] Given an innate predisposition certain environmental influences can be said to have served as precipitating events to bring his paranoia into the open.'[15]

Schwaab's power lies in that he doesn't lose himself in fantasy. He doesn't give a clear-cut explanation, but he shows – which is very valuable – Hitler was paranoid to the highest degree: without paranoia, no Holocaust. It is an observation of crucial importance. And we are in complete agreement with it. It is a pity that ordinary historians have paid no attention to Schwaab's work, in fact, it is a considerable omission. Schwaab's description of Hitler's mind is exceptionally good and is almost in exactly agreement with what has been said in this study about Hitler's psychopathology. We are now decades after Schwaab's publication. Meanwhile it has become clear that the circumstances in which Hitler lived during his first thirty years were triggering paranoia. We clarified these in Chapters 4, 5 and 12. Recall that Schwaab speaks about an innate tendency. We can agree with this. You could call this 'tendency' a vague and distant cause. Thanks to knowledge which has been gained in the meantime, we have been able to clarify this vague cause. We did that in Chapter 12, where we looked into the deepest roots of paranoia. What Schwaab calls an 'innate tendency' is already progress compared with most historians, who make no mention of hereditability. Schwaab also mentions 'certain environmental-influences'; he now remains vague, although what he says is true. There is something, however, which pervades his entire work and which is absolutely essential and with which we are in complete agreement. By this, I mean Hitler's extremely radical anti-Semitism. With this utmost anti-Semitism, he far exceeds every average anti-Semite. That is why Schwaab can only consider him extremely paranoid. One could call this a common-sense presumption.

In 1997, *Political Paranoia* by Robert Robins and Jerrold Post was released. Their book is not expressly a study about Adolf Hitler; only Chapter 11 is dedicated to him. The title of their work already suggests how they view Hitler, namely as a paranoid. They refer to the DSM-4 early on and name the central feature of the 'paranoid personality disorder': a pervasive mistrust and suspiciousness of others such that their motives are interpreted as malevolent. Robins and Post are not cautious with regard to the causes; they purposefully work out for themselves what the origin of paranoia is and do not hesitate to express robust statements about it.

To understand paranoia, they make use of insights on evolutionary psychology. From the evolutionary perspective, cooperation and deceit are already quite old. The authors refer to a study by animal behaviour experts who wondered whether – apart from cooperation – deceit plays a role in the behaviour of monkeys. The results of their research affirm this. Monkeys send false signals of reconciliation and become aggressive at the last moment. Survival-value is present in this capacity for deception. Furthermore, the ability to discover those false signals offers more chance of survival. In fact, there is a 'co-evolutionary struggle between deceiver and deceived'.[16]

If monkeys can deceive one another and recognise deceit in time now and then, then it is obvious that this power was present within the common ancestor of humans and apes. Therefore, man would not only be 'hard wired' to cooperate but also to deceive and to penetrate deception.[17]

In fact, suspicion has always been present.

A point of criticism that I would make about these authors is that deception is not paranoia, and neither is its recognition, but these qualities can be seen as a precursor or building block of paranoia. The authors call paranoia an innate tendency. In every culture there is unfounded distrust and therefore paranoia. In fact, paranoia, according to the authors, is 'part of the human condition'.[18]

We agree with these evolutionary insights, but we have gone into them much deeper ourselves in Chapter 12.

In some people, as explained by Robins and Post, there is a tendency towards paranoia. Psychologically unhealthy as well as healthy people may develop paranoid features in situations of unusual stress. Germs of a more primitive psychology remain within the personality, ready to be activated in times of stress: a stressful, diffuse and complex situation is simplified by using paranoid ideas to get a more manageable black-and-white image.[19]

Here, we see stress as a provoking factor, but the authors don't particularise the process. As far as Hitler is concerned, we have done this in Chapter 5, in particular.

Paranoia extends along a continuum from normal (adaptive) suspicious behaviour to severe psychiatric disorders, such as paranoid schizophrenia. Here, the authors approach paranoia dimensionally and not binarily as in the main section of the DSM: where one either has the abnormality or does not. In contrast, their starting point is 'normal adaptive suspicious behaviour', whereas ours, inspired by the DSM-5 (2013), is trust – a real polar opposite.

If a politician is too paranoid, he will not enjoy a long political life: He will fall short as a politician and be considered as downright crazy. Such a figure is an exception. The paranoid politician usually does not entirely take leave of reality. He is often fixated on one aspect. Because there is often a grain of truth to his statements and interpretations, he is not overly delusional; this politician is not seen to be psychiatrically disturbed; but it is precisely the manifestation of this type of paranoia (Hitler and Stalin are mentioned as examples) which is the most dangerous. One might say that the present paranoid traditions camouflage morbid paranoia.[20]

Up to this point, their insights and knowledge seem relevant to me. However, once they hone in on Hitler (he is one of many crazed politicians they discuss) the reader will notice that they unfortunately do not have much knowledge on the state of Hitler research in 1997. They rely on outdated publications; virtually everything they say about Hitler's course of life is obsolete. The second flaw is that they scrutinise Hitler using Freudian techniques. We now know that Freudian analysis is unreliable. Apparently, Robins and Post are immersed in the Freudian

Hitler during his Reichstag speech on 1 September 1939 He was justifying his invasion of Poland. He made no mention of the Jews. Later he would date his infamous annihilation prophecy of 30 January 1939 to 1 September 1939. (Image bank WO2 – NIOD)

German anti-Semitic poster The Jew is accused of causing wars. Hitler was convinced that Jews were the cause of the First and Second World Wars. They needed to pay for this. (Attributed to Everett Historical/ Shutterstock.com)

Photograph of Joseph Stalin in a Soviet newspaper on 24 June 1941
It reports Hitler's invasion of Russia, which had happened two days previously.
(Attributed to Oleg Golovnev/Shutterstock.com)

Triumphant German troops entering Minsk on 25 June 1941 As long as the war with the Soviet Union went according to Hitler's plan, he took no decision to murder all the European Jews. (Attributed to Everett Historical, royalty-free stock photograph)

The Wannsee Villa On 20 January 1942, in this beautiful house, the most horrifying meeting ever was held, under the command of Reinhard Heydrich. Agreement was reached in the General Government to kill the Jews in Europe by extermination through labour and by gassing. Hitler had already given 'the order' to kill the Jews a number of months previously. (Attributed to Electric Egg/Shutterstock.com)

Rudolf Höss The Auschwitz commander during his trial. He was hanged in 1947. (Image bank WO2 – NIOD)

A gas chamber in Auschwitz The Jews were told that they would be able to take a shower in this room. Almost 1,000 people could be gassed there at one time. As soon as the last victims had been squeezed into the room, the door was hermetically sealed. (Attributed to Brandon Fike/ Shutterstock.com)

A hole in the ceiling of the gas chamber Zyklon B was inserted though one of these. In some gas chambers there were four such holes (hatches which could be quickly opened and closed), allowing the substance to be dispersed from canisters. As soon as Zyklon B met the air, the crystals changed into extremely poisonous gas. (Attributed to Ramukanji/Shutterstock.com)

Two incineration ovens As soon as the Jews had been killed, they were straightaway taken to the incineration ovens. These often malfunctioned, so then the bodies were burnt in the open air. (Attributed to Brandon Fike/Shutterstock. com)

German prisoners of war at Stalingrad There was a direct link between the war with the Soviet Union, which was going badly for Hitler, and the decision to murder the Jews in Europe. (Attributed to Everett Historical/ Shutterstock.com)

Sir Winston Churchill
Hitler's great opponent.
(Pixabay license)

Willem Sassen He interviewed Eichmann in Argentina over a period of almost seven months. The conversations were recorded on a tape recorder. (Image bank WO2 – NIOD)

Eichmann in Jerusalem Here he is telling the judges the opposite of what he had told Sassen. (Public domain)

doctrine to such an extent that the criticism that has erupted since the 1980s has bounced off them. In fact, they don't prove Hitler was paranoid, they only assert it. Obviously, Hitler's extreme anti-Semitism and its genocidal consequences are sufficient to deem Hitler paranoid. In Chapter 8 of this study, it has been made clear that Hitler's anti-Semitism is only an indication of the paranoid style, as explained by Hofstadter, and it isn't automatically proof of clinical paranoia. They don't make this distinction. However, Hitler's anti-Semitism was so extreme, uncompromising, comprehensive and genocidal that they consider his behaviour and actions as outright paranoid. Edleff Schwaab did the same. This is in fact their anchor. In spite of its flaws, Robins and Post's book has special value: it appears to contain good starting points for further research, particularly its hypothesis that Hitler had a disposition for paranoia that developed later on. Their emphatic assertion that, of all people, paranoid politicians can bring about an ultimate catastrophe cannot simply be ignored. The fact that paranoia has always been among people and that the phenomenon has evolutionary ties is relevant information. We completely agree with these aspects. However, I think, their most relevant observation is this: 'Only paranoia is the quintessence of political psychopathology: political paranoids have no opponents or rivals, but enemies and enemies must not simply be defeated – they must be destroyed! There is no other mental disorder that will continue to have such profoundly destructive effects on human affairs.'[21] A psychopath as a dictator is a disaster, but he does not identify any non-existent enemies – a paranoid one does.

In 1998, one year after the publication of Robins and Post's book, Fritz Redlich published a study on Hitler. Redlich was a Jewish psychiatrist, born in Vienna in 1910, who at the age of 88 went public with his Hitler book. Redlich outlines a comprehensive psychopathological profile of Hitler.[22] The most prominent trait he mentions is Hitler's paranoid delusions and tendency towards suspicion.[23] Here, we see a researcher again – who is no historian like Schwaab and Robins and Post – connecting Hitler and paranoia. He concludes emphatically that Hitler's key psychological feature was paranoia and therefore he lays great emphasis on this. However, Redlich cannot get a good grip on a paranoid Hitler. He is vague and unconvincing about the causes. Redlich refers to Hitler's childhood, during which his suspiciousness may have arisen, and Redlich highlights the ambivalent relationship he had with his parents. One can hardly call these remarks an explanation – they lack specificity. However, he mentions one concrete example; the same one as in our Chapter 9. I quote Redlich: 'If Kubizek's comment is valid, Hitler's remarks after he failed the entrance exam for the Viennese Academy of Fine Arts that snares had been put out to get him is evidence that some suspiciousness existed in early adulthood.'[24] Redlich does not go on to look for other examples of unjustified suspiciousness in Hitler's private life. It goes without saying he sees Hitler's suspicion of Jews and the fact that he blamed them for all evil in the world. Although he calls Hitler's thinking about the Jews a delusion, in Hitler's days these thoughts were widely shared in Germany. And shared illusions are interpreted by experts differently than unshared illusions. Here, Redlich encounters what we called the paranoid style: hostile statements legitimised by a culture can be understood as normal expressions for the socio-cultural environment in which the personality finds itself.[25] Therefore, Redlich hesitates to call Hitler's anti-Semitism paranoid. He even says, 'Weird beliefs are not considered paranoid within their own cultures'.[26] It seems Redlich is not able to solve this problem, yet he maintains his observation that Hitler's paranoid delusions 'were Hitler's most significant psychopathological complex'.[27] He seeks some support from Robins and Post, but it doesn't help much, because they don't give a clear answer to the question why Hitler can be called a paranoid, as paranoid delusions belonged to the anti-Semitic culture in which he lived. In Chapters 8 and 9 we solved these problems. Finally, Redlich also reflects on a series of other diagnoses and then concludes, as he looks back with approval on the study by Robins and Post: 'For those who like short labels, political *paranoia* is the diagnosis. My own label is very similar: Hitler was a destructive, *paranoid* prophet.'[28]

Chapter 20

Evaluation and
Some New Remarks

Until now, many stories have been reviewed that explain Adolf Hitler's anti-Semitism. Some resemble each other, others are totally different. The most fitting explanation of Hitler's anti-Semitism is a story that is the most in-depth, explains all aspects of his anti-Semitism and is strongly anchored.

At the beginning of this study, we gave a proximate and later on an ultimate explanation. This explanation comprises two stories: the ultimate explanation is an exceptionally profound one in which *nature* also plays its part. We even travelled back to the Pleistocene period for this explanation. In the proximate explanation we put forward *nurture* and the direct causes of Hitler's delusional thinking, which ended in paranoia. In Chapter 10 the relationship between paranoia and anti-Semitism could be shown explicitly, and I could at last tell the explanatory story of Hitler's anti-Semitism. I did my best to anchor all the aspects as firmly as possible.

From there, we looked at the stories of traditional historians. We noticed that their explanations did not go any further than anti-Semitic influences from the environment. Of course, this influence is of importance, but at the same time it tells us nothing: History can explain anything by means of influence from the environment, so it doesn't give a specific answer. In this type of explanation, only *nurture* plays its part, and *nature* is completely absent. An addition is required in which dispositions or inherited characteristics of Hitler's personality are considered, interacting with nurture – i.e. the environment.

In the 1970s, psychohistorians focused heavily on Hitler's infancy and youth. Although they told fascinating and highly particular explanatory stories about the young Hitler, all their findings were based on an invalid theory, namely, Freud's theory. Correct interpretations cannot logically arise from an invalid theory.

In 1980, the DSM-III was published. In this impressive manual, Freud was rejected in the sense that no underlying psychopathology was used for diagnostics. The reason for this was that the explanations that did come forth differed greatly and these diagnostics told us more about the followers of this or that Freudian theory than about the truth of the explanation itself. Using the DSM-III, one could only check whether someone had a mental disorder or not. The manual tried to establish order in the chaos of competing schools of thought. In the latest edition, published in 2013, the DSM-5, there are still no causes mentioned for most mental disorders. Because of this, historians have been unable to use it as a tool to tell an explanatory story about Hitler's paranoia.

From the 1990s, more 'modern' psychological explanations have been offered about Hitler and his anti-Semitism. In this study, we have limited ourselves to discussing psychologists or psychiatrists who focus on paranoia in their explanations. This choice needs some clarification.

From the 1990s onward, a wide variety of psychological interpretations have been given: according to Jablow Hershman and Julian Lieb (1994) Hitler had bipolar disorder. Psychiatrist Michael Fitzgerald (2004) assumed Hitler was an 'autistic psychopath'. Hans-Joachim Neumann and Henrik Eberle (2009) concluded, based on the diaries of Theodor Morell, that there is no evidence of a mental disorder. Finally, in 2015 Norman Ohler explained Hitler's behaviour as the result of psychoactive drug use.[1]

It is possible Hitler had Asperger traits or that he showed behaviour consistent with bipolar disorder. Concerning Hitler's drug use, he was already extreme in his word and deeds before he began consuming them. All these so-called disorders hardly have any explanatory power as far as Hitler's extreme and genocidal anti-Semitism is concerned – whereas paranoia does! That's why, I have discussed the stories of Schwaab, Robins and Post, Redlich, who all emphasise paranoia.

If Hitler's strong paranoid traits do provide a good explanation for his extreme anti-Semitism, and if these add a complementary and deeper understanding than 'anti-Semitic influences from the environment', it is at least surprising that traditional historians have paid hardly any attention to paranoia. In 99 per cent of the publications by 'ordinary' historians one doesn't even come across the term. This omission becomes somewhat understandable, considering that the words 'paranoia' or 'paranoid' are well-known, but in-depth knowledge about the phenomenon is universally lacking. After the work of Schwaab, Robins and Post, and Redlich was published in the 1990s, there was enough information for traditional historians to see its importance. Alas, one will not find the names of these 'paranoia-researchers' in the traditional historians' bibliographies after 2000. The Freudian psychohistory of the 1970s, which was been cast in a bad light and from which historians dissociated themselves, has perhaps played a role in this.

Sir Ian Kershaw is an exception. He mentions Redlich in his bibliography. Whether he started consequently calling Hitler 'a paranoid anti-Semite' because of Redlich I don't know. He doesn't explain the paranoid aspect any further, let alone explain Hitler's paranoia. You cannot blame him for that. When he published his Hitler biography, there was – as I have said several times before – not much known about the causes of paranoia. Redlich also remains, as we have seen, vague about the cause of Hitler's paranoia. Until then, there simply hadn't been much research conducted.

This would change, however. Daniel Freeman and his research group in particular have conducted innovative research on the phenomenon from 2000 onwards and thanks to his work we now know more about the circumstances in which paranoia develops. One may say that an average historian lacks good and deep knowledge concerning paranoia in spite of the fact that more has become known about the underlying pathology. But historians will be historians and new knowledge about paranoia falls outside their scope. It often takes a long time before relevant knowledge seeps from one discipline into another. So, it is understandable they cannot use this new knowledge for profound clarification. However, if insight into a figure like Hitler increases by knowledge of the fact that Hitler had strong paranoid traits, then, in the Hitler research there is a robust omission, and it is necessary to make a link to psychopathology. We have done that. I dare say, without any doubt: without a paranoid Hitler, no Holocaust. So essential was his paranoia.

For me, it is difficult to accept that one of the most eminent Holocaust researchers, Peter Longerich, only mentions the word once in his recent Hitler biography, *Hitler* (München, 2015), even though he was given advice by psychologists and psychiatrists – they should have underlined its importance.[2] And when he finally mentions the word it is downplayed, whereas it should have been emphasised strongly. In Longerich's work *Holocaust* (2000) the search for a paranoid Hitler is in vain (the studies by Schwaab, Robins and Post, and Redlich had already been published). Longerich sees the Holocaust as a highly complicated decision process propelled forward step by step in which a series of points of escalation can be identified.[3] That is, 'The leadership at the centre and the executive organisations on the periphery radicalised one another through a reciprocal process.'[4] It is completely justified that he puts the Holocaust into a broad societal perspective, and that he explicitly includes the periphery, and with that our insight into the catastrophe increases. However, so-called mutual radicalisation would have been impossible without a paranoid Hitler. A paranoid Hitler is a necessary precondition for the process of reciprocal radicalisation. In fact, Hitler's paranoia was the starting point from which the process of radicalisation came forth. Again, without a paranoid Hitler, there would be no Holocaust.

Chapter 21

Hitler's Motives to Kill the European Jews

From the beginning of his political career Hitler had repeatedly made clear that the Jews had to be removed from Germany. In the 1920s his mind was full of genocidal fantasies. If you start reading his speeches from those years it doesn't take long before you encounter genocidal phrases. On 6 April 1920, he declared the Jews must be eradicated unrelentingly to the root.[1] Any means were permissible to achieve that goal, even a pact with the Devil. On 7 August, four months later, in Salzburg he declared one cannot eradicate a disease without killing the cause (Jewry). In *Mein Kampf*, published in 1925–6, he consistently compared the Jews to parasites, bacteria, harmful insects, vampires, fungi. This way he dehumanised the Jews and implicitly suggested a solution: a purifying genocide. Yet, in this period there is no trace of a conscious intention to kill the Jews, let alone making concrete plans for killing them. He stuck to genocidal remarks and fantasies.

When Hitler came to power in 1933, the Jews were 'stimulated' to emigrate. In the course of the 1930s this remained the formal policy – no murder. The Nisko-Lublin plan of October 1939 (expelling the Jews and resettling them in the Lublin region of Poland), the Madagascar plan of the summer of 1940 (transporting the European Jews to the island of Madagascar) and after that the plan – originating in about January 1941 – to deport the Jews to Russia, they all had genocidal traits, but the striving to kill all the West-European Jews was not immediate. Invading Russia in June 1941, Hitler had organised a war of annihilation, however, it is not probable that he had given an order to kill all the Barbarossa Jews. It was expected the war would be too short for that. The Trial of Major War Criminals in Nuremberg had shown that before the attack on Russia the leaders of the *Einsatzgruppen* had not received an order from Hitler to annihilate the Jews.[2] From August 1941 onwards, however, not only were the men of fighting age killed but now also women and children. The genocide of the Barbarossa Jews was a fact. The genocide of the West-European Jews started somewhat later. Before we give some thought to at what point in time Hitler issued the order or made the decision, I would like to first look at his motives. This is not a difficult matter, Hitler himself had mentioned them. That is, his conscious motives; the deeper paranoid and delusional ground from which they stemmed were not visible to him.

On 30 January 1939, Hitler made a mammoth speech lasting more than 2½ hours in the *Krollopera* in Berlin. It was exactly six years since he had come to power. He commemorated the take-over. He then made a prophecy regarding the Jews. This so-called prophecy encapsulates Hitler's most notorious words about the Jews, and every Hitler biography includes them. He announced his intention to kill the Jews if they didn't meet his demands. We encountered this prophecy when we discussed the work of Edleff Schwaab. Now it is quoted in a slightly different translation. On 30 January 1939 Hitler spoke threateningly:

> Today I want to be once again a prophet: if the international finance Jewry (*dem internationalen Finanzjudemtum*) inside and outside Europe should again succeed in plunging the nations of the world into a world war, then the result will not be the bolshevization of the earth and thereby the victory of the Jews, but the extermination (*Vernichtung*) of the Jewish race in Europe.[3]

Hitler wanted to prevent England and France, and at a later stage the US, from frustrating his imperialistic plans. By threatening to kill the Jews (he alluded, of course, to the Jews in his own territory and as such made them a bargaining chip: *ein Faustpfand*) he thought he would terrify the powerful Jewish *Drahtzieher* who acted behind the political scenes in France, England and the US. He supposed that, because of his threat, these nations (at this time especially France and England) would not act against Germany. That is, thanks to this threat, Hitler could now wage war unimpeded. However, if these nations opposed him, worse still, declared war on Germany, the international mighty Jews had ignored his warning and Hitler would punish their tribesmen in Europe, which meant: exterminating them. Here we see two closely connected motives for killing the Jews: if they do not listen to his warning and cause a new world war – he will exterminate them.

Two years later, on 30 January 1941, he repeated his prophecy in a slightly different form. He warns the Jews not to cause a new world war, however, if they do, he will finish completely the role of the Jews in Europe. Again, we see the same motives.

For the time being Hitler kept silent about the Jews with respect to killing them. However, from the end of October 1941, immediately prior to the beginning of the genocide of the European Jews, he made a couple of statements that once more indicated his motives for genocide. The reason for this was that the war in Russia was going badly.

On 25 October, Hitler was in the Führer Haupt Quartier, there he reminded Himmler and Heydrich of his notorious prophecy of 30 January 1939. After that he remarked: 'This Jewish race of criminals is responsible for two million dead people due to the [First] World War, now again hundreds of thousands ... who cares about our people? It is good the fright precedes us, that we eradicate the Jews.'[4] Hitler often covered himself in prophetic words speaking about the murder on the Jews, but in the abovementioned quote from 25 October, he clearly spoke about the eradication of the Jews in the here and now. He also mentions a new motive for the killing: the Jews have millions of deaths through the wars on their conscience; they must atone for them. On 13 December 1941, Hitler received the Nazi hierarchy in the old Reich Chancellery to discuss the new situation (being at war with the US). Goebbels recorded the key points of Hitler's speech to the prominent Nazis in his journal:

> The Führer is determined to settle with the Jews. He foretold then that [30 January 1939] if they again would bring about a world war, they would experience their own annihilation. These words were no hollow phrase. Now the world war is here, so their annihilation must be the necessary consequence . . . so those who caused it must pay for the bloody conflict with their own lives.[5]

Now Germany was at war with the US. The Jews had caused a new world war and they had remained deaf to the warnings of the *Führer*, so they had to be killed. The usefulness of the pawn (*das Faustpfand*) had ended. The time had come to take out the Jews. When Hitler spoke these words, the *Wehrmacht* in Russia was forced back. Worse still, the retreat threatened to change into a desperate escape in the style of Napoleon's Grande Armée in 1812.[6] The US was now also at war with Germany. The spectre of defeat must have loomed large before Hitler's eyes from mid-October (then things started to go horribly wrong for the *Wehrmacht* in Russia). Now the US, having endless resources, would fight Germany, so that nightmares about defeat must have become more terrifying to him. The way Hitler spoke about the Jews possibly started to change. On 2 January 1942, he declared, 'The Jew will not eradicate the European peoples; however, he will become the victim of his own attack.'[7] Twenty-eight days later, on 30 January 1942, he repeated this statement more extensively in his *Reichstag* speech.

> We are well aware that the war can only end by eradicating the Aryan peoples, or by the disappearance of Jewry from Europe. I already expressed this in the German Reichstag on 1 September 1939 . . . that this war will not end the way the Jews envisage, namely that the Aryan peoples will be eradicated [*ausgerottet*] in Europe, but that the result of this war will be the destruction of Jewry. For the first time, the real ancient Jewish law will be performed this time: an eye for eye, a tooth for a tooth.[8]

As we have seen, Hitler prophesied on 30 January 1939 that he would kill the Jews if they provoked a new world war. In October and December, he declared he wanted to murder them because they were the cause of the war with Germany, which spilled much German blood. All of a sudden, on 30 January 1942, he claimed that the Jews strove to eradicate the Aryan people. However, this would not happen because in the same sentence he remarked not the Aryans, but the Jews would be killed. What the Jews were pursuing, if they were triumphant, Hitler would instead bring on them – to eradicate them: an eye for an eye, a tooth for a tooth. Here, one can clearly see the delusional motive for revenge. At the same time, Hitler's fear of the Jews is becoming more manifest, 'The German people can be convinced of one thing: the events of 1918 will, as long as I live, never take place again; because I'll never lower the flag.'[9] In fact, he says, however much I get trapped by the enemy, I will always keep on fighting. Here, one hears a person who is afraid of defeat. Hitler also remarked in the same speech, 'How this year will finish, I don't know. If the war will end, nobody can say.'[10]

We see Hitler feeling insecure about the course of the war. He revealed himself to be very anxious and extremely vengeful towards the Jews. There were several reasons Hitler's words now hung so ominously in the air. The murder of the Jews in the extermination camp Chelmno was ongoing and camp Belzec was under construction, while the establishment of Treblinka and Sobibor was being planned and Auschwitz was preparing itself for genocide. Moreover, at the conference Am Grossen Wannsee 56–8, ten days earlier, on 20 January 1942, the following words were communicated: 'The evacuation of the Jews has now replaced emigration as a possible solution according to the approval of the Führer.' This message was not meant for a passive *Reichstag*, which served as a forum for world politics, but it was a clear announcement to active policy-makers – high representatives of the SS, party and bureaucracy – and 'evacuation' now meant 'killing' by gassing or by working (extermination by labour).[11]

Hitler's tone changed and his motives became clear. On 24 February 1942, we again hear the Jews want to exterminate the Aryan people.[12] This time Hitler clearly depicted what he was fighting against: the worldwide Jewish conspiracy which 'stretched from the bank buildings of the plutocratic world to the vaults of the Kremlin' and he would destroy that conspiracy and 'after eliminating this parasite [the Jews] a long time of reconciliation between the peoples will come and thereby true peace'.[13] Here we see something resembling a new motive, namely the striving for a long time of reconciliation between the peoples.

More than eight months later, he alludes to the murder that was occurring in the here and now. For this he had good reason.

On 8 November 1942, Germany was startled by the news that the Allied forces had landed in Morocco and Algeria. An atmosphere of gloom hung over Germany. This landing was an enormous defeat for Hitler, which weighed more heavily than the loss at the Battle of El Alamein. Normally, he would have remained silent in response to that kind of message, but he had already announced his speech in memory of the Beer Hall Putsch of 1923. And what did the narcissistic, military genius have to say? Of course, he repeated his notorious prophecy of January 1939 on that 8 November 1942. Now he added, 'The Jews had received my prophecies with laughter. From those who laughed at that time, many of them aren't laughing anymore and those who are still laughing will maybe not be doing that anymore.'[14] Now, before a global audience, Hitler's position was seriously weakened by the landing of the Allies in Africa. That sick mind couldn't do much more than say he was executing his threat: eliminating countless Jewish lives in extermination camps. Should he indeed lose the war against the Allies – Hitler's great anxiety – and should the defeat become a fact, and it seemed to be becoming a more possible reality, then he would still be defeated by the *Drahtzieher*. The powerful Jews would then – just as in 1918 – destroy Germany. However, before that day would come, Jews would no longer be laughing in Europe. The *Faustpfand* had been eradicated. Hitler would have taken long revenge on the world's Jewry – a revenge in advance. (I have taken the insight of 'a revenge beforehand' from Philippe Burrin's study *Hitler and the Jews. The Genesis of the Holocaust* (1994). We will go into this in more detail in a moment.)

Did Hitler have another motive to kill the *Faustpfand*? Yes! The Jews were, by virtue of their Jewishness, a deadly danger to the German people. He had already made this clear time and again, and since the 1920s Hitler's thoughts had not changed. Let us return to the Hitler of the 1920s.

Whatever a Jew does, it is always destructive to the non-Jew. The Jew cannot proceed in any other way, for his strivings stem from his blood.[15] He cannot help himself, his race predetermines his destructive impulses.[16] Whether a Jew is a leader of a democratic or socialistic party, or a prominent scientist, author or tradesman who markets his merchandise, he remains a Jew and therefore obsessed with one thought: how he can arrange world dominance for his people?[17]

So, whether a Jew is a mighty *Drahtzieher* in the US or in England, or a simple artisan in Germany or somewhere else in Europe, dangerous tendencies towards other peoples always stir within him. He is always aiming to plant perilous thoughts within people.[18]

What most Jews do, according to Hitler in the 1920s, is made clear in 'The Protocols of the Elders of Zion'. They reveal in a disgusting way the essence and activities of the Jews. The Protocols reveal all Jewish activities, in its rationale, and expose the Jew's ultimate aim. In this piece of writing, one reads what Jews unconsciously do.[19] Hitler speaks about 'doing unconsciously'; it seems as if many Jews are unaware of their own activities. However, most of the times he points out their concrete motives.

To live his countermining life, as stated by Hitler, the Jew must renounce his inner self in the public eye, so that he activates his ability to lie.[20] Any Jew is a liar – he is the master of the lie. Lies and deceit are weapons in his destructive struggle.[21] His greatness is situated in the destruction of man and his culture.[22]

Jewry is an anomaly of nature; therefore, it attacks basic healthy laws of the human race. The Jewish essence conflicts with nature's purpose, because the Jew himself doesn't struggle for existence, as he should, namely by the sword.[23] In fact, Jewry should not exist on earth.

What Hitler thought of the Jews in the 1920s remained the same afterwards. Only the circumstances changed. In the autumn of 1941, a cabal of Jews turned out to be all-powerful and caused, according to Hitler, immense harm to Germany. Moreover, the European Jews were now – more than ever – a danger. Thus, on 21 July 1941, Hitler said to the Croatian Marshal Kvaternik, 'for if only one state should tolerate for whatever reason one Jewish family in its land, then it would become a focal point of bacilli of a new countermining'.[24]

'Countermining' is a rather abstract word; however, events which took place in France in August and October 1941 elucidate it. In these months, the resistance assaulted the *Wehrmacht*. Of course, the conclusion was that Jews were behind it. In revenge French groups blew up six synagogues on the nights of 2 and 3 October. Heydrich approved this, as he wrote on 6 November after Hitler had forcefully designated the Jews as 'the culpable incendiary in Europe, one which must definitely disappear from Europe'.[25] The day before, on 5 November 1941, Hitler said to Himmler that:

> If I permitted that in a period in which the best men are dying at the front that criminals are kept alive, then I shifted up to the hilt the balance of a people at the cost of the good forces. . . . If a nation is endangered then the combatants can be robbed of their fruits by just a handful of criminals. It has happened to us in 1918. In such a case it is the best thing that anyone who assaults the people is shot to death.[26]

Here, Hitler alludes in a thinly veiled way to the 'November Criminals' (*Novemberverbrecher*): the Jews. In autumn 1941, the Jews were not only a *Faustpfand* but also formed – just like in 1918 – a fifth column. The Semite's dagger was again ready to be stabbed into the German back.

On 27 January 1942, Hitler repeated that the Jews must disappear from Europe. He added that in places where there were only a few Jews, they were most dangerous. They will always remain an element that turns people against each other.[27] That he continued to be absolutely convinced that the Jews were an anomaly of the natural order was evident from his February 1942 speech, 'As soon as there are no Jews anymore among people, natural order sets in again.'[28] Hitler was willing to ensure this; for on 22 February 1942, he said, 'The same war which Pasteur and Koch had to wage, must now be waged by us. Numerous diseases are caused by one bacillus: the Jew . . . We shall get healthy if we eliminate the Jew.'[29] Hitler's insights concerning how evil works in the world are, for us, obvious indications of his unwavering paranoid delusion.

So, Hitler himself has given insight into his motives for genocide. I sum them up here: 1. The *Drahtzieher* had not listened to his warnings, they had started a new war, therefore, they should be punished, that is their European tribesmen must be killed; 2. Again, the Jews had millions of deaths on their conscience; so they had to atone for these crimes; 3. Hitler was afraid of defeat and that the Jews would eradicate the Aryan people, however, he would exact revenge for this defeat in advance; 4. Hitler was afraid of the Jewish dagger, which was waiting to stab the German's back; by killing the Jews he would ward off this danger; 5. He wanted to stop the suffering of the world by eliminating the Jews, because they were undermining the natural order of things. He strove for reconciliation between peoples.

Let us dwell a moment on these motives. The question may arise: what are these motives anchored in? This time it is very simple: they are anchored in Hitler's own words. (Except the last part of motive 3, that is an interpretation.) The motives are valid if one assumes that Hitler believed he spoke the truth. There is no doubt Hitler was convinced his own statements were true. Therefore, Hitler's motives are convincingly anchored. Thus, we can be convinced that we have exposed Hitler's true motives.

It is significant that a lot of the aforementioned words date back to the end of October. By then, it must have become evident that the Russian campaign was a spectacular failure in comparison with what he had expected (Russia would collapse like a house of cards). Not by the greatest stretch of imagination could a fast victory be in sight. Hitler had to continue fighting in 1942 as if Germany had not already been beaten. From the second half of October, the phantom of defeat must have danced around more emphatically in his fantasies.

We have derived many motives for killing Jews from Hitler's words in the period from October 1941 to February 1942, but these did, of course, exist before this. Some of these were already in place in the 1920s. It is only because of circumstances changing in a negative way for him that he expressed his motives more clearly from October onwards.

Now, we will consider the most important motive – motive 3. It is worth examining more closely. The motive is as follows: Hitler was afraid of defeat and of the Jews eradicating the Aryan people. He would exact revenge for this defeat in advance, however. This is one aspect of Philippe Burrin's interpretation. I am quoting the last part of the paragraph in which Hitler's motive is expressed. I have emphasised the specific sentence in italic.

> By means of the somehow sacrificial death of the Jews, he was fanatically steeling himself to achieve victory, or fight to destruction. At the same time, and above all, he was expiating spilled German blood, and *avenging beforehand a possible defeat*. He would conduct this exercise of vengeance, as it turned out, with mounting determination as the situation worsened, and he advanced toward an apocalyptic end.[30]

Burrin's interpretation has been consciously noted and integrated into my own interpretation. It appears in the last sentence.

We need not repeat that Hitler was paranoid. He was a narcissist as well. The mixture of paranoia and narcissism is extremely dangerous. Hitler had styled himself as a latter-day Napoleon. In 1939, he was hailed as the greatest general of all time, which he did not doubt for a moment. Hitler believed in his own infallibility and considered himself a personality, who could not be replaced, as a polar star of curious humanity. Hitler had elevated himself to the company of Frederick the Great, Martin Luther, Richard Wagner and even Jesus Christ.[31] How would such a paranoid narcissist react to an enemy that not only worked against him but maybe even saw an opportunity to destroy him and the completion of his grandiose masterpiece from the second half of 1941 onwards? According to his paranoid cognitions everything that this paranoid narcissist had worked on since 1919 was threatened by destruction by this Jewish enemy, if Germany were to lose the war in Russia.

A looming defeat for Hitler, who had an awesome grandiose sense of self-importance and who was entirely engrossed in fantasies of endless success, power and brilliance, was absolutely intolerable.[32] Hitler had presented himself as a god and yet Germany faced the risk of losing another war. Actually, he saw this as impossible, but the threat was still present.

Again, how would such a man respond to this threat? How would such an extreme paranoid narcissist react to this?

Such a man wants to destroy his demonic bringers of bad luck, destroy and massacre them. There is only one possible answer in his opinion: ultimate revenge. In Hitler's perception, it was the Jews who supported those in power in London, Washington and Moscow and who were supportive of their military policy against Germany. And the European Jews were again – in Hitler's sick perception – a fifth column waiting for their chance, just like after the First World War, to plant a dagger in Germany's back. And these Jews threatened to beat Germany, just as in 1918.

The untouchable god is about to fall, but before his possible final downfall the guilty ones must pay and the hugely colossal demonic massacre on the Jewish archenemy must be completed before his own defeat became a fact. So, it was not an untouchable god who committed the genocide, but a deeply wounded paranoid narcissist, who retaliated beforehand.

I am emphasising Hitler's narcissism and paranoia.

Chapter 22

Was there a Killing Order?

We have seen what Hitler's motives were for the genocide of the Jews. We know that this genocide took place. Was its implementation set in motion by a clear order or clear decision from Hitler? Opinions differ widely about this. Given that there is simply no authentic genocide order by Hitler, it is justifiable to give informed and more or less speculative interpretations instead. There is however consensus about 1941 in particular being a crucial year in the path towards the Holocaust.

Researchers who believe that Hitler gave a clear command or took a clear decision to kill the European Jews differ greatly about the moment that this took place. To give a few examples: Richard Breitman (1991) dates the order to early 1941, Tobias Jersak (1999) in August 1941, Philippe Burrin (1994) in September 1941, Uwe Adam (1972) between September and November 1941, Edouard Husson (2005) in early November 1941, Sebastian Haffner (1978) in December 1941, L.J. Hartog (1997) also December 1941 and Christian Gerlach (1998) also dates it back to December. Christopher Browning (2003) sees two decisions: one in September and the other in October. It is noticeable that the majority date the order to the second half of 1941: it seems obvious that the failure of the war in Russia was strongly related to the order – if there was an order.

There are also researchers who think Hitler didn't issue an order at all. They emphasise local genocidal initiatives. Those in power in the lower echelons would have carried out murders of the Jews on their own initiative, while Hitler had nothing to do with it. In October 1941, 700 Jews were killed in this way in the Warthegau by the 'Sonderkommando Lange'. The *Gauleiter* Arthur Greiser started killing Jews in the second half of 1941 in the same unit. It was his undertaking. It seems that there were also initiatives in the autumn of 1941 in Galicia and Serbia by local leaders, in which killing Jews played a crucial role. There are more such examples, which strongly lead you to think that local leaders took the first steps towards killing Jews.[1]

In 1977, Martin Broszat wrote that it is highly probable there had never been an order to kill the Jews, although one cannot exclude it.[2] Hans Mommsen, however, had no doubts about this. In 1983, he simply drew the conclusion in his eye-catching article '*Die Realisierung der Utopischen*' ('The Realisation of the Unthinkable') that there had never been a *Führerbefehl* (*Führer's* order). According to him, one could even principally exclude the possibility that the policy of genocide was initiated by a direct *Weisung* (instruction) from the *Führer*.[3] The prominent researcher Götz Aly goes a step further, and claims in his book *Final Solution* (English edn 1999) that 'a *Führerbefehl* was not necessary' – because 'that would have been counterproductive'.[4] Ian Kershaw doubts whether a clear order was given, he writes, 'Hitler's "wish" may never have been expressed even to Himmler, as a precise, unequivocal directive, given on a specific occasion, to kill the European Jews. It would have sufficed to give a blanket authorisation to the Reichsführer-SS to proceed with the "final solution".[5] Peter Longerich disapproves of a single order. In his publication *Holocaust* (2000), we read, 'Any attempt to identify a decision taken at a single moment in time runs counter to the extreme complexity of the processes that were in fact taking place. The truth is that those with political responsibility propelled forward, step by step, a highly complicated decision-making process in which a series of points where it was escalated can be identified.'[6]

These two are the most prominent Hitler researchers. Peter Longerich, in particular, is the most influential figure in the area of the Holocaust. Longerich also points to another objection to a clear order. He says that all the territorial solutions (Lublin-Nisko reserve in 1939, Madagascar plan of 1940, deportation to the icy wastelands of Northern Russia) were also seen as the *Endlösung*, or final solution, because the ultimate aim of these plans was the destruction of all the Jews.[7] This might be true, but this doesn't address the fact that there must have been a point in time when the *Endlösung* using territorial solutions, which would have the side effect of (most) Jews dying at some indefinite time, changed into a more active policy which consisted of every Jew in Europe, man or woman, old or young, having to be killed in the near future. This change in policy meant that the Nazis stepped over a great divide. To do that, a clear decision must have been necessary, at least this seems to be a logical and self-evident thought. If this was the case, then locally limited murderous actions changed into a policy of general annihilation, legitimated in clear terms by Adolf Hitler.[8] Whether there are any sources to support this idea is the subject of the following chapter.

Chapter 23

The Killing Order – Three Sources

We have already seen that Hitler never wrote anything down, particularly if it might have been incriminating for him, because 'it could fall into the wrong hands'. Hitler would never, as Himmler did, have visited a death camp or given a speech, such as that of 6 October 1943 in Posen, in which Himmler spoke openly and explicitly about the genocide. There are at least three main sources, however, which show that Hitler did give a clear order for the genocide of the European Jews. The first source comprises the statements made by Adolf Eichmann, the second those of Rudolf Höss. There is an additional third source, the statements made by Heinrich Himmler in 1943 and 1944.

Sources always need to be approached critically. If people who have committed terrible crimes are brought before a judge, they won't speak the truth, but will say anything which they think might save them. We saw this during the trials of the *Einsatzgruppen* in the 1950s and 1960s in the Federal Republic of Germany. The accused had agreed amongst themselves that they would claim that they had received a clear order to kill all the Jews in the Soviet Union before the invasion of Russia. Later research showed that this order had definitely not been given at this point in time. This false claim was meant to allow them to shirk responsibility for the murders.[1]

Statements are more reliable if they are made in a situation in which those involved are not under duress, there is no chance of being prosecuted, receiving a prison sentence or the death penalty. We have a unique document here, in terms of the last point.

After his flight from Germany, Adolf Eichmann limited his contacts in Argentina to a circle of old SS comrades, including the journalist and ex-SS-er Willem Sassen and the publisher Eberhard Fritsch. Sassen needed money to support his family and this must have played a role in persuading Eichmann to agree to an interview. He agreed. They wanted to write a book, based on the interview, which was to be published by Fritsch's right-wing extremist publishing company. They planned to split the money two ways. The conversations started in April 1957 at the earliest and went on until at least mid-October.[2] The conversations were recorded on a tape recorder and then typed out by three different typists. Money certainly played a role for Eichmann, but he also had a few other motives for agreeing to the interview. He felt betrayed by his former comrades, who had stood trial in Nuremberg and who had accused him of all kinds of things. They had turned him into a Satan. He wanted to put the record straight, for example about Höss convincing the court that he, Eichmann, was responsible for introducing Zyklon B to Auschwitz. In addition, he said, his knowledge should serve as a source for future research, so that the past could be reconstructed well. The book was to be published after 1965, at which point his crimes would have passed the statute of limitations.[3]

Sassen had something other in mind than money: he wanted to reinterpret the *Endlösung* with the help of the former deportation expert. That reinterpretation entailed there having been no systematic destruction of the Jews by Adolf Hitler or by the Germans and that, above all, Hitler should have been free from any punishment. But who did kill the Jews in that case? These were just Jewish secret agents, according to this ridiculous story, who had perverted the *Gestapo*. So, it was the Zionists themselves who bore the moral responsibility for the mass murder of the Jews. That is how they were able to force an own state, scooping up a *Wiedergutmachung*. The destruction of the Jews therefore became a strictly internal Jewish situation, which poor Adolf Hitler was powerless to prevent from his bunker.[4]

In the 1950s, Eichmann was the only person who knew almost everything about the destruction of the Jews. He was the unequalled expert and Sassen wanted to turn him into a witness for the defence for his own absurd revisionist theories and, if that wasn't possible, work with him to minimise the number of Jewish victims.

Sassen was taking a risk by doing this, as naturally it was possible that Eichmann would tell other stories that Sassen wanted to hear. This was exactly what happened at the end of the conversations.

To begin with, Eichmann said what Sassen wanted to hear for a good while, but the urge still overtook him to tell his own version of 'history'. This urge came from Eichmann's purely national socialist view on history, which he held onto in Argentina with his heart and soul.

According to him, a war was taking place in history between the races. The race that was the most important enemy to the Germans were the Jewish one. Ultimately, only one race could win, and this was the German one, which meant that the Jews had to be eliminated.[5]

Towards the end of the interview, he gave a final explanation, which meant that Sassen's plan became null and void. The time had come for him to bid farewell to meeting Sassen's wishes. Hitler and his subordinates, so he said, had definitely committed genocide on the Jews, but they had not been very successful in their approach. They should have murdered 10.3 million Jews, but they had, 'unfortunately', only killed over 5 million. Eichmann himself had taken on a key role in this killing of a people, about which he said, I have no regrets and we did nothing wrong.[6] In the final stage of the conversations, he provoked Sassen even more by saying that he, Eichmann, was not at all interested in Sassen's aim: he didn't want to make it impossible to accuse Adolf Hitler and National Socialism of the Jewish genocide.[7] In other words, Eichmann didn't want to excuse Hitler for his evil deeds against the Jews. The murder of the Jews was a deeply German and justifiable business. For Sassen, he had thus become a worthless key witness for his correction of history.

Several things are now important in our investigation. The situation in which Eichmann told his story was safe for him. There was no pressure on him from a judge, he didn't need to fight for his life, there was no noose waiting for him.[8] What he said at the end of the conversation in the Dürer circle was exactly what he should never had said to a judge. So, there he was able to speak without any threat. As a result, it is these statements in particular that can be considered reliable. Eichmann wanted, or so he said, to serve historical research, but his so-called contribution grew out of an authentic National Socialist ideology.[9] This research in particular suddenly became less important after he had been kidnapped by the Mossad in 1960 and stood trial in Jerusalem. He and his lawyer did everything they could to prevent the Sassen transcripts from being admitted as evidence.[10] The fact that Eichmann was so radically opposed to acknowledging these transcripts also seems to increase the reliability of this source. Here we can see different anchors for the credibility of Eichmann's story in Argentina.

So, what did he have to say about the *Führerbefehl* in the final stages of his conversations with Sassen?

Unfortunately, we still have to wait a while to find out.

In 1960, straight away there were a number of difficulties regarding the Sassen tapes. When Eichmann was arrested, Sassen turned to the editors of the American magazine *Time/LIFE* and claimed that he had *the* Eichmann stories in his possession. The editors were very curious but wary. Before putting any money on the table and publishing the material, they naturally wanted to verify the authenticity of the stories and to avoid an enormous blunder. Two staff members of *Time/LIFE* visited Sassen to compare the tape recorder tapes with the transcripts and to confirm their authenticity. They established that the transcripts were a correct representation of what was on the tapes. Sassen was the anonymous ghost writer (for the time being). In November and December 1960, parts of the interview were published in two editions of the magazine with the title 'Eichmann tells his own damning story'. Part 1 had the subtitle: 'To sum it all up. I regret nothing'. Part 2 said: 'I transported them to the butcher'. (These were both Eichmann quotations.) The two articles, where he was himself speaking, were so damning for Eichmann that his lawyer Robert Servatius wanted to resign. He recovered, however, claiming that the article had been falsified and continued Eichmann's defence.[11]

Even before the policeman Avner Less began to interrogate Eichmann, the Israeli prosecutors had come into the possession of the transcripts. How remained unclear, Sassen may have sold the transcripts to the Mossad, but the prosecutors did not have the original source: the seventy-three tapes, and where these were remained unknown. The court needed to decide if the 798 pages of transcripts could be admitted as evidence. There was a lot of confusion and, finally, a compromise was achieved: only five pages would be admitted, namely the pages that Eichmann had approved with his signature in Argentina before his arrest and on which he had made corrections in his own handwriting.[12]

For us, however, it is important to know that all the tapes were recovered during the 1990s and are now split over three archives, in Koblenz in particular there is a lot of 'Argentinian material'. It might cause some amazement that all this material has not yet been published. The reason for this is that Eichmann is often difficult to understand on the tapes, he uses extraordinarily complicated sentences and his corrections to the tapes have been written down in his virtually illegible handwriting.

First, I will present some Eichmann quotations to illustrate the uncensored way in which he spoke. I am making use of both of the articles published by *Time/LIFE*. Both articles have been strongly edited in terms of the order of Eichmann's statements, but they do truthfully reflect what is on the tapes and what can be read in the transcripts.

How much time fate allows me to live, I do not know. I do know that someone must inform this generation. . . . I am writing this story in a time when I am in full possession of my physical and mental freedom, influenced or pressed by no one. May future historians be objective enough not to stray from the path of the true facts recorded here. . . . Where I was implicated in the physical annihilation of the Jews, I admit my participation freely and without pressure. After all, I was the one who transported the Jews to the camps. If I had not transported them, they would not have been delivered to the butcher.[13] . . . And on these grounds, you must understand me when I say: we would only have fulfilled our task if 10.3 million of the enemies [read: Jews] had been killed. Now that this has not happened, I must admit that the suffering and discomfort of our future generations has been made heavier. They may curse us.[14] . . . I must be completely honest with you, comrade Sassen, if we had killed 10.3 million Jews . . . then I would have been satisfied and would say, good, we have destroyed an enemy. . . . What I am saying to you is hard, I know, but I cannot tell you differently: this is the truth. Why would I lie?[15] There was no randomness in my work. . . . I could make allowances for anything but not delays in the transport schedule. Then I would have been guilty of other delays. Then I would have been the serving boy who was called to account for his actions. This was my main task after all.[16]

From the above quotations it is clear that various things have been taken from Eichmann's final declaration, supplemented by earlier statements. Above all, it is evident that he must have been a demonic anti-Semite. To the judges in Jerusalem, however, he denied his anti-Semitism. This was a colossal lie as can be seen from the above quote. In Jerusalem he tried to present himself as rescuer of Jews and on the subject of the extermination of the Jews he told the judges that this 'was the greatest crime in the history of mankind'.[17] Here, in Israel, a completely different Eichmann was speaking compared with the Eichmann who sat with Sassen in Argentina.

The Dutch writer Harry Mulisch and Jewish philosopher Hannah Arendt, who both reported on the trial in Jerusalem, couldn't see that he was hiding his demonic anti-Semitism behind the unconditional obedience to the leadership that he presented. He was not just an unthinking part in a totalitarian machine, as these two believed, he was a criminal, acting from an extremely powerful conviction, namely that of an ultra-radical anti-Semite. He told Sassen: 'I was not a normal recipient of orders, then I would have been an idiot, I was involved in developing them, I was an idealist.'[18]

By now, we have gained an insight into the way this source evolved. We know the circumstances in which Eichmann made his statements and we have already seen the results: he speaks in an uncensored way and is unusually open. It is now time to zoom in on the killing order itself. We quote him from the articles in *Time/LIFE*. First, he tells that he worked for the *Gestapo* and was involved in determining if someone was Jewish or German, but 'after the one-time German Führer gave the order for the physical annihilation of the Jews our duties shifted. We supervised Gestapo seizures of Jews and the trains that took them to their final destination.'[19] Further on in that article, Eichmann remarks, having stated which administrative tasks he had done with the *Gestapo* from 1935 onwards, that:

> In 1941 the Führer himself ordered the physical annihilation of the Jewish enemy. What made him take this step I do not know. But for one way the war in Russia was not going along in the Blitz fashion the High Command had planned. The ruinous struggle on two fronts had begun. And already Dr Chaim Weizmann, the world Zionist leader, had declared war on Germany in the name of Jewry. It was inevitable that the answer of the Führer would not be long in coming.[20]

Eichmann was sent to Minsk, Belzec, Chelmno (later also to Auschwitz and the other death camps) by *Gruppenführer* Müller, probably to prepare for the arrival of the Jews and he was a witness to executions.

> Müller wanted a report about the executions in Minsk. I went there and showed the local commanding officer my order. . . . [The Jews] walked the last 100 or 200 yards – they were not driven – then they jumped into the pit. . . . Then the men of the squad banged away into the pit with their rifles and machine pistols. Why did that scene linger so long in my memory? Perhaps because I had children myself. And there were children in that pit. I saw a woman hold a child of a year or two in the air, pleading. At that moment all I wanted to say was, 'Don't shoot, hand over the child. . . .' Then the child was hit. I was so close that later I found bits of brains spattered on my long leather coat. My driver helped me to remove them. . . . Having seen what I had in Minsk, I said this when I reported to Müller: 'The solution, *Gruppenführer*, was supposed to have been a political one. But now that the Führer has ordered a physical solution, obviously a physical solution it must be. But we cannot go on conducting executions as they were done in Minsk and, I believe in other places. Of necessity our men will be educated to become sadists. We cannot solve the Jewish problem by putting a bullet through the brain of a defenceless woman who is holding her child to be saved.'[21]

There are three remarks to be made about this quotation. Eichmann again names the killing order by Hitler, namely: 'the Führer has ordered a physical solution, obviously a physical solution it must be', which means genocide. It seems almost unthinkable that he was referring to something that had never been given to him with his remark about the killing order. When he appeared before the judge in Jerusalem you could still explain his claims about Hitler's final order as Eichmann's attempt to hide behind an order, but not here in Argentina.

The second remark is as follows: there seems to be some compassion in his words. It seems like he is concerned about the Jewish victims. But Eichmann is Eichmann and Bettina Stangneth interprets him as a witness of human suffering in a convincing way. The ordeal for him was not that people and children had to die, but that he had to see from close by, while he himself had two children. So, you can view his description not as a testimony to his empathy for the victims, but rather as proof that he himself was a victim. Stangneth calls this reaction 'horrendous self-pity'.[22] When he was in Auschwitz, he had no need whatsoever to see the destruction for himself, he found it bad enough that Höss described all the sights and smells to him.[23]

Now on to the third remark. His protest to Müller was not actually intended to stop the murder of the Jews. No, the genocide needed to be carried out by more 'humane' means. Who was this 'humane' for? It wasn't for the victims, but for the perpetrators. At the point that Eichmann was having this conversation with Müller, it had been known for a long time that the members of the *Einsatzgruppen*, who had been shooting thousands of Jews, even women and children from August 1941 onwards, had been developing psychological problems. They were looking for ways to protect the murderers from the direct death and dying which they themselves were causing. This is how the idea of the mobile gas vehicles and stationary gas chambers developed.

Through Eichmann's position and his frequent visits to the death camps, he was suddenly being confronted with the cruelties. In these cases, he had a method to shut himself off from them. He would recite a pious proverb, which would work as a mantra and distance him from the death and suffering.[24] At no point did he protest against the inhuman suffering of the Jewish victims. His focal point remained his anti-Semitism and the orders from the *Führer*. He repeated to Sassen: 'Everything, everything that happened after the prohibition of emigration (October 1941) regarding the solution for the Jewish question, took place based on a fundamental order by the Führer.'[25] Here, we hear about the notorious *Führerbefehl* from Eichmann's mouth in Argentina for the fourth time.

The second source for the *Führerbefehl* was Rudolf Höss, the camp commander in Auschwitz. Many Nazis committed suicide in the wake of the defeat or they cleaned themselves up if they appeared before a judge: mostly they, so they declared, had known nothing about the genocide or only very late, or they had done anything they could to save Jews or simply carried out orders, which were cast in stone. They remained silent about anything which was to their disadvantage.

Höss, however, was a completely different type of witness

He is reliable, simply because the man didn't want to lie and 'just' wanted to tell the truth. Because he had been responsible for carrying out the genocide in Auschwitz for three-and-a-half years and he described the extermination of Jews and other 'enemies' and 'inferior' people in great detail, his story is startling.

Martin Broszat published Höss's autobiography. In the introduction, he discusses this source at depth. Broszat remarks that the testimony of the camp commander is, at the very least, peculiar. Even before the International Military Tribunal (IMT) at Nuremberg, he showed himself to be helpful in a perplexing way and he didn't shy away from describing the annihilation of the Jews in great detail. In Nuremberg, his stories about the destruction in Auschwitz in front of judges, prosecutors, lawyers and victims were 'a deeply disturbing and paralysing sensation. . . . Even on the bench where the accused sat, [Höss's depiction of all the genocidal particularities] evoked a feeling of unease and horror, which had a long term effect.'[26] Later, the Auschwitz commander, after the IMT had extradited him to Cracow in Poland, turned out to be 'an extremely communicative prisoner with a conscience, who, using his unexpected accuracy and supported by a good memory, was able to answer most of the questions he was asked very precisely and correctly'.[27] He also volunteered extra details.

During his remand in Cracow in 1946 and 1947, Höss made extensive autobiographical notes. According to Broszat, they are striking 'because of their bookkeeper-like, precise functionality'.[28] He was a man 'who always served an authority, who always did his duty, as a bully or confessing culprit . . . to serve the cause'.[29] At the same time he described himself as sensitive and connected to nature and his horses. So, Höss ended his manuscript with these words: 'It is fine for the public to see me as a bloodthirsty beast, the murderer of millions – because how else could the masses see the commander of Auschwitz. The masses would not understand, that he also had a heart, that he was not bad.'[30]

The reliability of this source is simple: Höss simply did not want to lie. The fact that he did not lie about the events in Auschwitz has been shown by numerous other sources. His testimony has thus been confirmed by those who survived the camp, by Nazi testimonies from lower personnel and middle management, by higher figures such as Board and Aumeier, by the Auschwitz construction history archive and Auschwitz's location itself.[31]

Höss has the notification that Himmler (who was working on Hitler's orders) gave him the order to solve the Jewish problem. He mentioned this many, many times during the Nuremberg trials. He also mentioned this again in the essays that he wrote in Cracow and in his autobiography.[32] Again and again he claimed that he was given the order in the summer of 1941.[33]

Höss was a crucial source in the work of earlier researchers, both for the killing order as well as for dating it. As the functionalists gained influence, Höss became increasingly less reliable as a witness. Let us take a look at what he tells us in his autobiography. What he says there, matches almost word for word what he often stated under oath in front of the IMT.

> In the summer of 1941, I can't say the exact moment now, I was suddenly ordered to go to the Reichsführer SS in Berlin. . . . In contrast to his habit, he told me roughly the following, without the presence of an aide: The Führer has ordered a solution to the Jewish problem. We – the SS – have to carry out this order. The existing destruction locations in the East, are not capable of performing the large actions envisaged. That is why I have earmarked Auschwitz for this, firstly because of the favourable transportation circumstances, secondly because the earmarked area can be easily cut off and camouflaged. . . . It is hard and heavy work, that will require effort from the entire personality. . . . You must maintain strict silence about this order, even to your superiors. The Jews are the eternal enemy of the German people and need to be exterminated. Every Jew that we catch during the war has to be destroyed, without exception. If we are not successful in breaking the biological basis for the Jewish people, it will be the Jews who destroy the German people. After receiving this heavy order, I immediately travelled back to Auschwitz.[34]

Höss is being very clear. Just like Eichmann, he is saying that the *Führer* gave the order to kill the Jews. If we look at what we have seen earlier regarding his character and his willingness to work towards his own prosecution, it seems highly unlikely that he is lying here. At most, it is the correctness of his memory which could cause him problems. Many researchers refer to Karin Orth's article about Höss, where she presents three arguments against the dating of the killing order to the summer of 1941, as Höss claimed.[35] It is almost as if Orth was writing holy words in her article: you do not hear a word of criticism about her, and many researchers, who do not think much of a killing order, refer to her. Let us take a look at her three arguments.

The first argument reads: a killing order in the summer of 1941 does not fit the chronology of events. Orth says that you cannot speak of a systematic murder of Jews before the spring of 1942. The murder of Jews only began on a large scale in Auschwitz in the spring/summer of 1942. Why was it only then, she asks, while all of the conditions to do so had been met from September 1941? Historians who assume Höss's order in the summer of 1941, have never explained this gap, according to her, or even thought about it.[36] So, let's do that now.

First, we'll ask if there was a gap in time. The plan to build the Belzec camp and murder Jews there, was conceived in October 1941 and the first murders took place in March 1942. Between the plan to build the death camp and the start of the murders, there is a period of less than six months. If we date the start of the genocide of the Jews in Auschwitz to the spring of 1942 (Jews arrived in Auschwitz from nearby Beuthen on 15 February and were gassed immediately[37]), then the time between Himmler's order to Höss and these murders of Jews was a little more than six months. The difference with Belzec is minimal. In addition, you could speak of a gap in time if Himmler had ordered Höss to make immediate preparations, so that they could start with the genocide as quickly as possible. Neither Himmler's nor Höss's words show that there was any haste needed in building the extermination installations. He himself writes, when Eichmann visited him in Auschwitz, Himmler had not yet indicated the start of the genocide. 'Everything was still being prepared.'[38] When he returned to Berlin in November 1941, he was still unable to find out when the policy would be put into action.[39] Apparently, when he was informed by Himmler about the killing order in the summer of 1941, implementation was not such a matter of urgency: the order had been given in principle, but the order for the actual implementation for the murders hadn't and it might still take a while. So, it was possible to make preparations in an unhurried and relaxed manner. And it appears that is what happened.

On 3 September 1941, Karl Fritsch, Höss's subordinate, killed Russian prisoners of war with Zyklon B in the bunker of Block 11 of the Stammlager, which had been specially sealed up for this purpose. Fritsch was not satisfied (not all the Russians had died) and the chamber had to be aired for two days afterwards. He considered the mortuary at the crematorium, on the northern side of the Stammlager, to be more suitable, also because of its good ventilation system. In addition, it had a flat roof: it would not be difficult to make a few holes in it to throw the Zyklon B in. On

16 September 1941, the new gas chamber was put to the test: a transport of 900 Russian prisoners of war was killed without any problems.[40] Orth claims this murder, and this is her second argument, is separate from the *Endlösung der Judenfrage* (final solution to the Jewish question). According to her, it still fitted in the regime of concentration camps, in which the ill and Russian prisoners of war had been killed.[41] It may be the case that the murder of these two groups preceded the *Endlösung*, but there must have been a point at which this type of murder became a preparation for the genocide of the Jews. Orth does not clarify why this point had not yet been reached in September. Why could the gassings with Zyklon B on 3 and 16 September not be interpreted as an experiment to test if this method would also be suitable for the mass murder of the Jews? This is even more so, as Höss himself connects the gassing to the coming genocide. Zyklon B gas, according to Höss, worked so suddenly and strongly that it caused no suffocation effects and that 'reassured [him], because the mass destruction of the Jews needed to be started within a short space of time'.[42] If this is true, Höss and his henchmen did not stand still during 'Orth's gap'. There is also another argument for this, which has been strongly presented by Michael Thad Allen.

This American historian is of the opinion that there were already plans to build gas chambers to kill Jews in Auschwitz in October 1941. The first building contracts date back to 4 and 6 October 1941. On 21 and 22 October, Kurt Prüfer from Topf und Söhne came to visit Auschwitz (Topf and Sons were crematorium specialists from Erfurt). Kurt Prüfer was considering a special ventilation system for the mortuary to be built in Crematorium II with the *Zentral Bauleitung* from Auschwitz (Central Construction Management). A ventilation system in a mortuary in a concentration camp is nothing unusual of course. There are lots of corpses and you can reduce the stench of these to a minimum and the chance of spreading disease through flies by refreshing the air. However, in contrast to other mortuaries, 'the gentlemen' of the *Bauleitung* at Auschwitz and Topf and Söhne intended to make an enclosed ventilation system in the walls of the mortuary of the planned Crematorium II, where later Jews were to be gassed. In addition, they wanted to put the mortuary (the planned gas chamber) underground in the cellar, so that the noise of the suffocating, dying Jews would not be heard. This is because during the gassings on 3 and 16 September the victims had made so much noise that a large engine had to turned on to drown out their death cries. Because of the underground construction, the walls with their built-in air pipes also had to be made waterproof with a bitumen covering, because the water level at Auschwitz Birkenau was so high. All of these factors contributed to a great deal of extra work. According to Thad Allen, there is only one explanation for this extra work: the SS wanted to prevent victims struggling against death and gasping for breath and kicking external pipes to pieces or ripping them off, so that the installation would remain in operation. It seems unlikely that one would have developed such an advanced system in order to kill Russians from time to time or to liquidate other prisoners of war. Given that the discussions with Topf and Söhne about the internal ventilation system had already been started in October 1941, according to Michael Thad Allen, plans were already being made for the construction of a gigantic extermination installation using Zyklon B.[43] As has already been mentioned, ideas were being exchanged about this special construction in October 1941, but naturally there was also a period leading up to these conversations. The time between Himmler's order to Höss and actual preparations for mass murder now do not seem very long, Orth's gap seems increasingly to disappear and Himmler's order to Höss in the (late) summer of 1941 seems more credible.

The third argument that Orth gives against dating the order to Höss in the summer of 1941 is related to Höss's reference to the other destruction sites. (See quotation above.)

However, Orth stresses, the extermination camps in the East (Belzec, Treblinka, Sobibor) didn't yet exist.[44] In November of 1941, the construction of Belzec began and the camp became operational no earlier than March of 1942; the construction of Treblinka followed later, from spring 1942 until the beginning of the summer, and Sobibor appeared from April 1942. Therefore, according to Orth, the research literature tends to date Höss's statements a year later, so in 1942.[45]

This might have been the case in the 1990s, but after 2000, Höss virtually disappeared from research literature. From that point onwards, a great many Holocaust researchers made the generalisation that the man was so unreliable as a witness that he should also be ignored as a source. In fact, in recent works about the lead-up to the Holocaust, you no longer encounter him. This is unfortunately the result of a cognitive error, which can be quite simply demonstrated.

If someone tells a story about a real event, then one aspect may be untrue, but on the other hand, other aspects could be correct. It may even be the case that all the parts are correct, but there are some inconsistencies in the chronology. Research shows us in fact that it is much more difficult to remember *when* an event happened, or the date and time it occurred, than *what* happened, or the details of the events.[46] This means you should not be surprised if the chronology of Höss's story is incorrect. It is simply one of the guiding principles of how our memory works, that dates and times are badly recalled.

Let us now take a look into the events themselves, which are generally recalled more easily. Höss heard, or so he claimed, Hitler's order via Himmler, stating that all the Jews were to be killed. He speaks of a 'heavy order'. What Höss heard must have made a great impression on him. In this case, it is not just that events are recalled best, being a memory principle, but also that the information was horrific, highly unusual and he was going to be at the centre of it all. Such events, making a great impression on the individual, are recalled best of all. This has also been proved in solid scientific research.[47] Here again, we can speak of one of the guiding principles of memory. Based on this, it seems highly likely that Höss did indeed receive a killing order via Himmler and that he was well able to recall this in 1946 and 1947, when he stood trial in Nuremberg and Cracow.

By simply using knowledge about the rules about how the memory works, we have found a third reliable witness for a killing order from Hitler. We are not making the mistake of throwing the baby out with the bath water.

Let us now take a look at the problem of dating. We already know that memory has the most problems with this aspect and often proves itself unreliable on this point.

Höss himself dates the killing order to the summer of 1941. In his story, however, he mistakenly connects the order to the badly functioning extermination sites in 1942. We can indeed see him making errors here about the *when* aspect.

Incidentally, an initial order in July 1942 would have not made any sense. Höss had already been working on implementing the genocide for months at that point. It is impossible that he could have begun this without an order. So, he must have received one earlier. Now Höss's dating to the summer of 1941 begins to seem a little credible. Michael Thad Allen's explanation makes it even more plausible, as we have already seen.

One of the guiding principles in our memory clarifies why our memory has difficulties recalling when something happened: this is called the post hoc effect.[48] This means: later information is easily mixed up with earlier memories if they contain a lot of similarities.

Let us zoom in on July 1942, bearing these thoughts in mind.

On 17 and 18 July, Himmler visited Höss in Auschwitz and witnessed the whole destruction process of a transport of Dutch Jews who had arrived very recently.[49] One day earlier, on 16 July, Himmler had paid a visit to Hitler and they had decided to speed up the murder programme.[50] The new death camps had indeed been built at this time, but they weren't yet operating as desired: numerous problems had occurred.[51] During his visit to Auschwitz, Himmler told Höss that Eichmann's programme would proceed and that he (Höss) must ensure it was speeded up.[52] A few weeks after Himmler left Auschwitz, the number of crematoria increased from the original plan of one to four. Auschwitz then needed to play a more important part in the *Endlösung*, because the other extermination camps lacked sufficient capacity.[53]

Höss's memory of Himmler's visit to Auschwitz in 1942 could easily have been combined with his original memory of his own visit to Himmler in Berlin in the summer of 1941.

The reason for this is that both events share relevant aspects. It is the same Himmler talking to the same Höss and, in both cases, giving an order to kill the Jews. If there had been no similarities between both events, there could have been no possibility of mixing up the later event with the earlier one.

It now becomes possible to understand that, as a result of the post hoc effect, the events of July 1942 (Himmler speaking about the killing sites not being capable of performing the large actions that had been envisaged) could have been combined with the earlier killing order from 1941. Another aspect of the post hoc effect is that we tend to store such facts in our memories according to a causal relationship.[54] This seems self-evident from what we have read about Höss. According to him, he also received the killing order because the existing extermination sites were not functioning properly. As a result of this analysis, it becomes possible to look past the memory mistakes regarding the *when* aspect and to provide a correct image of the order of events.

It is quite possible that my story can confuse the reader. That is why I am repeating it here in a simpler summary. Höss received a killing order. We think this, because this made such a large impression on him and triggered emotions in him, which makes it unlikely that he could have forgotten it. Later information from 1942 became entangled with the original memory from 1941. What I am suggesting here in this summary is supported by the principles that guide how the memory works.

Karin Orth has presented three arguments against Höss's dating. We have found good reasons to doubt the validity of her three arguments and to therefore maintain Höss as a source for the *Führerbefehl* being given in the (late) summer of 1941.

The third source which informs us about Hitler's order to kill the Jews is Heinrich Himmler himself. Incidentally, there are no doubts about the authenticity of this source. Himmler's speeches were recorded on tape and are stored in the US national archives. Part of them can be heard on the Internet. Towards the end of the war, Himmler was unexpectedly open about the murder of the Jewish people, because he wanted to compromise the leaders of the Reich. He was making it clear to them that they were jointly responsible for the crime, for which there was no way back. This is how he tried to keep unity within Hitler's ranks. On 6 October 1943, Himmler made a long speech in Posen for the *Gau-und Reichsleiter* about the 'Jewish question'. Below are quoted two passages in which he speaks about implementing the genocide.

> I really am asking you just to listen and never to speak of what I am saying in this [most intimate] circle. The question has been raised to us: What should be done with the women and children? – I have decided, to find a completely clear solution for this as well. I considered it unjustifiable to exterminate the men – in other words, to kill them or have them killed – and to allow the children to grow up into people who would wreak their revenge on our sons and grandchildren. The heavy decision needed to be taken to let this people disappear from the face of the earth.[55]

It is striking that Himmler says: 'I have decided'. He is suggesting that he himself made this decision. In the last sentence of this quotation, he is becoming more abstract and speaking of 'the heavy decision'. He then continues: 'For our organisation, which had to carry out this task, this was the toughest thing we hitherto had to do.'[56] Now, he suddenly speaks of 'the toughest thing that "we" hitherto had to do' and seems to include himself in the 'we' and therefore point to an order from Hitler.[57] This text remains somewhat ambiguous. However, on 5 May 1944, Himmler became clearer in the presence of *Wehrmacht* generals in Sonthofen.

> The Jewish question in Germany and generally in the German occupied areas has been solved. It has been solved without compromise, in accordance with the life struggle of our people, which is about the existence of our blood . . . You may empathise with me, how heavy it has been to carry out this military order I was assigned, which I have followed and implemented out of obedience and complete conviction.[58]

Here Himmler is speaking literally of the 'military order which I was assigned'. In addition, he also states that he carried it out with obedience and conviction. There was only one man who could give him that order: Adolf Hitler.

On 24 May 1944, he spoke again to the generals and he said 'it [the Jewish question] was uncompromisingly solved after orders'. On 21 June 1944, he again addressed the generals and he almost reiterates what he said earlier, namely 'it was the most terrible task and the most terrible order which could have been given to an organisation'.[59] Here the same applies to his words: only Hitler could have issued that 'most terrible order' to eradicate the Jews.

What we hear here in 1943 and particularly in 1944 with Himmler is the same as we have heard from Eichmann and Höss. These two, however, date the order, Höss to the summer of 1941, Eichmann is rather unprecise when he speaks about the disastrous war on two fronts.

It is interesting to see what Ian Kershaw and Peter Longerich say about the Höss and Eichmann sources, as both researchers are of the opinion that it is highly probable that there is no question of one single order or decision. In Kershaw's Hitler biography (2009) Höss's testimony is omitted. He had dealt with Höss in his earlier biography of 2000 in a footnote, where he referred to Karin Orth, who, as we have seen, explains quite extensively why we cannot rely on Höss's words in her 1997 article. He says nothing about the Sassen tapes or transcripts, he doesn't refer to the many times that Eichmann spoke of the fundamental killing order on the tapes. Kershaw has missed something important here. And Peter Longerich? In my own opinion, he is one of the most erudite and prominent Holocaust researchers, a man who, just like Kershaw, plays a great role in Holocaust research and clearly demands respect. Longerich does deal with Höss. Longerich considers Höss's statements very dubious. And he considers this source too unreliable to believe in a killing order in the summer of 1941.[60] He too refers to the unreliable chronology of events which Höss reports, but he doesn't include the guiding principles of memory in his analysis. Even if his research didn't include how the memory works, it is still a fact that Höss states a clear killing order. In contrast to Kershaw, Longerich does react to Eichmann's claim that Hitler had issued the order for genocide. He does this by weighing Eichmann's statements to the judge in Jerusalem critically. Eichmann had been arrested by then and that is why Longerich distrusts Eichmann's information as he was fighting for his life in the courts in Jerusalem. Longerich says that it was in Eichmann's interest to date his trips to the execution sites as early as possible 'and to make them appear a result of a clear decision by the Führer to murder all the European Jews'.[61] Longerich concludes that Eichmann's statements *cannot* be seen as a key document, but that other sources should be used to reconstruct the process that led to the *Endlösung*. The point is, of course, that Longerich doesn't include the Sassen tapes in his analysis. It is precisely in these tapes and in *Time/LIFE* that Eichmann states, entirely freely and without any pressure whatsoever, just to repeat this, that there was a clear killing order. In addition, Eichmann dated the order early in the conversation with Sassen: Eichmann says 1941 and mentioned the setbacks in Russia (from August 1941 onwards) and – as said before – the so-called declaration of war on Germany by the Zionist leader Chaim Weizmann (in 1939) as the triggers for this. In the conversation with Sassen, Eichmann gains nothing by convincing Sassen that he was aware of an early decision by Hitler to kill the Jews and that he, Eichmann, already had to go to the execution sites as a result. He just told his SS comrade this because he thought he was reflecting the actual turn of events. As has been said, we don't hear anything from Longerich about this source. Again, we're seeing a researcher not discussing an important source which contradicts the contents of his paradigm. As long as Longerich and Kershaw cannot deal with the Sassen tapes on good grounds, we cannot accept their conclusions. The Sassen tapes, the transcripts and the article in *Time/LIFE* retain their status as reliable sources and are therefore important support for the killing order.

The order was no ordinary order, of course, and the word can conjure up incorrect images. It is useful to take a look into the nature of this order. Hitler will have communicated his decision to Himmler and Heydrich in complete secrecy: all the Western European Jews needed to be actively murdered. Hitler announced this message at a well-thought through moment. This was *the* major turning point of his Jewish policy. Now the diffuse genocidal initiatives could be fundamentally integrated into political policy, led from the centre, mainly by Himmler and Heydrich. Hitler's message was a clear statement to these two men. So, there was no question of an explicit order in Prussian tradition of obedience to the death, which needed to be implemented immediately. Hitler's announcement, however, being Hitler's words, bore the weight of an order. Himmler and Heydrich understood what they were expected to do. Now they started thinking about how the massive genocide could be carried out and only those who were directly involved were informed. In addition, it was deemed to be top secret. Where these two men did introduce Hitler's decision to others, they will have spoken of an 'order from the Führer', a *Führerbefehl*.

Now that Hitler had issued the order, a new, major project commenced. Its implementation was still tentative. And dependent on circumstances another thousand and one minor decisions had to be taken. However, these were only possible because Hitler had given the crucial order.

It is possible that Hitler's decision given to Himmler and Heydrich was a decision in principle, that could be retracted if the *Drahtzieher* in the US and England were to accommodate Hitler later. As soon as Hitler realised that the *Drahtzieher* would not let themselves be blackmailed, his decision became final. If there was indeed a decision in principle that later became final, then only two key decisions were taken by Hitler. We will look at this in the final chapter, which discusses the date of the killing order.

Chapter 24

The Killing Order: When?

Höss and Eichmann have already stated approximately when Hitler issued his *Führerbefehl*. Now we also want to determine the date of this order or these decisions. I can only suggest a motivated interpretation. After all, there is no authentic and dated written order by Hitler to kill the European Jews. In such a situation, you may speculate, but it has to be well motivated!

We will make use again of our knowledge about Hitler's paranoia to indicate approximately when he ordered the extermination of the European Jews, in whichever way that was.

Thus, to specify the timeframe in which Hitler gave his killing order, emphasis will again be placed on Adolf Hitler's personality. Let it be clear to the reader that I don't want to create the impression that one may limit the cause of the Holocaust to the story I am about to tell. I don't wish to speak out against the neo-functionalistic historiography of the Holocaust. In 1939–41, a growing consensus arose about eliminating the European Jews. Yes, there was a process of radicalisation during the course of 1941 and the process of 'working towards the *Führer*' maintained itself almost until the end. Because of the polycratic structure of the Reich, local SS men were able to develop genocidal initiatives without immediate orders by the *Führer*. There was a highly complicated decision-making process that radicalised itself step by step, which escalated more and more, with an increasing number of people becoming involved in 1941.[1] Insight into this offers the reader a broad perspective on the development of the Holocaust and ensures they will not fall into the trap of one monocausal explanation.

However, the significance of Hitler's paranoia is a little exposed fact. I think it would benefit from some attention being paid to it. It is possible that his paranoia weighed more heavily in the decision-making process than one thinks, perhaps to such a degree that we can even approximately date the order or decisions. As a result of his paranoia, Hitler believed the Jewish *Drahtzieher* could determine American foreign policy towards Germany. His threatening prophecy on 30 January 1939, is connected to this deep-rooted paranoid conviction. As long as, to his mind, the *Faustpfand* had blackmail value, an order to kill the Western European Jews would be counterproductive and was therefore improbable.

On 18 December 1940, Hitler made it clear to the top of the *Wehrmacht* that Russia must be conquered in a Blitzkrieg (*Barbarossa Weisung*). However, there was always a chance that the Jewish warmongers would successfully continue their initiatives. On 30 January 1941, he therefore repeated his previous prophecy in his *Reichstag* speech, with a slight difference: 'And I don't want to forget the warning I already gave in my Reichstag Speech on 1 September 1939 [Hitler purposefully misdates this: it was 30 January 1939]. Namely, the warning if the other world would be plunged into a World War by the Jews, the role of Jewry in Europe will be finished in its entirety.'[2] This time Hitler didn't confine himself to the accusation that the Jews are warmongers. No, in the above he reminds his audience of the vital fact that exactly two years before he had threatened he would kill the Jews.

Two years lie between the threat and the reminder. The question arises why Hitler now, on 30 January 1941, again referred to his old threat. We cannot look into Hitler's mind. The answer remains somewhat speculative; however, there is a similarity in both situations from which one can derive a possible explanation.

On 30 January 1939, Hitler was about to embark on new and risky adventures. His diplomatic and military conquests before 1939 (Saarland, Rhineland, Austria, Sudetenland) had a semblance of abiding by international law, but those after 30 January 1939 did not. In March 1939 he invaded the remainder of Czechoslovakia against all the promises he had made. In September he went to war with Poland. These were actions stemming from a lust for power and a longing for *Lebensraum*.

On 30 January 1941, Hitler was again about to embark on a new and grand adventure: he would attack Russia in the very near future. Just as two years before, he was apparently trying to put pressure on the powerful Jews in England and especially on those in the US. He simply reminded them of his old threat and hoped the *Drahtzieher* would keep England and the US in check. Possibly, he even hoped the *Drahtzieher* would persuade both these nations to make peace with Germany.

The aforementioned interpretation fits well with the psyche of a paranoid mind. Secondly, the point in time for the threat on 30 January 1941 was more significant for its effect than for any concrete implementation. This could come up for discussion later, if it turned out that the *Drahtzieher*

WHY DID HITLER HATE THE JEWS?

didn't care about his words. His threats from 1941 carried more weight than the one from 30 January 1939. In 1939, there were only 200,000 Jews under his dominion. Due to his conquests of Poland and Western European countries, he now reigned over more than 4 million Jews. Most of the 2 million Jews in Poland had been forced to leave their homes and were confined to ghettos. The *Faustpfand* had become more valuable and easier to manipulate. It is therefore possible that Hitler expected more from his threats this time. In 1941, as soon as he believed that his threat wouldn't have an effect on the US anymore, he would probably take his revenge, that is, issue the order for the genocide. It is quite conceivable that such a resentful and paranoid person, whose thoughts would immediately move to revenge and retaliation after receiving hard knocks, would act beyond words. However, at what point did he think threats would no longer be useful and would he instead translate his words into deeds? That idea could not have arisen overnight.

On 14 August 1941, the Atlantic Charter was issued. It was the result of the Churchill-Roosevelt meetings off the coast of Newfoundland. The eight principles that it included implied there was no place for Nazi-Germany in the post-war era. The *Faustpfand* must have lost much of its value. Through Roosevelt's shoot-on-sight order on 11 September 1941, which was an implicit declaration of war at sea to Hitler, the *Faustpfand* lost even more value. What remained of it after the end of the First Moscow Conference on 1 October 1941, which ensured military support (airplanes, tanks and lorries) for Russia?

Both the issuing of the Atlantic Charter and the shoot-on-sight order took place in the summer of 1941 and are consistent with Höss's story (that the order was given in the summer) and with that of Eichmann, in the sense that he says that it was issued shortly after the disastrous war on two fronts. It is possible that Hitler then took a decision in principle, the implementation of which depended on further developments.

Maybe Hitler threatened to kill the Jews in October for the last time before he indeed gave the definite order. He no longer warned of his notorious prophecy, rather he was showing the beginnings of the realisation of his threat. In the second half of October, the deportation of German Jews was openly taking place. Hitler did nothing to hide the deportations from public view: It seemed to be a public demonstration, so that everyone would know about it, especially abroad. International newspapers wrote extensively about it. The *Drahtzieher* could now draw their own conclusions concerning their tribesmen in Europe. However, shortly after the beginning of the deportations, perhaps the end of October, Hitler again saw no change in US foreign policy towards Germany.

This was a last-ditch effort, and now the fifth column (the Jews in Europe) would be seen and shown to be more dangerous. Using this assessment, we arrive at the upper time limit of the order: in fact, considering Hitler's paranoid logic, he could not have issued the order much later, or he now stated that the order had become definite.

Another clue may be found for the date of the order or message in the course of the war in Russia. To understand Hitler it is important to emphasise that he thought he was fighting against the Jews. I'd like to reiterate this point. The governments of the US and England (and Russia) were only masking the true policymakers: the Jews.

On 18 August 1941, Hitler was already considering defeat, it was going badly for the *Wehrmacht* in Russia. Hitler only tasted dust and ashes. He was hoping for a miracle: Stalin would offer peace or Churchill would fall from power.[3] Hitler recovered in September. At the end of that month, the *Wehrmacht* captured Kiev – a great triumph – and the Russian armies fell in the battles of Bransk and Wjasma about 10 October, another resounding success. These were the last great successes, however. From mid-October onwards, little positive news arrived from the Eastern Front. The rains had started, and the advance of the German armies was stymied by mud and therefore by a lack of supplies. In 1941, in his speech on 8 November, Hitler already seemed to be pointing the finger at the real culprits if the war were to be lost: the Jews.

As we have already seen, Hitler wanted to carry out a genocide of the Jews as a retaliation in advance of a possible German defeat; at the same time, he was eliminating the fifth column. Thus, the killing order must be directly related to the point in time at which he saw a possible defeat looming. In the second half of August, Hitler seemed to have seriously considered defeat for the first time. By the end of October, he was agonised by despair and uncertainty: A defeat would have dominated his fantasies. According to this reasoning, he must have given the order, in the period between mid-August and the end of October. Again, we see the end of October as the upper limit. Yet again, Hitler's paranoid interpretation was decisive. His fears of a defeat were real; he was convinced that – based on his stiff-necked paranoid views – that the Jews were behind all the violence of war. It is difficult to accept that such a delusion, which had no basis in reality, could have led to such a catastrophe.

Epilogue

At the start of this study, I presented a number of quotations from Hitler experts. The general theme was as follows: Hitler's anti-Semitism is a riddle which can never be solved. Now we have arrived at the end of this study, I think that a contribution has been made to explaining the origins of Hitler's anti-Semitism. It is up to the reader to judge to which extent this riddle has indeed been solved.

I hope that it has become clear how Hitler's hatred of the Jews led to the outcome of the Holocaust. I have consistently emphasised that the process which led to the widespread murder of the Jews is extremely complex. I have extracted one aspect and put it under the microscope from various angles. It is a legitimate choice to focus on one aspect of a process, particularly if you deem it a facet which has unjustly been paid too little attention. There are recent and weighty Hitler biographies which don't even mention the word 'paranoia'. I have repeatedly argued that this is a substantial omission.

Lastly, I have one final comment.

If one unmasks the motives of man's behaviour, it is often suggested that he could not have acted otherwise, that he was pre-determined. This is an illusion. Hitler was completely responsible for his enormous crimes. Hitler's own opinion about his responsibility is demonstrated by his words on 16 June 1941 written down by Joseph Goebbels: 'We are guilty of too many things that we must win the war, because, if we lose, our whole people and we ourselves first and foremost, with all we love, will be eradicated.' Here we see a man who knew exactly what he was doing, who knew he was executing a reign of terror, a man who knew he was fully culpable.

Notes

Chapter 2: The Detective

1. Robin George Collingwood, *The Idea of History* (Oxford, 1946), pp. 26–82.
2. Ibid., p. 237.

Chapter 3: The Nineteenth-Century Background: Anti-Semitic Traditions

1. Reinhard Rürup, *Emanzipation und Antisemitismus. Studien zur 'Judenfrage' der bürgerlichen Gesellschaft* (Göttingen, 1975), pp. 83, 100.
2. Jacobus Willem Oerlemans, 'Voor en tegen de vooruitgang. Sociale vooruitgang en radicalisering', in L. Wessels and A. Bosch (eds), *Veranderende grenzen. Nationalisme in Europa 1815–1919* (Nijmegen, 1992), p. 214. Rürup, p. 105.
3. Rürup, pp. 86, 90.
4. Jäckel, Eberhard and Axel Kuhn (eds), *Hitler. Sämtliche Aufzeichnungen* (Stuttgart, 1980) p. 199.
5. Margaret Hodgen, *Early anthropology in the sixteenth and seventeenth centuries* (Philadelphia, 1964), p. 417.
6. Ludolf Herbst, *Das nationalsozialistische Deutschland* 1933–1945 (Frankfurt, 1996), pp. 39, 40. George Mosse, *Rassismus. Ein Krankheitssymptom in der europäischen Geschichte des 19. und 20. Jahrhunderts* (Königstein, 1978), pp. 52–5.
7. Mosse, pp. 96–8. Herbst, p. 38. Saul Friedländer, *Das Dritte Reich und die Juden. Die Jahre der Verfolgung 1933–1939* (München, 1997), p. 103.
8. Chamberlain quoted in: Francis Ludwig Carsten, *The rise of fascism* (London, 1967), pp. 30, 31.
9. Herbst, pp. 45, 46. Carsten, p. 31. Mosse, pp. 99–101.

10. Norman Cohn, *Warrant for genocide. The myth of the Jewish world conspiracy and the protocols of the elders of Zion* (London, 1996), pp. 39, 40. Mosse, pp. 109, 110.
11. Rürup, p. 109.
12. Hans-Günther Zmarlik, 'Der Sozialdarwinismus in Deutschland als geschichtliches Problem', *VFZ* (1963), p. 262.
13. Ibid.
14. Brigitte Hamann, *Hitler's Wien. Lehrjahre eines Diktators* (München, 1998), pp. 344, 347, 352, 353, 490. Mosse, p. 130.
15. Carsten, pp. 35, 36. Hamann, *Hitlers Wien*, pp. 405, 411, 413, 417, 420. Mosse, p. 130. Friedrich Heer, *Der Glaube des Adolf Hitler. Anatomie einer politischen Religiosität* (Frankfurt, Berlin, 1989), pp. 105, 106, 112.
16. Adolf Hitler, *Mein Kampf* (München, 1942) (hereafter abbreviated as *MK*), pp. 130–2.
17. Herbst, pp. 46, 47.
18. Léon Poliakov, *Geschichte des Antisemitismus VII. Am Vorabend des Holocaust* (Worms, 1988), pp. 18, 19.
19. Herbst, p. 47.
20. Ibid., pp. 48, 49.
21. Quoted in Léon Poliakov, p. 23.
22. Herbst, p. 49.

Chapter 4: The Causes of Paranoia: The Proximate Level of Explanation

1. Daniel Freeman, 'Persecutory delusions: a cognitive perspective on understanding and treatment', *The Lancet* (2016), pp. 685, 686.
2. Daniel Freeman and Jason Freeman, *Paranoia the 21st-century fear* (Oxford, 2008), p. 73.
3. https://www.psych.ox.ac.uk/team/daniel-freeman.
4. Daniel and Jason Freeman, pp. 54, 56, 59, 73, 139, 159. Daniel Freeman, Jason Freeman and Philippa Garety, *Overcoming Paranoid and Suspicious Thoughts* (2nd edn, Oxford, 2016; digital version; this has different numbering than the physical book), pp. 41, 43, 44, 76–8, 94, 95. Daniel Freeman, pp. 685, 687.

Chapter 5: Adolf Hitler, 1889–1914

1. Hamann, *Hitler's Wien*, pp. 74–5.
2. August Kubizek, *Adolf Hitler. Mein Jugendfreund* (2nd edn, Graz and Göttingen, 1953), pp. 55, 57.

3. Volker Ullrich, *Adolf Hitler. Die Jahre des Aufstiegs 1889–1939* (Frankfurt am Main, 2013), p. 24.
4. Ian Kershaw, *Hitler* (London, 2009), p. 3.
5. *MK*, p. 1.
6. Ullrich, p. 28. Hamann, *Hitler's Wien*, p. 16.
7. *MK*, p. 4.
8. Hitler in Hamann, *Hitler's Wien*, p. 18.
9. Christa Schroeder, *Er war mein Chef. Aus dem Nachlaß der Sekretärin von Adolf Hitler* (5th edn, München, 2002), p. 34.
10. Quoted in Hamann, *Hitler's Wien*, p. 19.
11. Adolf Hitler, *Monologe im Führerhauptquartier 1941–1944* (München, 1980), p. 281.
12. Ullrich, p. 32.
13. *MK*, p. 6.
14. Bradley F. Smith, *Adolf Hitler. His Family, Childhood and Youth* (Stanford, 1967), pp. 56, 61.
15. Peter Longerich, *Hitler. Biographie* (München, 2015), pp. 18, 19.
16. Kubizek, p. 55. Schroeder, p. 63.
17. Hamann, *Hitler's Wien*, p. 20.
18. Bloch in Hamann, *Hitler's Wien*, p. 34.
19. Kubizek, pp. 53, 170.
20. *MK*, p. 16.
21. Mayrhofer in Hamann, *Hitler's Wien*, p. 31.
22. Hamann, *Hitler's Wien*, pp. 28, 29.
23. Longerich, *Hitler*, pp. 20–2. Hamann, *Hitler's Wien*, pp. 28, 29.
24. Hamann, pp. *Hitler's Wien*, 23–7.
25. Franz Jetzinger, *Hitlers Jugend. Phantasien, Lügen – und die Wahrheit* (Wenen, 1956), p. 105.
26. *MK*, pp. 7, 8.
27. Kubizek, pp. 23, 25.
28. Ibid., pp. 20, 23, 26, 42, 43.
29. Ibid., pp. 23, 34, 35, 36, 37, 40, 166, 186.
30. In the correspondence with the Hitler biographer Jetzinger, Stefanie writes that people often thought she was Jewish, while she was not – despite her maiden name. Jetzinger, p. 145. On the other hand, Anton Joachimstaler, in his documentary *The making of Adolf Hitler* (BBC 2, *Timewatch*, January, 2002), clearly proved that Stefanie Isak was Jewish using archive material.
31. Kubizek, pp. 79–81, 85, 87.
32. Ibid., p. 87.
33. Kubizek, p. 279. Jetzinger, p. 144.

34. Hamann, *Hitler's Wien*, p. 517.
35. Kubizek, p. 147. Longerich, *Hitler*, p. 27.
36. Hamann, *Hitler's Wien*, p. 52.
37. *MK*, pp. 18, 19.
38. Bloch in Hamann, p. 55. Kubizek, pp. 165, 166.
39. Ullrich, p. 40.
40. Longerich, *Hitler*, p. 28. Hamann, *Hitler's Wien*, pp. 56, 57.
41. Presemayer quoted in Hamann, *Hitler's Wien*, p. 59.
42. Hamann, pp. 59, 60.
43. Roller in Hamann, *Hitler's Wien*, p. 60.
44. Hamann, *Hitler's Wien*, p. 61.
45. Here Hamann paraphrases what Hitler would later quite openly tell *Gauleiter* Eduard Frauenfeld, Hamann, *Hitler's Wien*, p. 87.
46. Kubizek, pp. 10, 35, 44, 182.
47. Ibid., p. 190.
48. Ibid., pp. 27, 28, 29, 242.
49. Ibid, pp. 194, 195.
50. Hamann, *Hitler's Wien*, p. 58.
51. Kubizek, pp. 199, 200, 217, 218, 228.
52. Ibid., pp. 219, 220.
53. Ibid., pp. 37, 82, 205, 213, 215, 237, 273–6.
54. Ibid., p. 284.
55. Ibid., 281.
56. Wolfram Pyta, *Hitler, Der Künstler als Politiker und Feldherr* (München, 2015), pp. 12, 15.
57. Kubizek, pp. 285, 286. Hamann, *Hitler's Wien*, pp. 504–6.
58. Kubizek, p. 303, 312–15.
59. *MK*, pp. 40, 42.
60. Kershaw, *Hitler*, p. 29.
61. Jetzinger, p. 219.
62. Ibid., p. 220.
63. Reinhold Hanisch, 'I was Hitler's buddy', *The New Republic* (5 April 1939), pp. 239, 240. Hamann, *Hitler's Wien*, p. 225.
64. Hanisch, p. 240.
65. Jetzinger, p. 223.
66. Hanisch, pp. 241, 297, 298. Ullrich, pp. 54, 55. Hamann, *Hitler's Wien*, pp. 231, 232.
67. Hanisch, pp. 241, 242, 270, 297 (quote). Kershaw, *Hitler*, p. 35.
68. Hanisch, pp. 271, 272, 297.
69. Ibid., pp. 241, 272, 299, 300.
70. Hamann, *Hitler's Wien*, pp. 496–7.

71. Ibid., p. 272.
72. Quoted in Hamann, *Hitler's Wien*, p. 250.
73. Smith, pp. 8, 10.
74. Ibid., p. 149.
75. Birgit Schwarz, *Geniewahn: Hitler und die Kunst* (Wien, 2011), especially pp. 51–66.
76. Ibid., pp. 53, 57.
77. T. Kuipers, *Tijdschrift Voor Psychiatrie*, 37 (1995), p. 6.
78. Hamann, *Hitler's Wien*, pp. 518, 566, 567.
79. Ibid., pp. 568, 569.
80. Anna Popp in Anton Joachimsthaler, *Hitlers Weg begann in München* (München, 2000), p. 78.
81. Hans Schirmer in Joachimsthaler, pp. 84, 85.

Chapter 6: Adolf Hitler and the First World War

1. *MK*, p. 177.
2. Joachimsthaler, p. 129. Kershaw, *Hitler*, pp. 54, 55.
3. Joachimsthaler, pp. 129.
4. Werner Jochmann, *Adolf Hitler, Monologe im Führerhauptquartier 1941–1944* (Hamburg, 1980), p. 79.
5. Fritz Wiedemann, *Der Mann der Feldherr werden wollte. Erlebnisse und Erfahrungen des Vorgesetzten Hitlers im 1. Weltkrieg und seines späteren persönlichen Adjudanten* (n.p., 1964), p. 29.
6. Ibid., pp. 25–7, 33, 34, 209.
7. Longerich, *Hitler*, p. 48.
8. *MK*, p. 182.
9. Jäckel and Kuhn (eds), p. 69.
10. Ullrich, p. 78.
11. Amann quoted in Joachimsthaler, p. 158.
12. Ullrich, p. 76. Kershaw, *Hitler*, p. 55.
13. Longerich, *Hitler*, p. 51.
14. *MK*, p. 181.
15. Hitler, *Monologe*, p. 71.
16. Joachimsthaler, pp. 164, 165.
17. Ullrich, p. 83.
18. Joachimsthaler, p. 169.
19. Ibid., p. 171.
20. Hitler, *Monologe*, p. 132.
21. Longerich, *Hitler*, p. 53.

Chapter 7: From Pasewalk to Lechfeld

1. *MK*, pp. 222–5.
2. Kershaw, *Hitler*, pp. 68, 69.
3. Longerich, *Hitler*, p. 59.
4. *MK*, p. 226.
5. Ullrich, p. 109.
6. Guido Knopp, *Hitler, Een balans* (Amsterdam, 2000), pp. 136, 137.
7. Othmar Plöckinger, *Unter Soldaten und Agitatoren. Hitlers prägende Jahre im deutschen Militär* (München, 2013), pp. 44, 45.
8. Ibid., pp. 48, 49, 91.
9. Ibid., pp. 62–8.
10. Longerich, *Hitler*, p. 62. Plöckinger, p. 86.
11. Plöckinger has corrected the Hitler research on this issue as well. Until then, one assumed that Hitler had participated in the first course in June at Munich University, p. 100.
12. Karl Alexander von Müller, *Mars und Venus. Erinnerungen 1914–1919* (Munich, 1954), p. 338.
13. Jäckel and Kuhn (eds), p. 88.
14. Plöckinger, pp. 128, 129.

Chapter 8: The Method

1. Richard Hofstadter, *The Paranoid Style in American Politics and Other Essays* (New York, 1965), pp. 3, 4.
2. Ibid., p. 31.
3. Ibid., pp. 4, 14, 17, 29, 30.
4. DSM-5 (2013), p. 761.
5. Robert Robins and Jerald Post, *Political Paranoia, The Psychopolitics of Hatred* (New Haven, London, 1997), pp. 18, 19.
6. Daniel Freeman and Jason Freeman, pp. 8, 28, 38.
7. DSM-5 (2013), p. 649.

Chapter 9: Hitler and Paranoia

1. Kubizek, p. 197.
2. DSM-5 (2013), p. 649.
3. Kubizek, p. 131.
4. Ibid., pp. 217, 218.
5. DSM-5 (2013), p. 90.
6. Kubizek, pp. 20, 23, 26, 42.

7. Ibid., pp. 217. Quote on p. 228.
8. DSM-5 (2013), p. 649 .
9. Konrad Heiden, *Geschichte des Nationalsozialismus. Die Karriere einer Idee* (Berlin, 1932), pp. 61–3.
10. Ernst Hanfstaengl, *15 Jahre mit Hitler. Zwischen Weißem und Braunem Haus. Memoiren eines politischen Außenseiters* (München, 1970), p. 63.
11. DSM-5 (2013), p. 649.
12. Otto Alexander von Müller, *Im Wandel einer Welt. Erinnerungen Band drei 1919–1932* (München, 1966), p. 132.
13. Hanfstaengl, pp. 69, 70.
14. Ibid., pp. 81, 82.
15. Ibid., p. 264. The fact that Hitler never wrote anything down is also established by Christa Schroeder.
16. Ibid., pp. 74, 75. Heinrich Hoffmann, who was not present at the incident, gives a slightly different version. He claims that the photo reporter was a certain Pahl of the Associated Press. Hitler wanted to pay a high sum to that man on one condition, namely that he opened his camera on the spot to destroy the footage. This is what happened. Heinrich Hoffmann, *Hitler wie ich ihn sah. Aufzeichnungen seines Leibfotografen* (München, Berlin, 1974), p. 31.
17. Heinrich Hoffmann, p. 200.
18. DSM-5 (2013), p. 649.
19. Heinrich Hoffmann, p. 125.
20. Baldur von Schirach, *Ich glaubte an Hitler* (Hamburg, 1967), p. 107. Heinrich Hoffmann, p. 125.
21. Otto Dietrich, *12 Jahre mit Hitler* (München, 1955), p. 218.
22. Heinrich Hoffmann, p. 199.
23. H.A. Turner (ed.), *Hitler aus nächster Nähe. Aufzeichnungen eines Vertrauten 1929–1932* (Berlin, Vienna, 1978), p. 233.
24. Hanfstaengl, pp. 56, 267.
25. Friedrich Hoßbach, *Zwischen Wehrmacht und Hitler 1934–1938* (Hannover, 1949), pp. 24, 34.
26. Robins and Post, pp. 18, 19.
27. DSM-5 (2013), p. 649.
28. Robins and Post, p. 5.
29. Longerich, *Hitler*, pp. 406, 407.
30. Brigitte Hamann, *Winifred Wagner oder Hitlers Bayreuth* (München, 2002), pp. 325, 326.
31. DSM-5 (2013), p. 762.
32. Joseph Goebbels, *Tagebücher Band 3*, published by Ralf Reuth (München, 2003), p. 1026.

33. Hitler's fears for monarchist intrigues described by Hoβbach is set in the years 1934–8. In 1938 Hoβbach was distrusted by Hitler himself because of those intrigues. Hoβbach, p. 30.
34. Goebbels, p. 1040.
35. Franz Halder, *Kriegstagebuch Band III. Der Ruβlandfeldzug bis zum Marsch auf Stalingrad (22. 6. 1941–24. 9. 1942* (Stuttgart, 1964), p. 421.
36. Walter Warlimont, *Im Hauptquartier der deutschen Wehrmacht 1939–1945* (Frankfurt, 1962), p. 38.
37. Ibid., p. 48.
38. Ibid., pp. 48, 49.
39. Leni Riefenstahl, *Memoiren* (München, 1987), pp. 353, 354.
40. Pyta, pp. 298, 299.
41. DSM-5 (2013), p. 649.
42. Albert Speer, *Erinnerungen* (1969, repr. Berlin, 1979), p. 208.
43. Ibid., p. 208.
44. Max Domarus, *Hitler. Reden und Proklamationen. Kommentiert von einem deutschen Zeitgenossen* (Würzburg, 1962–3), pp. 2033, 2035. Heinz Linge, *Bis zum Untergang. Als Chef des persönlichen Dienstes bei Hitler* (München, Berlin, 1980), pp. 97, 98.
45. Warlimont, p. 385.
46. Ibid., p. 111.
47. Heinz Guderian, *Erinnerungen eines Soldaten* (Heidelberg 1950; 4th edn. Neckargemünd, 1960), pp. 296, 310, 338, 402.
48. Goebbels, pp. 2036, 2037.
49. Albert Kesselring, *Soldat bis zum letzten Tag* (Bonn, 1953), pp. 386, 387.
50. Goebbels, p. 2173.
51. Schroeder, p. 208.
52. Ibid., p. 210.
53. David Irving, *Die geheimen Tagebücher des Dr. Morell, Leibarzt Adolf Hitlers* (München, 1983), p. 22.
54. Ibid., p. 206.
55. Ibid., pp. 276, 277.
56. Erich Kempka, *Die letzten Tage mit Adolf Hitler* (Oldendorf, 1975), p. 71.
57. Linge, p. 250.
58. Traudl Junge, *Tot het laatste uur. Het intrigerende levensverhaal van Hitlers secretaresse* (Baarn, 2002), p. 209.
59. Schroeder, p. 225.
60. *Desk Reference DSM-5* (London and Washington, 2013), p. 322.
61. Peter Hoffmann, *Hitler's personal security* (London, 1979), p. 265.
62. Goebbels, p. 364.

Chapter 10: The Anti-Semitic Turnaround

1. Daniel Freeman and Jason Freeman, pp. 43, 51, 111.
2. Jäckel and Kuhn (eds), p. 88.
3. Theodore Millon, Seth Grossman, Carrie Millon, Sarah Meagher and Rowena Ramnath, *Personality Disorders in Modern Life* (2nd edn, Hoboken, 2004), p. 2.
4. DSM-5 (2013), p. 647.
5. Millon et al., p. 36.
6. Quoted in Peter van Koppen, Harald Merckelbach, Marko Jelicic and Jan de Keijser, *Reizen met mijn rechter. Psychologie van het recht* (Deventer, 2010), p. 340.
7. Daniel Freeman and Jason Freeman, pp. 43, 51, 111.

Chapter 11: The Lethal Consequences of Hitler's Paranoia

1. Daniel Freeman and Jason Freeman, p. 80.
2. Ibid., p. 39.
3. *MK*, pp. 69, 70.
4. Ibid., p. 358.
5. Hitler quoted in Domarus, p. 1821.
6. Ibid., p. 1829.
7. Ibid., pp. 2236, 2237.

Chapter 12: Nature and Paranoia: The Deepest Roots of Paranoia

1. Randolph Nesse, 'The smoke detector principle', *Annals New York Academy of Science* (New York, n.d.). In this article, he elaborates on this principle. I have derived the quote from the Internet: https://www.randolphnesse.com/articles/smoke-detector.
2. Frans de Waal, *De Bonobo en de tien geboden. De moraal is ouder dan de mens* (2015), p. 69.
3. Ibid., p. 71.
4. Jessica Hamzelou, the *New Scientist* (16 March 2010).
5. On the Internet, one can find a lot of information about the so-called Gombe Chimpanzee War.
6. Cecie Starr and Ralph Taggart, *Biology. The Unity and Diversity of Life* (7th edn, n.p., 1997), p. 476.
7. *Nature*, Vol. 546, pp. 293–6 (8 June 2017).
8. Max Planck Gesellschaft, 7 June 2017 (quote).

WHY DID HITLER HATE THE JEWS?

9. Robin Dunfar, *Grooming, Gossip and the Evolution of Language* (digital version, n.p., n.d.), p. 138.
10. Peter Richerson and Robert Boyd, *Not by Genes Alone. How Culture Transformed Human Evolution* (Chicago, 2005), pp. 195–7.
11. Ibid., p. 200.
12. Yuval Noah Harari, *Sapiens: A Brief History of Humankind* (London, 2014), p. 23.
13. Ibid., pp. 26, 40, 41.
14. Ibid., pp. 67, 68.
15. Lance Workman and Will Reader, *Evolutionary psychology* (Cambridge, 2014), quotes, pp. 281, 284.
16. Raymond Fancher, *Pioneers of Psychology* (3rd edn, London and New York, 1996), pp. 226, 227. The mathematician Gauss described this curve in 1809 with a formula that has played an important role in both descriptive and mathematical statistics. This model describes many natural phenomena.

Chapter 14: Provisional Incantation of Fear and Narcissism

1. Eberhard Jäckel, *Hitlers Weltanschauung. Entwurf einer Herrschaft* (Stuttgart 1981), p. 60.

Chapter 15: Other Interpretations

1. Collingwood, p. 237.
2. Ibid., p. 269.

Chapter 16: The Viennese Interpretation

1. Joachimsthaler, p. 36.
2. Konrad Heiden, *Adolf Hitler. Das Zeitalter der Verantwortungslosigkeit* (Zürich 1936), pp. 39, 40.
3. John Lukacs, *Hitler en de geschiedenis* (Amsterdam, 1999), p. 20.
4. Alan Bullock, *Hitler: A Study in Tyranny* (London, 1952), p. 34.
5. Brigitte Hamann clarified this in her impressive biography about Hitler: *Hitler's Wien.*
6. Raymond Nickerson, 'Confirmation Bias: a Ubiquitous Phenomenon in Many Guises', *Review of General Psychology* (1998), pp. 177, 187, 201.
7. Jäckel and Kuhn (eds), pp. 64–9.

8. Kershaw, *Hitler*, p. 41. Here I refer to Kershaw's edition from 2009, but the text is exactly the same as the one in his biography from 1998. Joachimsthaler, pp. 157, 172.
9. In Jäckel and Kuhn (eds), fifty-nine documents are listed until this date (letters, postcards and poems).

Chapter 17: More Recent Publications

1. Thus, Rudolph Binion already emphasised in 1976, that Hitler's hatred of Jews only became manifest in 1918 in Pasewalk – so not in Vienna. *Hitler among the Germans* (New York, 1976), pp. 19, 20, 21, 129, 130. In John Toland's work one also strongly doubts whether Hitler was already an anti-Semite in Vienna. Toland seems to date the transformation to the end of the First World War. John Toland, *Adolf Hitler* (New York, 1976), pp. 45, 47, 50, 66.
2. Hamann, *Hitler's Wien*, p. 502.
3. Brigitte Hamann, 'Einer von ganz unten', *Der Spiegel* 21 (2001), p. 137.
4. Kershaw, *Hitler*, p. 37.
5. Ibid., p. 41.
6. Ibid., p. 42.
7. Kubizek, p. 162. Hamann, *Hitler's Wien*, p. 34.
8. Hitler quoted in Hamann, *Hitler's Wien*, p. 56.
9. *Timewatch* (2015) and *Timewatch* (2002).
10. Nickerson, p. 187.
11. Kershaw, *Hitler*, p. 43.
12. Ibid., p. 41.
13. Ibid., p. 44.
14. Hamann, *Hitler's Wien*, p. 498.
15. Joachimsthaler, p. 157. Jäckel and Kuhn (eds), p. 69.
16. Binion, p. 19.
17. Kershaw, *Hitler*, p. 44.
18. Ibid., p. 58.
19. Ibid., pp. 63, 64.
20. Ibid., p. 64.
21. Ralf Georg Reuth, *Hitlers Judenhass Klischee und Wirklichkeit* (München, 2009).
22. Ibid., p. 206.
23. Ullrich, p. 11.
24. Ibid., p. 12.
25. Ibid., p. 101.
26. Ibid., p. 421.

27. Ibid., p. 421.
28. DSM-5 (2013), p. 649.
29. Pyta, pp. 10, 13, 14, 30, 138, 285, 327, 374, 508.
30. Longerich, *Hitler*.
31. Ibid., pp. 67–72.
32. Ibid., p. 72.
33. Ibid., p. 172.
34. Ibid., p. 910.
35. Ibid., p. 172.
36. Ibid., p. 88.

Chapter 18: Freudian Psychohistory

1. Peter Gay, *Sigmund Freud. Zijn leven en werk* (Baarn, 1989), pp. 249–54.
2. Lloyd DeMause, *Foundations of psychohistory* (New York, 1982), p. 85.
3. Ibid., pp. 87, 88, 90, 91.
4. Andreas Hillgruber, 'Tendenzen, Ergebnisse und Perspektiven der gegenwärtigen Hitler-Forschung', *Historische Zeitschrift* (München, 1978), p. 609.
5. Walter C. Langer, *The Mind of Adolf Hitler: The Secret Wartime Report* (New York, 1972). Erich Fromm, *The anatomy of human destructiveness* (New York, 1973). Rudolph Binion, *Hitler Among the Germans* (New York, 1976). Robert Waite, *The psychopathic God: Adolf Hitler* (New York, 1977).
6. Elisabeth Loftus, *The myth of the repressed memory* (New York, 1994).
7. David Stannard, *Shrinking history. On Freud and the Failure of Psychohistory* (New York, Oxford, 1980).

Chapter 19: More Modern Psychological Research

1. The twenty-five pairs are divided into five broad domains, known as the Big Five. These five large domains were originally based exclusively on the analysis of adjectives in dictionaries with which hundreds of personality traits were indicated. The choice for dictionaries is clear: There is no other place where one can find such a wide range of adjectives to describe persons. After a factor analysis, underlying variables came to light, which were finally distributed into the Big Five on the basis of similarity. The said twenty-five couples were all validated and were also found in various cultures. The empirical basis is therefore solid.
2. DSM-5 (2013), p. 780.

3. Ibid., p. 773.
4. Ibid., p. xli.
5. Ibid., p. 20.
6. Edleff Schwaab, *Hitler's Mind. A Plunge into Madness* (New York, 1992), p. 63. On this page one also reads the quote from *MK*.
7. Ibid., p. 70.
8. Ibid., p. 79.
9. Ibid., p. 84.
10. Ibid., p. 85.
11. Ibid., p. 139.
12. Ibid., p. 147.
13. Ibid., p. 151.
14. Ibid., p. 120.
15. Ibid., p. 85.
16. Robins and Post, pp. 73, 74.
17. Ibid., pp. 3, 69, 89.
18. Ibid., p. 3.
19. Ibid., pp. 89, 93.
20. Ibid., pp. 3–6, 19.
21. Ibid., pp. 5, 6.
22. Fritz Redlich, *Hitler, Diagnoses of a Destructive Prophet* (Oxford, 1998), pp. 255–339.
23. Ibid., pp. 293, 294.
24. Ibid., p. 294.
25. DSM-5 (2013) p. 761.
26. Redlich, p. 295.
27. Ibid., p. 293.
28. Ibid., p. 335.

Chapter 20: Evaluation and Some New Remarks

1. Wikipedia; see Psychopathography of Adolf Hitler.
2. Longerich, *Hitler*, p. 910.
3. Peter Longerich, *Holocaust. The Nazi Persecution and Murder of the Jews* (München, 2000), p. 6.
4. Ibid., p. 426.

Chapter 21: Hitler's Motives to Kill the European Jews

1. Hitler in Jäckel and Kuhn (eds), p. 176.
2. Longerich, *Holocaust*, pp. 187, 189.

3. Hitler quoted in Domarus, p. 1058.
4. Hitler, *Monologe*, p. 106.
5. Quoted in Christopher Browning, *Entfesselung der Endlösung: Nationalsozialistische Judenpolitik 1939–1942* (München, 2003), p. 582.
6. Tom Notten, Go2War2.nl, *Uitgestelde slag om Moskou*, p. 24.
7. Hitler in Domarus, p. 1821.
8. Ibid., p. 1829.
9. Ibid., p. 1830.
10. Ibid., p. 1833.
11. Quoted in Peter Longerich (ed.), *Die Ermordung der Europäischen Juden* (n.p., 1990), p. 85.
12. Hitler in Domarus, p. 1844.
13. Ibid.
14. Ibid., p. 1937.
15. *MK*, pp. 428, 751.
16. Ibid., pp. 310, 372, 428.
17. Hitler in Jäckel and Kuhn (eds), p. 199.
18. *MK*, p. 149.
19. Ibid., p. 337.
20. Ibid., p. 335.
21. Ibid., p. 386.
22. Ibid., p. 387.
23. Ibid., p. 149.
24. Hitler quoted in Browning, *Entfesselung der Endlösung,* p. 455.
25. Philippe Burrin, *Hitler and the Jews. The Genesis of the Holocaust* (n.p., 1994), p. 124. Peter Longerich, *Politik der Vernichtung. Eine Gesamtdarstellung der nationalsozialistische Judenverfolgung* (München, 1998), pp. 436, 439.
26. Hitler, *Monologe*, p. 126.
27. Ibid., p. 241.
28. Ibid., p. 280.
29. Ibid., p. 293.
30. Burrin, p. 147.
31. Peter Range Ross, *The Year that Made Hitler: 1924* (New York, 2016), pp. 63, 117, 218, 233, 234. For almost all these narcissistic statements, made by Hitler about himself, the author refers to *MK*.
32. This self-image of a narcissist is outlined by the DSM-5 (2013), p. 670.

Chapter 22: Was there a Killing Order?

1. Longerich, *Holocaust*, pp. 290, 294, 300, 301, 302.

2. Martin Broszat, 'Hitler und die Genesis der "Endlösung"', *Vierteljahrshefte für Zeitgeschichte*, 25 (1977), pp. 739–75.
3. Hans Mommsen, 'Die Realisierung des Utopischen: Die "Endlösung der Judenfrage" im "Dritten Reich"', in *Geschichte und Gesellschaft* (Berlin, 1983), pp. 394, 417.
4. Götz Aly, *'Endlösung' Völkerverschiebung und der Mord an den europäischen Juden* (Frankfurt am Main, 2002), p. 390.
5. Ian Kershaw, *Fateful choices. Ten decisions that changed the world 1940–1941* (London, 2007), p. 468.
6. Longerich, *Holocaust*, p. 6.
7. Ibid., p. 424.
8. Christopher Browning in Dan Stone (ed.), *The Historiography of the Holocaust* (London, 2005), pp. 187, 188. Saul Friedländer, *Die Jahre der Vernichtung. Das Dritte Reich und die Juden* (München, 2006), pp. 314, 315.

Chapter 23: The Killing Order – Three Sources

1. Longerich, *Holocaust*, pp. 187–91.
2. Bettina Stangneth, *Eichmann Before Jerusalem. The Unexamined Life of a Mass Murderer* (New York, 2015), p. 246.
3. Irmtrud Wojak, *Eichmanns Memoiren. Ein kritischer Essay* (Frankfurt am Main, 2001), pp. 21, 22, 24, 25, 47, 50. Irmtrud Wojak listened to all of the tapes and compared them to the transcripts. In the abovementioned book, she reports on her findings. You can hear Eichmann calling Rudolf Höss a liar straight from his own mouth in the KRO programme *Profiel Willem Sassen: de biograaf van Eichmann* (11 May 2005); *Profile Willem Sassen: Eichmann's biographer* (11 May 2005). Parts of the interview can also be heard on YouTube: 'Eichmann – The Sassen Tapes 1 and 2'.
4. Stangneth, p. 181.
5. Ibid., 216.
6. Ibid., p. 303.
7. Ibid., p. 506, footnote 292.
8. Wojak, pp. 45, 49, 50, 56, 57, 81, 90, 91.
9. Eichmann direct on tape. KRO programme (11 May 2005).
10. Wojak, pp. 53, 55, 56.
11. Ibid., pp. 51, 53.
12. Ibid., pp. 48, 54, 55, 56.
13. Eichmann quoted in *Time/LIFE* (Chicago, November 1960), p. 21.
14. Eichmann direct on tape. KRO programme (11 May 2005).
15. Ibid. Eichmann quoted in Wojak, pp. 64, 65.

16. Eichmann direct on tape. YouTube, 'Eichmann – The Sassen Tapes 1 and 2'. Eichmann quoted in Wojak, p. 199.

17. Eichann in Wojak, p. 75.

18. Eichann in Wojak, p. 195.

19. Eichmann quoted in *Time/LIFE*, p. 21.

20. Ibid., p. 24.

21. Eichmann directly on tape. KRO programme (11 May 2005). Eichmann in *Time/LIFE*, p. 102.

22. Stangneth, pp. 278, 281.

23. Ibid., pp. 277, 278.

24. Ibid., p. 281.

25. Eichmann quoted in Wojak, p. 207.

26. Martin Broszat (ed.), *Kommandant in Auchwitz. Autobiographische Aufzeichnungen des Rudolf Höss* (München, 2011), p. 18.

27. Ibid., p. 10.

28. Ibid., p. 11.

29. Ibid., p. 13.

30. Ibid., p. 235.

31. Robert Jan van Pelt, *The case for Auschwitz. Evidence from the Irving Trial* (Bloomington, 2002), pp. 253, 254.

32. Ibid., p. 254.

33. Ibid.

34. Höss in Broszat (ed.), *Kommandant in Auchwitz*, p. 237.

35. Karin Orth, 'Rudolf Höss und "die Endlösung der Judenfrage". Drei Argumente gegen deren Datierung auf den Sommer 1941', *Werkstattgeschichte* (1997), p. 18.

36. Ibid., p. 48.

37. Danuta Czech, *Kalendarium der Ereignisse im Konzentrationslager Auschwitz-Birkenau 1939–1945* (Hamburg, 2008), pp. 174, 175.

38. Höss in Broszat (ed.), *Kommandant in Auchwitz*, p. 239.

39. Ibid.

40. Déborah Dwork and Robert Jan van Pelt, *Auschwitz* (New York, London, 2008), pp. 292, 293. Czech, p. 122.

41. Orth, p. 51.

42. Höss in Broszat (ed.), *Kommandant in Auchwitz*, pp. 189, 190.

43. Michael Thad Allen, 'The devil in the details', *Holocaust and Genocide Studies* (2002), pp. 193, 198, 199 and Michael Thad Allen, 'Anfänge der Menschenvernichtung in Auschwitz, Oktober 1941', *Vierteljahrshefte für Zeitgeschichte* (Heft 4/Oktober 2003), pp. 572, 573.

44. Orth, p. 52.

45. Ibid., p. 53.

46. H.F.M. Crombag, P.J. van Koppen and W.A. Wagenaar, *Dubieuze zaken. De psychologie van het strafrechtelijk bewijs* (Amsterdam, 1992), p. 272.
47. Van Koppen et al., pp. 457–8.
48. Crombag et al., pp. 280, 281.
49. Czech, pp. 250, 251.
50. Christopher Browning, *Der Weg zur 'Endlösung' Entscheidungen und Täter* (Bonn, 1998), p. 153.
51. Ibid., p. 152.
52. Czech, p. 251. Höss in Broszat (ed.), *Kommandant in Auchwitz*, p. 279. Browning, *Der Weg zur 'Endlösung' Entscheidungen und Täter*, p. 154.
53. Browning, *Der Weg zur 'Endlösung' Entscheidungen und Täter*, p. 154.
54. Crombag et al., pp. 280, 281.
55. Https://de.wikipedia.org/wiki/Posener_Reden.
56. Ibid.
57. Peter Longerich, *Der ungeschriebene Befehl. Hitler und der Weg zur Endlösung* (München, 2001), p. 189. Here Longerich underlines the quotes 'I have decided' and the 'toughest thing we hitherto had to do'.
58. Ibid.
59. Https://forum.codoh.com/viewtopic.php?t=7225.
60. Peter Longerich, *Holocaust*, pp. 261, 262.
61. Ibid., p. 263.

Chapter 24: The Killing Order: When?

1. Longerich, *Holocaust*, p. 6.
2. Hitler in Domarus, pp. 1663, 1664.
3. Goebbels, pp. 1656–8.

Bibliography

Allen, Michael Thad, 'The devil in the details', *Holocaust and Genocide Studies* (Oxford, 2002)

Allen, Michael Thad, 'Anfänge der Menschenvernichtung in Auschwitz, Oktober 1941', *Vierteljahrshefte für Zeitgeschichte* (Heft 4/Oktober 2003)

Aly, Götz, *'Endlösung' Völkerverschiebung und der Mord an den europäischen Juden* (Frankfurt am Main, 2002)

Binion, Rudolph, *Hitler among the Germans* (New York, 1976)

Boehm, Christopher, 'The moral consequences of social selection', *Behaviour* 151 (2014)

Broszat, Martin (ed.), *Kommandant in Auchwitz. Autobiographische Aufzeichnungen des Rudolf Höss* (München, 2011)

Broszat, Martin, 'Hitler und die Genesis der "Endlösung"', *Vierteljahrshefte für Zeitgeschichte*, 25 (1977)

Browning, Christopher, *Der Weg zur 'Endlösung' Entscheidungen und Täter* (Bonn, 1998)

Browning, Christopher, *Entfesselung der Endlösung: Nationalsozialistische Judenpolitik 1939–1942* (München, 2003)

Bullock, Alan, *Hitler: A Study in Tyranny* (London, 1952)

Burrin, Philippe, *Hitler and the Jews. The Genesis of the Holocaust* (n.p., 1994)

Carsten, Francis Ludwig, *The rise of fascism* (London, 1967)

Cohn, Norman, *Warrant for genocide. The myth of the Jewish world conspiracy and the protocols of the elders of Zion* (London, 1996)

Collingwood, Robin George, *The Idea of History* (Oxford, 1946)

Crombag, H.F.M., P.J. van Koppen and W.A. Wagenaar, *Dubieuze zaken. De psychologie van het strafrechtelijk bewijs* (Amsterdam, 1992)

Czech, Danuta, *Kalendarium der Ereignisse im Konzentrationslager Auschwitz-Birkenau 1939–1945* (Hamburg, 2008)

Damasio, António, *Descartes' Error: Emotion, Reason, and the Human Brain* (n.p., 1994)

DeMause, Lloyd, *Foundations of psychohistory* (New York, 1982)

Desk Reference DSM-5 (London and Washington, 2013)

Deuerlein, Ernst, *Hitler. Eine politische Biographie* (München, 1969)

Diagnostic Statistical Manual of Mental Disorders (DSM-5) (London and Washington, 2013)

Dietrich, Ottto, *12 Jahre mit Hitler* (München, 1955)

Domarus, Max, *Hitler. Reden und Proklamationen. Kommentiert von einem deutschen Zeitgenossen*, Band I-IV (Würzburg, 1962–3)

Dunfar, Robin, *Grooming, Gossip and the Evolution of Language* (Faber and Faber, digital version, n.p., n.d.)

Dwork, Déborah and Robert Jan van Pelt, *Auschwitz* (New York and London, 2008)

Eichmann, Adolf, 'Eichmann's Confessions' in *Time*/LIFE (Chicago, 1960)

Fancher, Raymond, *Pioneers of Psychology* (3rd edn, London and New York, 1996)

Fest, Joachim, *Hitler* (Berlin, 1973)

Freeman, Daniel, 'Persecutory delusions: a cognitive perspective on understanding and treatment', *The Lancet* (2016)

Freeman, Daniel and Jason Freeman, *Paranoia the 21st-century fear* (Oxford, 2008)

Freeman, Daniel, Jason Freeman and Philippa Garety, *Overcoming Paranoid and Suspicious Thoughts* (2nd edn, Oxford, 2016)

Friedländer, Saul, *Das Dritte Reich und die Juden. Die Jahre der Verfolgung 1933–1939* (München, 2000)

Friedländer, Saul, *Die Jahre der Vernichtung. Das Dritte Reich und die Juden 1939–1945* (München, 2006)

Friedländer, Saul, *The Years of Extermination. Nazi Germany and the Jews 1939–1945* (e-book)

Fromm, Erich, *The Anatomy of human destructiveness* (New York, 1973)

Gay, Peter, *Sigmund Freud. Zijn leven en werk* (Baarn, 1989)

Gisevius, Hans Bernd, *Adolf Hitler. Versuch einer Deutung* (München, 1963)

Goebbels, Joseph, *Tagebücher, Band 1–5*, published by Ralf Reuth (München, 2003)

Guderian, Heinz, *Erinnerungen eines Soldaten* (Heidelberg, 1950; 4th edn, Neckargemünd, 1960)

Haidt, Jonathan, *The righteous mind. Why good people are divided by politics and religion* (New York, 2012)

Halder, Franz, *Kriegstagebuch Band III. Der Rußlandfeldzug bis zum Marsch auf Stalingrad (22. 6. 1941–24. 9. 1942)* (Stuttgart, 1964)

Hamann, Brigitte, *Hitler's Wien. Lehrjahre eines Diktators* (8th edn, München, 1998)

Hamann, Brigitte, 'Einer von ganz unten' in: *Der Spiegel* 21 (2001)

Hamann, Brigitte, *Winifred Wagner oder Hitlers Bayreuth* (München, 2002)

Hamzelou, Jessica, *The New Scientist* (16 March 2010)

Hanfstaengl, Ernst, *15 Jahre mit Hitler. Zwischen Weißem und Braunem Haus. Memoiren eines politischen Außenseiters* (München, 1970)

Hanisch, Reinhold, 'I was Hitler's buddy', *The New Republic* (5 April 1939)

Harari, Yuval Noah, *Sapiens: A Brief History of Humankind* (London, 2014)

Heer, Friedrich, *Der Glaube des Adolf Hitler. Anatomie einer politischen Religiosität* (Frankfurt, Berlin, 1989)

Heiden, Konrad, *Geschichte des Nationalsozialismus. Die Karriere einer Idee* (Berlin, 1932)

Heiden, Konrad, *Adolf Hitler. Das Zeitalter der Verantwortungslosigkeit* (Zürich, 1936)

Herbst, Ludolf, *Das nationalsozialistische Deutschland 1933–1945* (Frankfurt, 1996)

Hertog, Peter den, *Hitlers Schutkleur. De Oorsprong van zijn Antisemitisme* (Amsterdam, 2005)

Hertog, Peter den, *Adolf Hitler Ontmaskerd. Het bevel tot Vernietiging van de Europese Joden geanalyseerd* (Soesterberg, 2012)

Hillgruber, Andreas, 'Tendenzen, Ergebnisse und Perspektiven der gegenwärtigen Hitler-Forschung', *Historische Zeitschrift* (München, 1978)

Hitler, Adolf, *Mein Kampf* (München, 1942)

Hitler, Adolf, *Monologe im Führerhauptquartier 1941–1944*, published by Werner Jochmann (München, 1980)

Hodgen, Margaret, *Early anthropology in the sixteenth and seventeenth centuries* (Philadelphia, 1964)

Hoffmann, Heinrich, *Hitler wie ich ihn sah. Aufzeichnungen seines Leibfotografen* (München, Berlin, 1974)

Hoffmann, Peter, *Hitler's personal security* (London, 1979)

Hofstadter, Richard, *The Paranoid Style in American Politics and Other Essays* (New York, 1965)

Hoßbach, Friedrich, *Zwischen Wehrmacht und Hitler 1934–1938* (Hannover, 1949)

Husson, Edouard, *'Nous pouvons vivre sans les Juifs'. Novembre 1941. Quand et comment ils décidèrent de la Solution nationale* (n.p., 2005)

Irving, David, *Die geheimen Tagebücher des Dr. Morell, Leibarzt Adolf Hitlers* (München, 1983)

Jäckel, Eberhard and Axel Kuhn (eds), *Hitler. Sämtliche Aufzeichnungen* (Stuttgart, 1980)

Jäckel, Eberhard, *Hitlers Weltanschauung. Entwurf einer Herrschaft* (Stuttgart, 1981)

Jetzinger, Franz, *Hitlers Jugend. Phantasien, Lügen – und die Wahrheit* (Wien, 1956)

Joachimsthaler, Anton, *Hitlers Weg begann in München* (München, 2000)

Junge, Traudl, *Tot het laatste uur. Het intrigerende levensverhaal van Hitlers secretaresse* (Baarn, 2002)

Kempka, Erich, *Die letzten Tage mit Adolf Hitler* (Oldendorf, 1975)

Kershaw, Ian, *Fateful choices. Ten decisions that changed the world 1940–1941* (London, 2007)

Kershaw, Ian, *Hitler* (London, 2009)

Kesselring, Albert, *Soldat bis zum letzten Tag* (Bonn, 1953)

Knopp, Guido, *Hitler. Een balans* (Amsterdam, 2000)

Koppen, Peter van, *Overtuigend bewijs. Indammen van rechterlijke dwalingen* (Amsterdam, 2011)

Koppen, Peter van, Harald Merckelbach, Marko Jelicic and Jan de Keijser, *Reizen met mijn rechter. Psychologie van het recht* (Deventer, 2010)

Kubizek, August, *Adolf Hitler. Mein Jugendfreund* (2nd edn, Graz and Göttingen, 1953)

Kuipers, T., *Territorial Aspects of the Paranoid Psychosis* (Utrecht, 1995)

Lang, Jochen von (ed.), *Eichmann Interrogated. Transcripts from the Archives from the Israeli Police* (New York, 1999)

Langbein, Hermann, *People in Auschwitz* (London, 2004)

Langer, Walter C., *The Mind of Adolf Hitler: The Secret Wartime Report* (New York, 1972)

Linge, Heinz, *Bis zum Untergang. Als Chef des persönlichen Dienstes bei Hitler* (München, Berlin, 1980)

Loftus, Elisabeth, *The myth of the repressed memory* (New York, 1994)

Longerich, Peter (ed.), *Die Ermordung der Europäischen Juden* (n.p., 1990)

Longerich, Peter, *Politik der Vernichtung. Eine Gesamtdarstellung der nationalsozialistische Judenverfolgung* (München, 1998)

Longerich, Peter, *Holocaust. The Nazi Persecution and Murder of the Jews* (München, 2000)

Longerich, Peter. *Der ungeschriebene Befehl. Hitler und der Weg zur Endlösung* (München, 2001)

Longerich, Peter, *Hitler. Biographie* (München, 2015)

Lukacs, John, *Hitler en de geschiedenis* (Amsterdam, 1999)

Maser, Werner, *Adolf Hitler. Legende, Mythos, Wirklichkeit* (München, 1971)

Millon, Theodore, Seth Grossman, Carrie Millon, Sarah Meagher and Rowena Ramnath, *Personality Disorders in Modern Life* (2nd edn, Hoboken, 2004)

Mommsen, Hans 'Die Realisiering des Utopischen: Die "Endlösung der Judenfrage" im "Dritten Reich"', in *Geschichte und Gesellschaft* (Berlin, 1983)

Mosse, George, *Rassismus. Ein Krankheitssymptom in der europäischen Geschichte des 19. und 20. Jahrhunderts* (Königstein, 1978)

Müller, Karl Alexander von, *Mars und Venus. Erinnerungen 1914–1919* (Munich, 1954)

Müller, Otto Alexander, *Im Wandel einer Welt. Erinnerungen. Band drei 1919–1932* (München, 1966)

Nesse, Randolph, 'The smoke detector principle', *Annals New York Academy of Science* (New York, n.d.)

Nickerson, Raymond, 'Confirmation Bias: a Ubiquitous Phenomenon in many Guises', *Review of General Psychology* (1998)

Orth, Karin, 'Rudolf Höss und "die Endlösung der Judenfrage". Drei Argumente gegen deren Datierung auf den Sommer 1941', *Werkstattgeschichte* (1997)

Pelt, Robert Jan van, *The case for Auschwitz. Evidence from the Irving Trial* (Bloomington, 2002)

Plöckinger, Othmar, *Unter Soldaten und Agitatoren. Hitlers prägende Jahre im deutschen Militär* (München, 2013)

Poliakov, Léon, *Geschichte des Antisemitismus VII. Am Vorabend des Holocaust* (Worms, 1988)

Pyta, Wolfram, *Hitler, Der Künstler als Politiker und Feldherr. Eine Herrschaftsanalyse* (München, 2015)

Redlich, Fritz, *Hitler, Diagnoses of a Destructive Prophet* (Oxford, 1998)

Reuth, Ralf Georg, *Hitlers Judenhass Klischee und Wirklichkeit* (München, 2009)

Richerson, Peter and Robert Boyd, *Not by Genes Alone. How Culture Transformed Human Evolution* (Chicago, 2005)

Riefenstahl, Reni, *Memoiren* (München, 1987)

Robins, Robert and Jerald Post, *Political Paranoia, The Psychopolitics of Hatred* (New Haven, London, 1997)

Ross, Peter Range, *The Year That Made Hitler: 1924* (New York, 2016)

Rürup, Reinhard, *Emanzipation und Antisemitismus. Studien zur 'Judenfrage' der bürgerlichen Gesellschaft* (Göttingen, 1975)

Schirach, Baldur von, *Ich glaubte an Hitler* (Hamburg, 1967)

Schroeder, Christa, *Er war mein Chef. Aus dem Nachlaß der Sekretärin von Adolf Hitler* (5th edn, München, 2002)

Schwaab, Edleff, *Hitler's Mind. A Plunge into Madness* (New York, 1992)

Schwarz, Birgit, *Geniewahn: Hitler und die Kunst* (Wien, 2011)

Smith, Bradley F., *Adolf Hitler: His Family, Childhood, and Youth* (Stanford, 1967)

Smith, Bradley and Agnes Peterson, *Heinrich Himmler: Geheimreden 1933 bis 1945 und andere Ansprachen* (Frankfurt am Main, 1974)

Speer, Albert, *Erinnerungen* (1969, repr. Berlin, 1979)

Stangneth, Bettina, *Eichmann Before Jerusalem. The Unexamined Life of a Mass Murderer* (New York, 2015)

Stannard, David, *Shrinking history. On Freud and the Failure of Psychohistory* (New York, Oxford, 1980)

Starr, Cecie and Ralph Taggart, *Biology. The Unity and Diversity of Life* (7th edn, n.p., 1997)

Stone, Dan (ed.), *The Historiography of the Holocaust* (London, 2005)

Toland, John, *Adolf Hitler* (New York, 1976)

Turner. H.A. (ed.), *Hitler aus nächster Nähe. Aufzeichnungen eines Vertrauten 1929–1932* (Berlin, Vienna, 1978)

Ullrich, Volker, *Adolf Hitler. Die Jahre des Aufstiegs 1889–1939* (Frankfurt am Main, 2013)

Waal, Frans de, *De Bonobo en de tien geboden. De moraal is ouder dan de mens* (n.p., 2015)

Waal, Frans de, *The Bonobo and the Atheist: In Search of Humanism Among the Primates* (New York and London, 2014)

Wagenaar, Willem and Hans Crombag, *The Popular Policeman and Other Cases. Psychological Perspectives on Legal Evidence* (Amsterdam, 2005)

Waite, Robert. *The psychopathic God: Adolf Hitler* (New York, 1977)

Warlimont, Walter, *Im Hauptquartier der deutschen Wehrmacht 1939–1945* (Frankfurt, 1962)

Wiedemann, Fritz, *Der Mann der Feldherr werden wollte. Erlebnisse und Erfahrungen des Vorgesetzten im 1. Weltkrieg und seines späteren Persönlichen Adjudanten* (n.p., 1964)

Wojak, Irmtrud, *Eichmanns Memoiren. Ein kritischer Essay* (Frankfurt am Main, 2001)

Work, Déborah and Robert Jan van Pelt, *Auschwitz* (New York, London, 2008)

Workman, Lance and Will Reader, *Evolutionary psychology* (Cambridge, 2014)

Zmarlik, Hans-Günther, 'Der Sozialdarwinismus in Deutschland als geschichtliches Problem', *VFZ* (1963)

Index